The Episcopal Church and Its Work

THE CHURCH'S TEACHING

I

THE HOLY SCRIPTURES

II

CHAPTERS IN CHURCH HISTORY

III

THE FAITH OF THE CHURCH

IV

THE WORSHIP OF THE CHURCH

VI

THE EPISCOPAL CHURCH AND ITS WORK

In Preparation

V CHRISTIAN LIVING

VOLUME SIX

The Episcopal Church and Its Work

POWEL MILLS DAWLEY

With the collaboration of James Thayer Addison and with the assistance of the Authors' Committee of the Department of Christian Education of The Protestant Episcopal Church

GREENWICH · CONNECTICUT · 1955

LIBRARY OF CONGRESS CARD CATALOG NUMBER: 55-6354

PRINTED IN THE UNITED STATES OF AMERICA

BY THE COLONIAL PRESS INC., CLINTON, MASSACHUSETTS

DESIGNED BY STEFAN SALTER

Foreword

This book is Volume VI in THE CHURCH'S TEACHING. As it goes to press, the fifth volume, *Christian Living,* is being prepared, and upon its appearance the series will be complete.

After treating the faith and practice of the Church and their foundations in the Scriptures and in tradition, it is fitting that the final volume in the series should be concerned with the present structure and activity of the Episcopal Church. The first section of the book establishes a link with Volume II, *Chapters in Church History,* by expanding the material to be found there on the history of our own Church and relating it to the present day scene.

No volume in this series is intended to be used as a textbook for a Church school course. Each volume is designed to be used by older students and adults, both in general reading and in adult study groups. All six volumes will find their primary place as resource books in relation to the total teaching program of the Church. Every course of study for children and adults will lean upon these six works for the knowledge of our common heritage. The popularity and usefulness of the first four volumes as general books for all Episcopalians has already been attested by their immense sales. Each volume in the series should find its way ultimately into every home in the Church.

It is appropriate that the author of *Chapters in Church History* should be the one to write *The Episcopal Church and Its Work.* In this task Dr. Dawley has been assisted by the members of the Authors' Committee and has received many helpful suggestions from a host of readers throughout the country. We are deeply indebted to the late James Thayer Addison for extensive preliminary work on Part III.

DAVID R. HUNTER
JOHN HEUSS
Co-Chairmen, The Authors' Committee

Preface

The purpose of this final volume in THE CHURCH'S TEACHING series is to provide an introduction to the heritage, character, and work of the Episcopal Church. While earlier volumes have dealt with the Holy Scriptures, Church history, the Church's faith and worship, and Christian living, it is in the context of the Episcopal Church that these central elements of the Christian tradition make their claims upon us. The series, therefore, appropriately concludes with a description of the nature and activity of the Episcopal Church. Like the other volumes, this book is necessarily selective in its treatment of the subject. Limitations of space allow little more than an introduction to our Church life, though an attempt is made to give at least some mention to all matters of significant importance. None of the books in THE CHURCH'S TEACHING series is exhaustive; in every case some aspects of the subject matter must be pursued in further reading, and for that reason a list of suggested books is included in the appendix of each volume. This will be especially true in the first part of this volume where the history of the Episcopal Church is necessarily summarized in a few chapters, and in the final part where space permits no adequate description or discussion of the work of many organizations, societies, and agencies in the Episcopal Church.

Work on the preparatory notes for this volume was begun shortly after all six books in THE CHURCH'S TEACHING series were planned. At that time the writing was to be done by collaboration between the present author and the late James Thayer Addison. For some years Professor of the History of Religions and Missions in the Episcopal Theological School, and later vice-president of the National Council and director of its overseas missionary work, Dr. Addison was singularly equipped by both interest and experience to contribute much to this volume. Many of his writings are well known and widely used throughout the Church, in particular *Our Expanding Church,* the story of our missionary enterprise, and *The Episcopal Church in the United States 1789-1931,* a popular standard text.

Dr. Addison's sudden death, early in 1953, prevented the completion of his collaboration on the chapters of this book. Since that time both the plan and contents of the volume have been altered by decisions of the Authors' Committee, and in its present form the book is much expanded beyond the outlines on which Dr. Addison and I at first worked together. Wherever possible I have used both his notes and the preliminary drafts he had completed, and through the necessary revisions I have sought to retain the emphasis he placed upon certain essential matters in the life of our Church. This is especially true in those sections of Part I that follow the general outline of his book on the history of the Episcopal Church, and in the portions of Part III which deal with the missionary work of the Church and the activities of the National Council. For such inadequacies as this book may have, Dr. Addison is not responsible, but any virtues it may possess should recall him to memory as one whose years of unselfish and devoted labor inspired successive generations of pupils and friends to seek, as he did, to give their best to the Church they serve.

The greater part of the text of this volume, like that of others in the series, has been read in manuscript by large numbers of clergy and lay people. Their helpful comments and suggestions have assisted immensely in bringing the work to completion, and for both their time and interest the members of the Authors' Committee are deeply grateful. Without the assistance that has been so generously given by so many throughout the Church, no volume in this series could have achieved the usefulness demonstrated in them all.

POWEL MILLS DAWLEY

Contents

PART ONE

The Heritage of the Episcopal Church

CHAPTER ONE

The Anglican Tradition

EPISCOPALIANS are often aware that they share a heritage which is distinctive in Christendom. Embodied in our faith, worship, and church order is a Christian tradition sturdy enough to embrace diversities as old as the New Testament itself, creative enough to hold these diversities together in a unity that bears the promise of a fuller apprehension of Christian truth. We begin our exploration of the life and work of the Episcopal Church, therefore, by recalling the nature of our Anglican Tradition.

People are sometimes led to think that Christians in the modern world are divided into a bewildering array of distinct and separate Churches, hopelessly sundered from one another in unhappy competition. This is hardly an accurate picture of Christendom. The fact is that nearly all Christian Churches belong to one of a few great families. That is, they fall into groups, often because of their common origins or similar essential doctrines. Within these groups their relation to one another, whether close or distant, is primarily a family relationship of those who have inherited similar traditions. However internal differences may have impaired their fellowship, or a combination of time and circumstances made them "cousinly" Churches instead of "sister" Churches, they are still more closely akin within the family than to those Churches in a different group.

The most closely knit family is that of the Roman Catholic Churches in every land—indeed, so nearly related are they as to form a single Church instead of a family of separate members. This is partly the result of the last four hundred years of Roman Catholic history. Since the Reformation the central power or supremacy of the Roman Pope, both in church government (what is called "ecclesiastical jurisdiction") and in the determination of right belief (by use of "papal infallibility"), has increased to the point where it imposes a single papal or *Roman* tradition upon what was once a freer family of Catholic Churches.

More truly a family of different member Churches are the Eastern Catholics of the Orthodox Churches, some in close fellowship with each other, others severed from family unity by the remains of ancient theological quarrels. All, however, share in recognizably similar traditions of faith, order, and worship; together they form that vast portion of Christendom known as Eastern Orthodoxy.

The chief families of Protestant Churches are those sharing the traditions of Lutheranism, Methodism, Calvinism (the Reformed and Presbyterian Churches), and Independency. Here there is a wide variety within the various groups. Both Baptists and Congregationalists, for example, belong to the family of Independent Churches, though their differences make them seem only distantly related. They share, however, in the characteristic Independent principle of the autonomy of each local church or congregation. In other words, their family unity is one based on a common form of church government—*polity* or "church order" as it is sometimes called.

It is clear that the unifying principles among these great families of Churches may be different. Members of the group that has inherited the traditions of Independency find kinship in their similar church order; their doctrines, on the other hand, may differ at some points. In contrast, Lutheran Churches are bound together by the priority given in all of them to specific Lutheran doctrines; their forms of church order or manner of worship may be quite different. A striking illustration of this is offered by the differences between a typical Lutheran Church in the United States with its familiar aspect of American Protestantism and the Lutheran State Church of Sweden with its bishops and hierarchy in the apostolic succession and the stately rites of its High Mass.

[Episcopalians belong to a Church that is a member of the family known as the *Anglican* Churches or *The Anglican Communion*. The word "Anglican" is here used to describe those Churches that derived from the Church of England and its expansion overseas, and which share in the common traditions of faith, church order, and worship that are distinctively theirs. Thus *Anglican* is in one sense a neutral word. It does not imply adherence to the teachings of a particular churchman or theologian, as does "Lutheran" or "Calvinist"; rather it signifies that Christian tradition which became the ethos of the Church of England and spread thence to become the distinguishing mark of a vast world-wide Communion of Churches.]

A striking characteristic of the Anglican tradition is its combination in a single church life of Christian elements sometimes sharply divided by the words "Catholic" and "Protestant." The Anglican Communion is, as the Anglican Congress of 1954 affirmed, "a fellowshp of Churches at one and the same time Catholic in seeking to do justice to the wholeness of Christian truth, in emphasizing continuity through the Episcopate and in retaining the historic Creeds and Sacraments of undivided Christendom; and Evangelical in its commission to proclaim the Gospel and in its emphasis on personal faith in Jesus Christ as Saviour . . ." Congress statements made plain the vocation which this unique heritage places before all Anglicans: "If Anglicanism did not preserve variety in unity, it would make a poorer contribution to the Church Universal. It is our costly responsibility to hold together these loyalties in mutual forbearance, trust and co-operation in the Church's work and mission." [1]

To understand more fully the unique traditions of the Episcopal Church, or the place in Christendom of the Anglican family of Churches, we must explore briefly the history of the Church of England in which this heritage is rooted.[2]

CHRISTIANITY IN ENGLAND

Christianity first came to Britain when the island was a Roman province. While the story of the evangelization of the British folk is now lost to us in its details, by the beginning of the third century of the Christian era there was a Church organized and established among the Romanized Britons. The invasions of the Germanic barbarians who overran the Roman Empire in the fifth century nearly destroyed the British Church. Yet once the invading Anglo-Saxons had settled down and made England theirs, St. Aidan and other Celtic missionaries from the North, and

---

[1] The report of the Editorial Committee: "Our Vocation," *Anglican Congress 1954: Report of Proceedings* (Greenwich: The Seabury Press, 1954), page 195.

[2] More detailed treatment of the history of the Church of England will be found in Volume II of THE CHURCH'S TEACHING series, *Chapters in Church History* (Greenwich: The Seabury Press, 1950), pages 91-188.

St. Augustine and his companions from Rome gradually conquered the Saxon tribesmen for the Church of Christ. Near the end of the seventh century the Saxon Church embarked upon its four hundred years of development before the Norman conquest, a Church closely identified with the life of the Saxon people and ultimately strong enough to absorb the invading Danes who threatened the Saxon state in its later years.

The life of the Saxon Church was virtually as long as the time span that separates us from Christopher Columbus' voyages of discovery. During all those centuries few of the characteristics we associate with the later papal Church of the Middle Ages were present in England. Largely owing to the heritage of Celtic scholarship and devotion, English church life flowered in an intellectual and spiritual renaissance in the eighth century, the influence of which spread to the Continent in the days of Charlemagne and helped to bring Europe out of a dark age. English missionaries played a large part in the conversion of northern Europe and Scandinavia in these years. Furthermore, it was the unity of a single Church that helped to weld the divided Anglo-Saxon tribal states into a single English nation. The Church of England is, in fact, not only older than the kingdom, but also the chief architect of its existence. The foundations of a vigorous national Church were thus laid in the ancient Saxon heritage of Englishmen.

After the conquest of Saxon England by the Normans, Christianity in England became an integral part of the developing papal system in the West. Though the Saxon Church had shown great reverence towards Rome, the extension of the Pope's immediate and direct authority into every corner of the life of the Catholic Church did not take place until the Saxon period in English history had passed. The result was that the comparative isolation of the self-contained island people bred an independence of spirit that was never wholly extinguished during the Middle Ages. Like every other regional Church in medieval Europe, the spiritual loyalty of the Church of England to the papacy was seldom questioned, papal canon law was received and enforced in England, and the powers of the Pope were strongly exerted there as elsewhere. There was, however, intermittent resistance to the attempts of the Pope to assert temporal authority in medieval England; conflicts between Crown and Church were frequent.

A coherent national self-consciousness, owing something perhaps to the old Saxon spirit of independence, emerged in the last years of the Middle Ages, increasing the resentment Englishmen harbored towards the interference of the papacy in matters regarded as within the sphere of the jurisdiction of the Crown, the government, or the English Church itself. By the eve of the Reformation many Englishmen saw the papal power as an unwarranted and alien authority, attempting to exert itself over their own rights and customs. The exorbitant papal taxation was viewed as draining large sums of money from the incomes of England's Church to be expended on political designs of the Popes that were often hostile to the nation's interests on the Continent. Add to these factors the continued corruption in both the institutional and religious life of the papal Church; the Renaissance awakening in which men sought emancipation from the shackles of tradition, in the political and commercial world quite as much as in that of art and learning; the political changes in which the old medieval Christian Commonwealth was fragmented into the modern nation-states;

and the rise of the Christian New Learning by which men of the fifteenth and sixteenth centuries called the papal Church into judgment from the basis of their new knowledge of the Scriptures and the Early Church—and there in summary lay the chief causes of the Reformation.

The first phase of the English Reformation began when King Henry VIII was embroiled in a bitter quarrel with the Pope because of the latter's refusal to annul the royal marriage to Katherine of Aragon. The quarrel was the nation's as well as the king's. Englishmen believed the continued security and prosperity of the realm to be bound up with the peaceful accession of a Tudor prince, and unless means were found to permit Henry VIII a marriage that would give England a male heir to the throne the nation's future might be gravely imperiled by civil strife or foreign interference. Royal annulments were common, and the reluctance of the Pope to grant Henry VIII a sentence often handed down by the papacy was the occasion that brought the deeper and more serious forces of the Reformation into action.

The unique feature of the English Reformation was that at the outset it was not a religious revolution but a constitutional crisis. King and Parliament repudiated the papal authority in England, affirming the popular belief that the nation of old had been rightly free from alien interference. Only by a usurpation of power unsanctioned in Scripture, unknown in the early history of Christianity, and rejected by the great Eastern Orthodox Communion, had medieval Popes denied the English Church its independence and the English Crown its responsibilities for the spiritual welfare of the nation. Legislation in Parliament righted this, turning the Church *in* England into the Church *of* England, while the English Convocation of the Clergy solemnly declared that the Roman pontiff had no more authority in England than any other foreign bishop. But for all the increase of royal power in the life of the Church, Henry VIII had no intention of making any essential alteration in the Catholic religion of his country. His actions had made the Church in England a national Catholic Church, separated from the papacy, but, as the parliamentary statutes expressly made plain, with no intention to "decline or vary from . . . the ancient Catholic faith of Christendom." Thus from the beginning the English Church at the Reformation made no break with its own past. Continuity in the faith, order, and structure of the Church became the first clearly emerging mark of Anglicanism.

The second stage of the English Reformation occupied the twelve years of the reigns of Edward VI and Mary I. During the first half of this period Protestant influence was strong, and radical changes were attempted in the faith and practice of the English Church. Much influenced by the religious revolt of Luther, Calvin, and others on the Continent, the Edwardian reformers turned the church services into English, repudiated portions of the old canon law, abandoned a large number of Catholic customs and usages, placed a new emphasis on the Evangelical doctrines of Continental Protestantism, and tried to lead the Church of England along the religious paths followed in Germany and in Switzerland. But in fact a great many of the changes were both unpopular and due less to the honest zeal of the religious reformers than to the avarice and ambitions of the unscrupulous councillors who ruled in the name of Edward VI. A small class of prosperous merchants and landowners skillfully manipulated the forces of religious unrest to serve their designs to break the power of the Church and confiscate its wealth and endowments.

When the accession of Mary I put an unexpected end to this chaos, the six years following were those in which the Catholic Queen attempted to turn the clock back twenty-five years. Formal obedience to the papacy was restored, the Reformation changes swept away, and many of the leading reformers condemned to death or imprisonment. But Mary's reign, marked as it was by an alliance with the hated Spaniards and the unforgettable courage in which Englishmen went to the stake for their religious convictions, was a failure. The nation which had been reluctant to adopt the extremes of Edwardian Protestantism was equally repelled by Marian papalism. Out of the reign of Edward VI, however, came Archbishop Cranmer's *Book of Common Prayer,* to stand side by side with the English Bible which Henry VIII had authorized, twin foundation stones of future Anglicanism. The Prayer Book, with its translation of the historic liturgy of the Catholic Church into the language of the people, and its revision of the ancient services that purged them of erroneous medieval doctrines and restored their Scriptural character, was the chief legacy of this second phase of the English Reformation.

The third and crucial phase of reform in England was that during the long reign of Henry VIII's last surviving child, Queen Elizabeth I. The "Elizabethan Settlement," as it is called, determined the shape of emerging Anglicanism, and the unique marks of the Anglican tradition are the result of Elizabeth's judicious and statesmanlike settlement of the vexing religious controversy. Comprehension was the Queen's aim, a policy that was necessarily accompanied by a certain tolerance and forbearance unusual amid the passions of sixteenth-century religious conflict. A settlement was brought out of the experiences of the quarter-century past sufficiently coherent to be administered with firmness and vigor when necessary, yet broad and flexible enough to command the spiritual loyalty of virtually the entire nation. Conciliating her Catholic subjects, Elizabeth I was careful to preserve unbroken the institutional and spiritual continuity of the English Church with its own past. No break was allowed in the apostolic succession of English bishops, and everywhere the traditions of the past molded the minds of Anglicans. Furthermore, the Queen made it plain that the Crown's ecclesiastical supremacy was only that responsibility for the Church's welfare with which all Christian princes were charged; it did not permit her "to define, decide or determine any article or point of the Christian faith and religion, or to change any ancient ceremony of the Church from the form received and observed by the Catholic and Apostolic Church."

On the other hand, the gains of the Reformation were secured. The *Book of Common Prayer,* with such alterations as would remove the exclusively Protestant interpretations which the Edwardian reformers had tried to give some disputed doctrines, was established as the standard of faith and practice. The religious reorientation of the nation continued, and from a medieval piety narrowly centered upon the sacrifice of the Mass Englishmen were turned towards far wider spiritual horizons. Anglican piety gradually became thoroughly Scriptural, but Bible and Church were not set against each other. The appeal of the Church of England was to both Scripture and tradition—"the word of God and the primitive Church"—or, as the *Canons of 1571* put it, "to observe and believe that which is agreeable to the doctrine of the Old Testament and the New, and that which the Catholic fathers and ancient Bishops have gathered out of that doctrine." It was this grasp upon the centrality of the Scriptures within the continuing life of the Church that brought Anglicanism its precious freedom from the confining restraints of sixteenth-century Protestant dogma, bound its integrity inseparably with sound learning, and made it possible for later generations to perceive truth in more than one emphasis within the total Christian tradition.

Such was the settlement stoutly defended by Elizabeth I and her bishops against the onslaughts of a small group of obdurate papists on one hand and a zealous Puritan minority on the other. And during these years a whole generation of Englishmen grew up, bred within the comprehensive limits of the Elizabethan Church and nurtured upon the spirituality of the Prayer Book. What that generation embraced was a Christian tradition still recognizably continuous with the Catholic order England had known for centuries, now enriched and widened by the religious and intellectual challenges that came to men in the Reformation. Perhaps the uniquely distinctive feature of the whole movement of reform in the English Church was the achievement of a synthesis between the Christian elements in the Renaissance awakening and the truth that was preserved and transmitted through the medieval order. There Anglicanism finds its justification. If that synthesis has given rise to tensions in the post-Reformation history of Anglicanism, they are encouraging signs of the continued exploration of the whole truth which the Anglican tradition attempts to embrace.

Such was the Anglicanism that spread through the family of independent Churches which came into being as a result of the overseas expansion of the Church of England in modern times. Outside the British Isles the first of those Churches was our own Protestant Episcopal Church, whose life in the American colonies began almost simultaneously with the end of the Elizabethan era. Through the eighteenth and nineteenth centuries the Churches overseas grew, each gradually becoming independent of the mother Church yet linked together by the bonds of the same heritage of faith, order, and worship. Today they are still growing in strength and in numbers as the Anglican Communion bears witness in the world to its unique embodiment of the Christian tradition.

THE CHURCHES OF THE ANGLICAN COMMUNION

In the Anglican family of Churches today there are fourteen independent Churches or Provinces, varying greatly in size and strength, some of them closely associated with the Anglo-Saxon heritage of their members, others truly indigenous in lands of African, Indian, and other non-Western cultures. The racial and ethnic backgrounds of Anglicans today are as wide as the world scene itself.

Four Churches are located in the British Isles—the *Church of England,* with its two ecclesiastical provinces of Canterbury and York; the *Church in Wales,* the historic Church of the Cymric nation, consisting of the Welsh dioceses which were restored in 1920 to an autonomy that dates back to the ancient British Church of the third century; the *Church of Ireland,* like that in Wales, tracing its lineage through the centuries of Celtic Christianity, now a disestablished and self-governing Church made up of the two provinces of Armagh and Dublin; and the *Episcopal Church in Scotland,* a small body of Scottish Episcopalians descended from those who clung heroically to their traditions during the decades of persecution after 1689 when the established Church of Scotland became a presbyterian church. It was from the bishops of this Scottish Episcopal Church that our American Church received its first episcopal orders in the consecration of Samuel Seabury at Aberdeen in 1784.

Outside the British Isles the oldest Anglican Church is the Protestant Episcopal Church in the United States. Almost as old is the *Church of England in Canada* whose first diocese, Nova Scotia, was founded in 1787, partly under the stimulus of the large number of Anglicans among the American Loyalists who migrated to the Canadian maritime provinces at the close of the Revolutionary War. Charles Inglis, rector of Trinity Church, New York, for example, became the first Anglican bishop in Canada. Today the Canadian Church, with twenty-eight dioceses grouped into four ecclesiastical provinces, each with its archbishop, has an independent organization very similar to that of our own Episcopal Church.

The overseas expansion of the Church of England brought Anglican dioceses into being in all the former dominions of the British Empire, now separate members of the British Commonwealth of nations. In Australia the dioceses have been formed into the *Church of England in Australia and Tasmania,* more closely associated constitutionally with the mother Church of England than any of the other autonomous Anglican Churches. Like its neighbor, the *Church of the Province of New Zealand,* the Australian Church is an example of the transplanting of Anglicanism into an English colonial scene. The New Zealand Church, however, seizing the opportunities for evangelism presented by the Maori folk of New Zealand and the natives of the far-flung islands of Melanesia and Polynesia, has made itself the Church of thousands of primitive Pacific peoples.

The non-English character of some Churches of the Anglican Communion may be seen in the *Church of India, Pakistan, Burma and Ceylon* and, to a lesser degree, in the *Church of the Province of the West Indies,* both of which had their origins in the effort to keep the Church with Englishmen in their colonial migrations, but in which the subsequent progress of evangelizing native non-Christians has been so great as to give the Churches a truly indigenous appearance. This characteristic of some Anglican provinces, however, is most fully apparent in the two independent Churches in the Far East: the *Nippon Sei Ko Kwai* (the Holy Catholic Church of Japan) and the *Chung Hua Sheng Kung Hui* (the Holy Catholic Church in China), both of which have grown from dioceses that were at first missionary areas of the English, American, or Canadian Churches.

The extraordinary spread of Anglicanism through the continent of Africa has been largely owing to the activity of the famous missionary societies of the Church of England: the Society for the Propagation of the Gospel, the Church Missionary Society, and the Universities Mission to Central Africa. The chain of Anglican dioceses that stretches from Egypt down to the Cape of Good Hope, from Sierra Leone across to Mombasa, contains hundreds of native clergy and many thousands of African communicants. In Uganda, for example, there are nearly 150 native clergy and 97,500 communicants, while on the other side of the continent in Nigeria there are 75 African clergy and 55,000 confirmed members of the Church—and these are but two of the numerous areas of the Church's missionary work in Africa.[3]

Many of the African dioceses are under the jurisdiction of the Archbishop of Canterbury—missionary districts of the Church of England, we should call them—like other scattered Anglican dioceses in various parts of the world: Bermuda, Gibraltar, Iran, Singapore, Borneo, and South America. Two groups of dioceses, however, in different parts of the continent of Africa have united to form separate and self-governing Churches. These comprise the *Church of the Province of South Africa* and the *Church of the Province of West Africa.* In process of formation is still a third autonomous Church in Central Africa, and before many years the strong missions in East Africa will likely be brought together in yet another Anglican Province.

As might be expected, these different member Churches of the Anglican family show a wide variety within their essential unity. The freedom and flexibility that is part of their Anglican heritage has been fully explored in each local or national scene. In church government, for example, there is much variation, especially in the matter of lay participation. In the Convocation of the English Church the layman has no place, though he is admitted to a voice in many ecclesiastical affairs through the Church Asembly; in the American General Convention, on the other hand, lay representation in the House of Deputies is as great as that of the clergy. In some Anglican Churches bishops are elected by their diocesan conventions; in others there is a special electoral college for the selection of members of the episco-

[3] The Episcopal Church maintains the Missionary District of Liberia in West Africa. The Australian Church has supported the growth of the mission in Central Tanganyika.

pate; in England the continued establishment of the Church makes the nomination of bishops the responsibility of the Crown. Canon law likewise differs markedly among the Churches of the Anglican Communion, and most of the independent Churches have revised from time to time the Prayer Book in which their common heritage of faith and worship is enshrined.

Each Church makes its own particular contribution to the life and thought of the whole Communion, as has been evident in recent Lambeth Conferences of Anglican bishops and in the Anglican Congress of 1954. The day is long past when some of the older Anglican Churches regarded the newer bodies as "colonial" dioceses, out of whose life and experiences little could come of interest or value to the mother Churches. Today it is recognized on all sides that each member Church brings particular gifts to the whole Communion. The strong traditions of the Church of England and its vivid consciousness of the significance of a national Church, the scholarly contributions of Irish Anglicans, the unswerving loyalty of the Scottish Episcopalian minority to their religious heritage, the missionary fervour of the Africans, the conservatism of Canadian Anglicanism, the genius of American Episcopalians for effective organization of the Church's work, the reminder of Indian spirituality that the Church is called to holiness—such things, and there are many more of them, enrich the whole Anglican Communion and stretch the horizons of each member Church by the example of others.

ANGLICAN UNITY

The close fellowship that is maintained among the Churches of the Anglican Communion springs from a shared heritage of faith, church order, and ways of worship. Alike these Churches cling to the principle of the necessary continuity of the Church with its own past, chiefly maintained by the unbroken continuance of the apostolic ministry of bishops. Anglicans everywhere use the historic Creeds of undivided Christendom; they retain the ancient Sacraments as the central acts of worship in the life of individuals and of the Christian community. They find doctrine necessary for salvation only that which may be proved from the Scriptures through which we have access to the Word of God; they proclaim the Gospel of the redemption of all men in Jesus Christ alone.

Uniformity of belief concerning this common heritage of faith and order is not imposed upon Anglicans by any central ecclesiastical authority. Anglicanism inherits its view of authority from the earliest ages of Christianity. Ultimately it is the authority of God alone that challenges every man—that of the Eternal Father, the Incarnate Son, and the guiding and empowering Spirit, mediated through the ministry of the Word and the Sacraments. His authority comes to us through the Scriptures, constantly interpreted in the life of the Church; through the traditions of faith, order, and worship thus created; and through the very freedom in which man responds to truth, a sign of the continuing experience of the Holy Spirit among the faithful people in His Church. Such a view combines authority and freedom in a dynamic relationship that is characteristic of the New Testament and the mark of Catholic Christianity in the true sense of that term.

The chief external bond of Anglican unity is the *Book of Common Prayer* which embodies not only the ways of Anglican worship, but also the central traditions of doctrine and order that all the Churches share. While there are variations in Prayer Book rites in different parts of the Communion, in all essentials they remain the same. Unity of faith is experienced through unity in corporate worship. For example, however much may be unfamiliar to him, the American Episcopalian is spiritually at home in the worship of the Church of England, while the Anglican from India or Japan is no stranger at the altars of the American or Canadian Churches.

On other levels there are a number of agencies of unity and instruments of common action that strengthen the bonds of Anglicanism and assist its Churches to do their work together. Cycles of intercessory prayer bring the needs and remembrances of each Church into the prayer life of others; the journal *Pan-Anglican,* edited and published in America, increases the knowledge Anglican Churches have of the inner life of one another; and St. Augustine's College at Canterbury, a central house of studies for clergy and students from over the whole Communion, makes possible a continuous interchange of thought. By a multitude of other means, both formal and informal, Anglican fellowship is strengthened among the Churches: personal contacts among the bishops and clergy, exchanges of pulpits and parochial cures, visits of scholars and lecturers, education of students in the seminaries or theological colleges of other Churches, inter-Church consulting committees for the exploration of different aspects of their common work, the assumption by one Church of financial assistance to another—these means and many others are in constant use.

Two institutions have emerged out of the life of the world-wide Anglican Communion to play perhaps the chief role in shaping common thought and action among the Churches. The first is the *Lambeth Conference,* a gathering of Anglican bishops from all over the world held at Lambeth Palace, the residence of the Archbishop of Canterbury, every ten years, unless postponed by unusual circumstances. Since the first conference in 1867, these meetings of bishops have gradually assumed great importance in the life of the Communion. The Lambeth Conference is not a constitutional body, nor does it jeopardize in any way the independence of each Church. Its authority is simply that adhering to the common decisions of the Anglican episcopate. The assembled bishops each time publish an Encyclical Letter—a message to be read in all Anglican congregations—and a Report containing not only the resolutions of the bishops, but also the findings of committees which have studied carefully moral problems; ecumenical relations; the needs of Christian education and evangelism; various social, political, and economic issues on which the Church is called to speak; and other subjects of concern to Anglican Churches.

The other institution, similar in the scope of its interests but differing in that it includes representation of clerical and lay delegates equal to that of bishops, is the *Anglican Congress.* Only two such assemblies have been held, a tentative and experimental one in England in 1908 and the recent more effectively organized congress at Minneapolis in 1954. Like the Lambeth Conference, the second Anglican Congress has published a Report of Proceedings, containing addresses made before the delegates by a number of churchmen from different parts of the Communion, and a group of findings and resolutions upon many aspects of the subjects presented for discussion. The overwhelming success of the 1954 Congress in every respect has made it very likely that in the future such meetings of Anglican representatives will be held in the intervals between Lambeth Conferences. The American Episcopal Church, under whose auspices the recent congress was held, may well be proud of its initiative in making successful an institution which in years to come will undoubtedly play a decisive part in enabling the Anglican witness in Christendom to be more articulate and influential.

CHAPTER TWO

Anglicanism in Colonial America

THE HISTORY of the Protestant Episcopal Church as a self-governing member of the Anglican Communion begins with its organization as a Church independent of the mother Church of England during the years immediately following the American Revolution. But the history of its whole life stretches back for many years before that. Roughly three hundred and fifty years have elapsed since the first Anglican parishes were formed in the English settlements along the American coast. For approximately half that time the Anglican Church in America was a collection of overseas parishes that were part of the Church of England; during the other half it has been the separate and independent Protestant Episcopal Church. To try to understand the distinctive elements in the life of the Episcopal Church without exploring its colonial history would be as grave an omission as to begin the story of the American nation without regard to the long years of colonial development.

However great the constitutional changes that freed the Anglican congregations in the United States from English ecclesiastical control and united them into a group of new dioceses, within the inner life of the American parishes there was an unbroken spiritual continuity of faith and practice. "This Church," wrote the American leaders in 1789, "is far from intending to depart from the Church of England in any essential point of doctrine, discipline, or worship." It was with deep affection that our founding fathers acknowledged their spiritual loyalty to the mother Church, to which, they affirmed, "the Protestant Episcopal Church in these States is indebted, under God, for her first foundation and a long continuance of nursing care and protection." [1] That "first foundation" took place in 1607 and links the beginnings of the American Church with the early years of Stuart England.

THE VIRGINIA ESTABLISHMENT

The Church of England had barely emerged from the most critical period of the Reformation—Queen Elizabeth I had been dead only four years—when Anglicanism took permanent root on the shores of North America. England in 1607 was astir with activities that led to the diverse developments in her political and economic, religious and cultural life in this century. James I had embarked upon the long struggle of the Stuart monarchs with Puritans and Parliaments; Shakespeare had just finished a new play entitled *Macbeth;* scholars were hard at work on a new English translation of the Bible—our familiar *King James Version* —that would have a profound effect upon the piety and the language of English-speaking peoples. In the early spring of that year a little company of Englishmen settled at Jamestown in Virginia. There, wrote Captain John Smith, "we did hang an awning (which is an old sail) to three or four trees . . . till we cut planks, our pulpit a bar of wood nailed to two neighboring trees. This was our church till we built a homely thing like a barn . . . yet we had daily Common

[1] See the Preface to the *Book of Common Prayer.*

Prayer morning and evening, every Sunday two sermons, and every three months the Holy Communion." Anglicanism, having barely emerged from its formative period during which the first generation of Elizabethans had been reared in the piety of the *Book of Common Prayer,* was thus carried at once across the seas to begin the long association of the Episcopal Church with American life.

The ministrations of Robert Hunt, chaplain to the Virginia colonists, were not the first Prayer Book services in North America. Almost simultaneously with the settlement in Virginia, Anglican worship was conducted on Monhegan Island off the coast of Maine for the hardy folk temporarily settled there by Sir Fernando Gorges and Chief Justice Popham. A few years before, the shores of Buzzard's Bay were the scenes of similar ministrations to Gosnold's company, and still earlier were the religious activities in the ill-fated Roanoke Colony. Anglican chaplains accompanying the Elizabethan adventures celebrated the Holy Communion for the men of Humphrey Gilbert's expedition in Newfoundland in 1582, for Francis Drake's company on the California coast in 1579, and for Martin Frobisher's people on Kodlunarn off Baffin Land in 1578. But all these were isolated instances of Anglican worship. They are of more antiquarian interest than historical significance. The Virginia colony became the first permanent Anglican settlement, and in the crude shelter that was their chapel there was planted in America the tradition which is embodied today in every parish of the Episcopal Church.

The Virginia colony was a transplantation to the American wilderness of all that was familiar to the settlers at home. As far as frontier conditions permitted, English institutions were simply carried across the ocean. The Virginia

Church, therefore, was established in 1619 by the colonists on the same basis as it existed in the mother country, though inevitably there were modifications imposed by the circumstances of colonial life. From the early injunctions issued for the settlers—that "the Word and service of God be preached, planted, and used . . . according to the rites and doctrines of the Church of England"—down through the years of government first by the Virginia Company and later under royal governors, Anglicanism was in a privileged position, "established" by law. The geographical parishes of the Church were the units of colonial civil administration, instead of the townships familiar in New England; the Church and its clergy were supported partly by grants of farm land—"glebe," as it was called—and the imposition of a tithe or tax on the staple crop, tobacco, its payment enforced by law.

Ecclesiastical supervision of the Virginia clergy was eventually entrusted to the Bishop of London. It was an unsatisfactory arrangement from every point of view, and in the end proved disastrous to the Church. Though successive Bishops of London, especially in the eighteenth century, made earnest attempts from time to time to regulate the religious affairs of the Virginia colony, particularly in the matter of providing zealous and devoted ministers and encouraging the enforcement of ecclesiastical discipline, no effective oversight could be exercised by an authority three thousand miles distant and wholly unfamiliar with the problems of frontier life. Bishops attempted to ease this situation by dispatching deputies—"commissaries"—to America who would act for them in nearly all functions save those of administering Confirmation and ordaining men to the ministry. But few commissaries found it possible to enforce discipline without the coercive power of canon law, and much of their time was spent warning and exhorting the clergy and quarreling with the local civil authorities. Commissary Blair in Virginia was perhaps the best known deputy there in the whole colonial period, but today he is remembered less for any outstanding success in his attempts to reinvigorate church life than for his notable achievement in the foundation of William and Mary College.

One important result of the close connection between the Church and the colonial government in Virginia was the large measure of control of church affairs that fell into the hands of the governor. There being no bishop, at the outset he appointed clergymen to vacancies or instituted those who were selected and presented by the vestries. Moreover, in the absence of church courts the civil authorities necessarily assumed legal and juridical control over some areas of church life. Pioneer conditions inevitably stimulated the increase of lay leadership and responsibility in the Church, and gradually the vestries came to hold powers in respect to appointments, properties, and church government that were enormously increased over those of the old churchwardens in England.

PURITAN NEW ENGLAND

In the northern colonies of New England, and especially in Massachusetts, the Church faced an opposition unknown elsewhere in America. The settlers in New England brought with them a fanatical dislike of the established Church of the mother country. Indeed, large numbers of them came across the Atlantic solely to find freedom to pattern their religious and community life after the models of Calvinist Geneva or the Reformation cities of the Rhineland and the Low Countries. The Pilgrims who landed at Plymouth were Separatists, reckoning the English Church so incompletely reformed as to be no true Church at all. The settlers in the Massachusetts Bay Colony were Puritans, eager to refashion the Anglican settlement along lines they believed to be prescribed in the Scriptural plan for the Church. Despite their own differences, Puritans and Pilgrims alike detested the Prayer Book, rejected government by bishops, and deplored the evident continuity of the Church of England with the Church of the Middle Ages. They organized their communities on congregational principles and "established" their Church with even greater intolerance than that about which they had complained at home. No dissent was allowed by people who themselves had migrated to find spiritual freedom.

The establishment and growth of Anglican parishes in Massachusetts was, therefore, necessarily slow. Clergy who used the liturgy or defended the principles of the Church of England were at first expelled from the settlements. Not until after 1688 did some measure of toleration, enforced by the royal government, permit the erection of King's Chapel in Boston. Even then, Puritan preachers scornfully labeled it a "High Place" with its "Priests of Baal," while Increase Mather roundly declared Anglican worship to be papistical and idolatrous. As a result of this early Puritan opposition, it was not until the first years of the eighteenth century that Anglicans came to enjoy any real freedom or occupy a significant place in the life of the Massachusetts colony. By that time Puritan Congregationalism, with its singular adaptability to the conditions of pioneer life, was deeply entrenched in the northern area. Anglican parishes were ultimately formed there in all the chief centers, but in contrast to Virginia they were never the churches of the bulk of the population. Their membership was often regarded as that of folk of wealth and quality, those later suspected of loyalty to the Crown during the struggle for independence.

The situation in New Hampshire and Maine—the latter a frontier region annexed to the Massachusetts colony—was very similar. In Rhode Island, however, where the principles of religious liberty and the separation of Church and State were the guiding convictions of its founders, Anglican parishes were formed without opposition in the beginning of the eighteenth century. Their growth was rapid, and within a few decades Newport, Bristol, Providence, Warwick, and Narragansett all had flourishing churches.

The Connecticut colony, founded by settlers from Massachusetts, was originally as hostile to the Church of England as the first Puritans had been. But after toleration was granted in 1708, the slow growth of Anglican parishes was abruptly accelerated by the famous incident of the "Yale Converts." In 1722, to the dismay of the Congregational leaders, Timothy Cutler, President of Yale College, Daniel Brown, an instructor, and five other well-known ministers openly proclaimed their doubts concerning the validity of their orders and their uneasiness at not being in "visible communion with an Episcopal Church." Four of the converts, including Cutler and Samuel Johnson (later to be the first President of King's College in New York), soon left for England to seek episcopal ordination. Through their study of the writings of the great Anglican divines the flavor of seventeenth-century high churchmanship was imparted to a newly stimulated Anglican Church in Connecticut. Its increase in the colony was steady. By 1742 there were fourteen parishes; at the outbreak of the Revolution there were forty churches and twenty resident clergymen. Such was the strength of colonial Anglicanism in Connecticut that it was destined to play a leading and significant part in the organization of the independent Episcopal Church.

THE OTHER COLONIES

In South Carolina the Church of England was established and public support provided for its clergy and buildings, though toleration was afforded to dissenters to worship as they pleased. The colony was never as much dominated by Anglicanism as Virginia; Protestant congregations numbered among their members over half the population, and were particularly strong in the western frontier areas. In North Carolina, with its fewer settled communities, the Church was slow to gain a foothold. Its technical establishment was not effectively implemented, and Anglicans remained a minority group among the Baptists, Quakers, and Presbyterians. A similar situation existed in Georgia, the other southern colony, where as late as 1769 there were only two Anglican churches, at Savannah and Augusta.

In the Middle Atlantic areas, on the other hand, the Church was stronger. While not numerous throughout Pennsylvania and Delaware, Anglicans nevertheless formed an influential group in the larger towns of both colonies. Christ Church, Philadelphia, destined to become the leading parish of the area, was founded in 1695. In the neighboring colony of Maryland a large amount of religious liberty, as in Pennsylvania, was permitted by the proprietors, though chiefly in order that Roman Catholics might enjoy freedom of worship. Anglican parishes were established side by side with the churches of other denominations. When, however, in the last years of the seventeenth century, the proprietary government of the Roman Catholic Calverts was overthrown by the Protestant majority of the settlers and Maryland became a royal colony, the local assembly established the Church of England by law. Following the Virginia pattern, the province was divided into parishes, vestries were organized, and the support of the clergy was provided by a tobacco tithe. The colonial legislature, under the influence of a zealous Anglican royal governor, actually attempted to make Prayer Book worship compulsory for all the people, but Parliament rejected this action as contrary to England's Toleration Act of 1689 which allowed dissenters to have their own places of worship. Never popular, the Church establishment in Maryland was more of a hindrance than a help to the spread of Anglicanism. The formation of congregations was slow during the eighteenth century, and the Church in Maryland did not rise to the dominating position occupied by its adjacent neighbor in Virginia.

New York and New Jersey offer the best examples of Anglican strength in the middle colonies. The early Dutch regime in the former had attempted to exclude all forms of church life except that of the Dutch Reformed Church, but the people of New Netherland proved more tolerant than their government. As a result, by 1664, when the Dutch territories became the English colony of New York, large numbers of the settlers held different religious views. In 1693, however, the New York colonial assembly passed an act creating a limited establishment of the Church of England. "Sufficient Protestant Ministers," a phrase interpreted by the governors to mean Anglican clergymen, were to be supported in the counties of New York, Richmond, Westchester, and Queens. No establishment was erected in Kings,

Dutchess, Orange, Albany, or Suffolk counties, where the population was chiefly made up of the Dutch Reformed or English dissenters. The first Anglican parish to be organized was that of Trinity Church, New York, four years later.

The early years of the eighteenth century witnessed a steady growth of Church of England congregations in the colony. Trinity Church, enriched by large grants of land which were later to prove immensely valuable, began the establishment of its famous chapels, while new parishes came into existence in Westchester and on Staten Island, at Rye, Hempstead, and other places in the counties of the establishment, as well as among the Hudson River settlements. To the credit of the Anglicans of New York is the foundation of King's College, chartered in 1754, which remained under the control of churchmen until after the Revolution. Even today its successor, Columbia University, retains some vestiges of the traditional association with the Episcopal Church.

In New Jersey the Anglican Church appeared late, chiefly because the northern area of the colony had been under strong Dutch and Puritan influences, while the southwestern section was subject to control by the Quakers. In the first quarter of the eighteenth century beginnings were made at Burlington, Amboy, Elizabeth, and some other centers, and within a few decades Anglican congregations were spread to all the chief towns. Much of the increasing strength of Anglicanism here in the years just before the Revolutionary War was owing to the devoted efforts of missionaries sent out from England by the Society for the Propagation of the Gospel—indeed, in other colonies as well as in New Jersey the work of the Society's clergymen forms one of the most important chapters in the history of Colonial Anglicanism.

THE VENERABLE SOCIETY

The "Venerable Society," or, as it is commonly called, the "S.P.G.," was founded in England in 1701, largely as a result of the representations of a zealous clergyman, Thomas Bray, who after an extended visit to the colonies pressed for the provision and support of more clergy in America. His interest in establishing theological and classical libraries for the training of the clergy and the religious and cultural improvement of the people of the colonies matured in the formation of the *Society for the Promotion of Christian Knowledge;* his concern for the support of the Church and the maintenance of clergymen in places where no colonial establishment provided for them bore fruit in the *Society for the Propagation of the Gospel.*

The interests of both societies were broader than merely the financial support of Anglican ministers or the dissemination of religious literature. Clergy, catechists, and teachers were sent out to the West Indies and other British colonies as well as to North America, schools and colleges were started, and libraries were provided, both for the use of the clergy and for the enrichment of educational institutions. Harvard College, for example, was twice the recipient of "goodly gifts" of books from the S.P.G., while grants were also made to Yale. Dean Berkeley's gift to the latter college, largely in response to the entreaty of Samuel Johnson, a "Yale Convert" and an S.P.G. missionary in Connecticut, was once described as "the best collection of books which had ever been brought at one time to America." The major objective of the societies founded by Dr. Bray and his associates was to fill the intellectual and spiritual needs in the American colonies on the broadest possible scale.

More than three hundred and fifty S.P.G. missionaries, on the whole a disciplined body of educated and devoted Anglican priests, labored in America from 1701 to 1776, constantly under the direction of the Society at home, establishing missions, maturing them into self-supporting parishes, and building the Anglican tradition firmly into American religious life. Their fields of work were largely in the areas where no colonial establishment of the Church provided its support—in the New England provinces, parts of New York, New Jersey, and the middle colonies, and occasionally in the far South. While it is probably true to say that continuous support by the S.P.G. sustained the life of the Anglican Church in many areas of the colonies where Anglicans were in a minority, the ultimate accomplishment was more than merely keeping the Church alive. The real success of the Society's missionaries is attested by the loyalty and devotion in which Episcopalians preserved their church life despite the withdrawal of all S.P.G. support after the American Revolution.

COLONIAL CHURCH LIFE

Anglican church life in the American colonies reflected many of the patterns in the eighteenth century Church of England. Public worship, for example, was marked by a restraint and simplicity that often approximated a formalism we should regard today as depressingly barren. The parson and his clerk conducted the services from their desks below the pulpit with little participation on the part of the congregation. Hymns were few; metrical psalms were monotonously sung by singers placed in a gallery or other seats near the rear of the church. The center of attention was usually the pulpit, where the hourglass stood to time the long sermons. Morning Prayer, the Litany, and Ante-Communion—the Communion Service to the Creed—was the normal form of Sunday morning worship, while the Holy Communion itself was celebrated once a quarter, or in some places, every month. Congregations were largely drawn from the upper classes of colonial society, lawyers, doctors and other professional men, prosperous landowners and merchants, government and military officials. Naturally the more flourishing Anglican parishes were in the cities and larger towns where these groups formed a substantial part of the population.

To some degree the gradual growth of the Colonial Church and its importance in the chief centers is reflected in the church buildings. While most seventeenth century structures have perished or been extensively rebuilt, a few examples of the earliest Anglican architecture remain, notably the Tower at Jamestown, St. Luke's Church, Isle of Wight, both in Virginia, and Trinity Church, Dortchester County, Maryland. A large number of small churches, unprepossessing on the outside save in their proportions, but attractive in their interior line and simplicity, still remain to testify to the relative prosperity of the Church in the eighteenth century. Pohick Church, Virginia, St. Michael's in Marblehead, Massachusetts, and St. Paul's, Wickford, Rhode Island, are typical examples of churches that were numerous along the Atlantic seaboard. Far more impressive are the "great churches" of Colonial Anglicanism with their spacious proportions and paneled interiors, the wide box pews and high pulpits—often "three-deckers," the ample graceful galleries and pleasing white woodwork, relieved by the glint of brass and crystal chandeliers, the blazoned colors of the Royal Arms, and the black and gold accents of the

Ten Commandments and the Lord's Prayer painted over the Communion table. Some of these large churches, like Christ Church, Philadelphia, or St. Paul's Chapel, New York, show marked baroque influences; others, like Trinity Church at Newport, Rhode Island, or Christ Church ("Old North") in Boston, betray suggestions of Wren design, especially in their tall spires. Together with such others as Bruton Parish Church, Williamsburg, Christ Church, Alexandria, St. Michael's, Charleston, King's Chapel, Boston, and St. Peter's, Philadelphia, they give evidence of the close identification of Anglicanism with the educated and prosperous people of the chief towns.

Yet however much American Anglicanism mirrored features of the Church of England at home, the colonial circumstances imposed a number of modifications upon the patterns of church life and exercised a strong influence upon the thinking of church members. Most striking, perhaps, was the fact that the Colonial Church lacked almost all the organization now familiar to Episcopalians. The parishes were not even grouped together into dioceses. On the contrary, each church was virtually an independent congregation, and elements of local congregational government were strong. Except for the supervision exercised by the S.P.G. over missions and parishes that received its support, the seat of all ecclesiastical authority was across the Atlantic in London. Technically the American churches were under the jurisdiction of the Bishop of London; practically this meant an authority too far distant to be of any assistance in the growth and development of the Church. The Bishop's commissaries could not provide the kind of oversight, ministration, and leadership that is a bishop's function. Despite all efforts made to remedy this situation, both on the part of earnest Anglicans in the colonies and devoted S.P.G. missionaries, or by many farsighted English bishops, direct episcopal care was never provided for the colonial parishes. No bishop was sent to America; no dioceses were organized. Strong opposition from dissenters here and in England, fears that the coming of bishops might bring the imposition of a State Church, the inability of most men on both sides of the Atlantic to conceive the episcopal office in any other terms than those familiar in eighteenth-century England—these and other factors combined to frustrate every attempt made to send out bishops and organize the isolated and separate congregations into dioceses.

Crippling as it was to the growth and advance of the Church, the absence of bishops throws into sharp relief the earnest and stubborn loyalty with which the American Anglicans maintained their Church. For more than a century and a half the Colonial Church clung tenaciously to its hold in American life, its native American clergy forced to undertake the costly and hazardous journey to England for ordination, its people denied Confirmation, its evangelism retarded by the lack of co-ordinated effort and the vision that episcopal leadership provides—indeed, the wonder is that the Anglican Church in the colonies was not only able to survive, but actually to extend itself slowly but surely in the face of these difficulties.

In this situation a large measure of local independence and initiative was bred in the parishes. The laity through the parochial vestries came to occupy an essential and significant place in church government, and many of the elements which give the Protestant Episcopal Church its democratic and constitutional character among Anglican Churches today are owing to the circumstances of colonial and pioneer life in the early American scene.

Equally important was the influence exercised upon American Anglicans by the religious atmosphere that surrounded them. America became a haven for the free-thinking and radical elements in Protestant Christianity, people who were denied freedom to believe as they would, not only by the Roman Catholic states, but also by the more conservative Reformation Churches of Protestant countries. Both Lutheranism and the Reformed Church (Presbyterian or Calvinist), where dominant or established in Europe, refused to tolerate radical religious minorities except under severe disabilities, and the immigrants who poured into the colonies in the eighteenth century were largely non-English—Germans, Huguenots, and Scotch-Irish. They brought with them their numerous religious loyalties, in some cases shortly to be abandoned under the strain of pioneer conditions, in others soon to be exchanged for the newest sectarian allegiance offered by itinerant preachers. At the same time, the prevailing rationalism among educated people in the colonies loosened the hold that orthodox Christianity had maintained, both in Puritan New England and in Anglican Virginia. Everywhere men sat lightly to the strong religious convictions of their grandfathers, many of them finally drifting into the ranks of the unchurched thousands who formed such a large part of the population during the last decades before the American Revolution. Repeated revivalist movements stirred masses of people for a short time, but the lasting result of these popular revivals was generally a leveling social influence, the wider acceptance of social and political equality as a religious principle rather than any significant spiritual and moral reinvigoration of the older Churches.

Out of this chaotic scene the typical American of the Revolutionary era began to emerge as a self-reliant individualist, far more readily drawn to a Church conceived as a voluntary and local association of like-minded believers, where social equality and individual initiative were the virtues inseparable from successful life in the land of promise in the wilderness. Deeds, not creeds, were important; a man's religion was his private concern. Inevitably American Anglicans were affected by these currents of thought, as well as by the thinly disguised Deism characteristic of the time. On one hand they frequently suffered the undisguised hostility of the peoples of non-English origin; on the other they themselves absorbed more than a little of the typical individualistic American spirit.

REVOLUTION AND INDEPENDENCE

The American Revolution plunged the Colonial Church into a crisis that rapidly became sheer disaster. Thousands of American Loyalists—"Tories," as they were called—conscientiously believed that the colonies should remain in union with the mother country, and for this conviction they suffered indignities, deprivations, and severe persecution at the hands of earnest Patriots. In the northern colonies where many of the Loyalists were Anglicans, their flight to Canada and other British dominions not only cost American civic life a large number of its ablest and most prosperous citizens, but also deprived the Anglican congregations of the greater number of their leading members. Parishes were completely disorganized. Acute financial distress resulted from the destruction of church property and the necessary withdrawal of funds from the S.P.G.

The sufferings of the clergy were especially severe. The majority of them outside the South were Loyalists, a result of their political conservatism and, in some cases, their English birth and education. Many in the North were missionaries of the S.P.G., and for most of these men their ordination oath of allegiance to the Crown was an insuperable obstacle to their support of the cause of independence. Reviled as Tories, branded as traitors by the newssheets and broadsides that stirred up popular indignation and mob violence against them, repudiated by many of the laity by whom the problem of conscientious loyalty was not so keenly felt, the Anglican clergy were treated with a cruel harshness that forms one of the least attractive chapters in American history. Mistreated, their property confiscated, their churches wrecked, they were silenced, imprisoned, and banished. Many of them accompanied the Loyalists to the Canadian maritime provinces or to the West Indies.

In the central and southern colonies the financial distress was almost equally great, for everywhere the civil establishments guaranteeing the support of the Church were terminated by the newly independent states. But in these areas the great majority of both the laity and the clergy were in sympathy with the Patriot cause. The clergy interpreted their oath as one to maintain not necessarily the Crown, but the duly constituted civil authority. This was now embodied in the provisional governments of the former colonies and in the Continental Congress. The largest section of Anglicanism south of New York, therefore, though suffering reverses and laboring under the handicap of suspicion of disloyalty, retained some semblance of order through the years of the Revolutionary War.

It was from this area that the first impetus towards reorganization came at the conclusion of the strife. While in each new state the Anglican congregations embarked on the task of finding paths by which they could be formed into a state association or, as we should say, a diocese, it was from William White, rector of Christ Church, Philadelphia, that there came the first proposals for a federal or national Church. He advocated the creation of a union or federation of the separate Churches existing in each of the former colonies, along the lines of confederation that were being explored by American statesmen to find a basis for the political union of the independent states into a single nation. White's wisdom and energy launched the American parishes upon a bold experiment—the formation of a free and independent Anglican Church, the first of its kind outside the British Isles, and one that was destined to serve as a model for the other autonomous Churches of the Anglican Communion that were later to come into being. It was at this point of courageous experiment that the local initiative and sense of responsibility which had developed under the conditions of colonial life played its part in bringing the movement to a successful conclusion.

Meanwhile in Connecticut plans were made to obtain the episcopate, a step that appeared imperative to the clergy there. They felt, and rightly, that the presence of a bishop was primary to the continuation of Anglican church life. However remote, the Bishop of London and his brother bishops in England had provided the essential episcopal background to Colonial Anglicanism. But the anomaly of an Episcopal Church without bishops could not be long maintained. Consequently, Samuel Seabury, a Connecticut-born clergyman and graduate of Yale College, a former Loyalist who had been driven from his parish and served with the

King's forces as a chaplain, was chosen bishop and sent to England to seek consecration. Though Seabury was courteously received, the existing ecclesiastical laws prevented the Archbishop of Canterbury from consecrating a man who was no longer able to take the oaths of supremacy and allegiance. Seabury turned then to the bishops of the Scottish Episcopal Church, successors to those who nearly a century before had refused their oath to William III at the time when James II was forced into exile. They belonged to a small but free Episcopal Church which had found its spiritual strength and integrity through years of bitter persecution. No legal barrier prevented the Scotch bishops from extending the episcopate to America, and on November 14, 1784, in a little chapel in Aberdeen, Seabury was consecrated by Bishops Kilgour, Petrie, and Skinner. By the summer of 1785 he was back in the Connecticut Church, and for the first time Anglican ordinations were held in America.

During Seabury's absence, the efforts of White and William Smith of Maryland to bring the separate Churches in each state into a single national Episcopal Church had made some progress. Following a conference in New Brunswick, New Jersey, a meeting widely representative of the state Churches was held in New York in October, 1784. Adopting a declaration of principles that was later embodied in the Church's constitution, the delegates at New York summoned a general or national convention of the Protestant Episcopal Church to meet at Philadelphia in 1785.[2]

[2] The name "Protestant Episcopal" had been officially adopted by the Church in Maryland at a conference in 1780. The phrase had been previously in use to describe the position of the Church of England—"Protestant" to affirm its adherence to Anglican Reformation principles and distinguish it from Roman Catholicism; "Episcopal" to affirm its traditional church order and mark it off from Protestantism of the Reformed or sectarian types.

STEPS TOWARDS A NATIONAL CHURCH

It was at once evident at the convention in 1785 that the unity of the Churches in the different states was the chief problem. No delegates came to this meeting from New England, North Carolina, or Georgia. In the latter states the Church was apparently too weak to respond; in the former, Connecticut churchmen refused to attend a convention that had made no provision for the presidency of a bishop, and Massachusetts Episcopalians either shared their view or found the distance too great to travel. Yet the group that met in Philadelphia took the first steps towards completing the work begun by William White. Committees were appointed to draft a constitution for the federation of the Churches in the states, and to revise the *Book of Common Prayer*. The convention presented a memorial to the English archbishops and bishops requesting them to confer episcopal orders upon such men as were chosen bishops by the conventions in each state.

The English bishops responded to the request by securing the passage of an act in Parliament allowing them to consecrate men without requiring the oaths of loyalty and canonical obedience imposed upon English candidates for consecration. But before consenting to perform such consecrations, the English bishops made known their strong objections to the revisions that were proposed for the new American Prayer Book and the very restricted position that was given to bishops in the Church's new Constitution. Some alterations in the English Prayer Book of 1662 which had been in use in the colonies were, of course, necessary—such as the conversion of the old prayers for the King into supplications for the civil magistrates of the states. Others, such as alterations in phraseology that removed obsolete words and the addition of new occasional prayers, were desirable. But the English churchmen feared that proposals to omit the Athanasian and Nicene Creeds, to make permissive the use of the sign of the cross in Baptism, and to remove from that service all expressions of baptismal regeneration—as well as other less important changes—were such as would come close to a departure from the Anglican tradition. In reply to their objections a convention held in 1786 restored most of traditional usages and material which had been omitted from "The Proposed Book," an action made easier by the fact that the proposals were already thoroughly unpopular among American churchmen. No barrier now stood in the way of further extension of the episcopate, and on February 4, 1787, William White of Pennsylvania and Samuel Provoost of New York were consecrated in Lambeth Chapel by the Archbishop of Canterbury, the Bishop of Bath and Wells, and the Bishop of Peterborough.

The unity of American Episcopalians was, however, still impeded by serious disagreements among church people in different areas. The high churchmen of New England, particularly in Connecticut, looked with some distrust upon their brethren in the southern Churches, partly because of the sweeping doctrinal modifications that had characterized "The Proposed Book," and partly because of the large share given to the laity in the councils and government of the Church there. On the other hand, many Episcopalians outside New England viewed with suspicion the prelatical pomp they imagined to surround the episcopal office in Connecticut. Personal prejudices and ignorance complicated these uneasy relationships. Bishop Provoost of New York, for example, who had been a vigorous champion of independence during the Revolution, detested all Tories in general and Bishop Seabury in particular, refusing to have any dealing with him whatsoever. Furthermore, others shared Provoost's groundless suspicion that Seabury's episcopal orders, derived as they were from the Scottish bishops, were irregular if not invalid. In these circumstances the decisive convention was that which met in Philadelphia in 1789. There in a series of sessions held from the end of July to the middle of October, unity was at last found, and the bold experiment of the formation of an independent Anglican Church was carried to a successful conclusion.

THE CONVENTION OF 1789

The famous General Convention of 1789 cleared away the ignorance, suspicion, and prejudice that stood in the way of the union of the Churches in the different states into a single national Episcopal Church. A unanimous resolution affirming the validity of Seabury's consecration won the adherence of New Englanders, while the recognition of the separate functions of both the episcopate and the lay order in the government of the Church brought together those who feared on one hand an authoritarian prelacy, or on the other, the submergence of traditional episcopal powers in a church order largely shaped out of presbyterian and congregational elements. The Convention of 1789 adopted a *Constitution,* agreed upon and ratified a body of *Canons,* and published an American *Book of Common Prayer.* These became the foundation documents in the structure and life of the new national Church.

The Constitution of 1789 provided for a General Convention that would be representative of the Church in the various states, for the participation of lay deputies therein, for the election and jurisdiction of bishops, for the admission of an Episcopal Church in any state to union with the national Church, for the education, ordination, and discipline of the clergy, and for the use of the new Prayer Book. These constitutional provisions were amplified and extended in the seventeen canons that formed the first enactments of canon law in the American Church.[3]

The Prayer Book adopted in 1789, though containing no departure from essential Anglican doctrine, discipline, or principles of worship, was nevertheless a thorough revision of the English 1662 Book. The "State Prayers" were altered, liturgical language was modernized, and obsolete words omitted; the Athanasian Creed was dropped from use; the lesser saints' days were eliminated from the Calendar; the form of Absolution in the office for the Visitation of the Sick was abandoned; several changes were made in Morning and Evening Prayer and in some of the Occasional Offices; and new prayers or Forms of Prayer were added.

The chief change, however, was that made in the Communion Service. In place of the central Consecration Prayer of the Holy Communion in the English *Book of Common Prayer,* the American liturgy employed the form generally used in the Scottish Episcopal Church, a prayer very close to that in Archbishop Cranmer's first Prayer Book of 1549. This change was owing both to the intrinsic merit of the Scottish Communion Office and also to the influence, among others, of Bishop Seabury who, faithful to an agreement with his Scottish consecrators, had used the prayer in the *Order for the Holy Communion,* issued in 1786 for use in his diocese. The change greatly enhanced the beauty and

[3] The Constitution and canon law of the Episcopal Church are discussed in Chapter IV.

enriched the meaning of the liturgy, bringing into the American Communion Service not only the western Latin tradition through the 1549 Prayer Book, but also such elements of Eastern Orthodox liturgies as had been incorporated into the Scottish revision.[4]

With these enactments of the 1789 Convention the federation of state Churches in a single American Episcopal Church was accomplished. Within a few years local organization was completed in nearly all the dioceses and bishops consecrated for most of them.[5] The newly independent Church of the Anglican Communion embarked upon its autonomous life as the Protestant Episcopal Church.

---

[4] The American *Book of Common Prayer* was again revised in 1892 and in 1928. For a more detailed discussion of the Prayer Book of 1789 and its subsequent revisions see Volume IV of this series, *The Worship of the Church* (Greenwich: The Seabury Press, 1952), pages 67-94; and *Chapters in Church History*, pages 167-176, 224-225.

[5] James Madison was consecrated for Virginia by the English bishops in 1790, and the four American bishops then consecrated Thomas Claggett for Maryland in 1792. Three years later Robert Smith was made Bishop of South Carolina, and in 1797 Edward Bass was consecrated for Massachusetts. Rhode Island temporarily received the episcopal care of Bishops Seabury and Bass, later joining New Hampshire and Vermont in the short-lived Eastern Diocese; Delaware, New Jersey, and North Carolina for some years received the episcopal ministrations of bishops in adjoining areas; Georgia received its first bishop in 1841.

CHAPTER THREE

The Protestant Episcopal Church

FOR TWENTY years after the Convention of 1789 the Episcopal Church, its strength seemingly spent by the tremendous effort of reorganization, lapsed into lethargy and inaction. Spiritual vitality was at a low ebb in the Church; economic distress was acute. With the loss of the former S.P.G. revenues in the North and the disendowment of the colonial establishments in the South, the long and painful process of educating Episcopalians to support their Church by voluntary offerings was begun. Crippled by the loss of potential lay leaders among the emigrating Loyalists and hampered by a severe shortage of clergy, the Church was slow to recover from the disastrous effects of the recent war.

Nor were the times propitious for the Church's recovery and expansion. A strong social and political restlessness, combined with severe economic depression in some areas, was the legacy of the Revolution. These decades witnessed a clash between social classes in America, the conservative Federalists fearful of the radical influences that spread from the French Revolution, their republican or Jacobin opponents welcoming every unorthodox opinion, both political and religious. Deism was a popular creed among the educated; Tom Paine's *The Age of Reason* was avidly read on all sides. In most of the Churches there was a sharp decline of spiritual influence and strength. Moreover, the general insecurity was increased by the westward movement of large numbers of people from the seaboard states. The call of the frontier was strong, and the vast reaches of territory beyond the Alleghenies beckoned alluringly to the pioneer spirit in the American citizenry. What was to become one of the greatest migrations of people in modern history was already under way, temporarily disrupting and impoverishing the older communities in the East.

The Church during these two decades received little or no inspired leadership from its first bishops. William White, a saintly scholar, was not an aggressive figure, while Samuel Seabury, vigorous enough, died in 1796. Bishop Provoost showed little enthusiasm for Church affairs in New York, resigning in 1801 to occupy himself with botanical studies. Claggett of Maryland discovered the diocese in so deplorable a condition, its churches neglected, its clergy unable to be supported, that he despaired of accomplishing anything at all. Bishop Madison of Virginia did not even try. After one visitation of his congregations, he devoted himself entirely to his presidential duties at William and Mary College.

Reprehensible though we may consider the inactivity of these churchmen, it must be remembered that they and their immediate successors—Edward Bass in Massachusetts, Benjamin Moore in New York, Abraham Jarvis in Connecticut, and others—had to learn how to exercise the episcopal office with which they were clothed. We sometimes judge them harshly because we now look back upon the lost opportunities with full knowledge of the crucial role of episcopal leadership in the reinvigoration of the Church's life. There were no models before these first bishops of an episcopate fully and effectively exercised under the conditions of

American life. They were all rectors of parishes—necessarily so to ensure their support—and their duties as bishops often seemed to them to be limited to ordinations and occasional services of Confirmation. Indeed, one diocesan convention resolved that "the duty and office of a bishop differs in nothing from that of other priests, except in the power of ordination and confirmation and the right of presidency in ecclesiastical synods." Bishop White himself protested against "the supposition in the minds of many, that a bishop should always be engaged in visitations." They did not know how to meet the challenges of their own environment or the needs and appeals of Episcopalians who were moving through the passes of the mountains with thousands of others into Ohio, the western parts of Pennsylvania and Virginia, Kentucky, and Tennessee.

REVIVAL AND EXPANSION

The year 1811 is generally taken to mark the beginning of a revival in the life of the Episcopal Church; for on May 29 of that year in Trinity Church, New York, the first of a new generation of episcopal leaders were consecrated: John Henry Hobart of New York and Alexander Viets Griswold of New England. These two bishops, unlike in their outlook upon the Church, yet one in their evangelistic zeal and concern for its expansion, provided a new kind of leadership: devoted, selfless, and farsighted. Nor were Griswold and Hobart the only men who roused the Church from lethargy and led the way to a recovery of strength and influence. Richard Channing Moore in Virginia and Philander Chase in the Mid-West devoted themselves to the same end; Theodore Dehon stirred the South Carolina diocese with his vigorous sacramental teaching and strong emphasis on the unique traditions of Anglicanism; John Ravenscroft, a vivid and unconventional personality, devoted to high church principles, revitalized the parishes of North Carolina and increased their number from four to twenty-seven; Thomas Brownell carried on the work begun so well by Bishop Seabury in Connecticut. A glance at some of these churchmen of a new generation reveals the transformation wrought in their extension of the outreach of the Episcopal Church.

Alexander Viets Griswold, a Connecticut farmer's son, largely self-educated by heroic application to the studies necessary to the ministry, was ordained by Seabury in 1795. For sixteen years he labored faithfully in parishes in Connecticut and Rhode Island, underpaid, working cheerfully at farm labor and school teaching to eke out his small stipend, enduring every hardship to carry on his earnest and effective ministry. The group that elected him bishop in 1810 represented the so-called Eastern Diocese, an alliance of the dioceses of Rhode Island, Massachusetts, New Hampshire, and Vermont. Scarcely more than a fictional entity, the Eastern Diocese was simply a means whereby four New England dioceses (later five, when Maine was admitted as a state) could share one bishop among them. To the oversight of this vast area Griswold was called, responding with the humble devotion and whole-hearted consecration that characterized his ministry. The difficulties of the task were not lessened by the fact that, like his predecessors in the first generation of bishops, he remained rector of a parish —first at Bristol, and later at Salem—until he moved to Boston in 1835, soon by seniority to become Presiding Bishop.

Griswold was an ardent representative of that group

known as "evangelical men," those of Evangelical churchmanship whose main emphasis was on an active, personal faith in their Lord, and the necessity of a conversion experience of conscious submission to Christ. Their piety was of a warm, emotional kind; their zeal was directed towards an enthusiastic response to the missionary challenge. Though a loyal churchman, like most Evangelicals of the time, Griswold felt a sense of close kinship with the Protestant Churches, especially in the missionary task common to them all, and an impatience with partisan disputes. "Whether I am called High Church or Low Church," he declared, "I am altogether indifferent; for I cannot easily decide which I most dislike." This indecision did not prevent him from harboring the worst suspicions of high churchmen who were influenced by the theological and devotional aspects of the new Oxford Movement that sought to recall the Church of England to its Catholic heritage. "There is a sect," he warned, "lately sprung up among us called Puseyites, or Low Papists, who have, chiefly in England, written and preached and published much against the Reformation . . ."

These matters were peripheral to Griswold's main concern: the care of all the churches of northern and eastern New England. To this he devoted himself indefatigably, traveling constantly, confirming and ordaining, founding new parishes and missions, seeking better means for the education and support of his clergy, never sparing himself, and everywhere bringing new life and courage to the scattered Episcopal congregations.

In the person of Bishop Griswold, as he came riding horseback through the winter snows, jolting over the rough roads in coach or wagon, sailing along the rocky coasts, or later in life braving the uncertainties and hazards of a journey by the new "steam-cars," there came faith and renewed resolution into the churches of the Northeast. His earnest piety and gentle Christian character bred a new respect for the Episcopal Church in areas traditionally hostile or indifferent to Anglicanism. In the end Griswold's success was best measured by the dissolution of his temporary Eastern Diocese. Vermont was so strengthened by his work that in 1832 it secured its own bishop, John Henry Hopkins; and after Griswold's death Manton Eastburn succeeded him in Massachusetts, John Henshaw in Rhode Island, Carlton Chase in New Hampshire, and George Burgess in Maine.

Like Griswold, Richard Channing Moore, elected Bishop of Virginia and rector of the Monumental Church in Richmond in 1814, was an Evangelical, a gentle and persuasive preacher, staunchly devoted to the informal prayer-meetings that some thought "irregular and methodistical," but equally loyal to the Prayer Book, whose liturgy he described as "combining with the soundest sense the purest and most sublimated devotion" and whose rubrics he ordered obeyed "without the least deviation." Under the impact of Moore's eloquent and zealous leadership, the Virginia Church was lifted out of the slough of Bishop Madison's neglect. Churches were re-opened, new parishes established, the clergy increased from seven to nearly a hundred during his episcopate, and Virginia set well on the road to that expansion of church life which was to make her future dioceses one of the strongest centers of the Episcopal Church in the United States.

John Henry Hobart, brought up in Christ Church, Philadelphia, a graduate of Princeton, ordained in 1798 by Bishop White and consecrated Assistant Bishop of New York with Griswold in 1811, was a churchman of a different stamp.[1] His convictions were fervently high church. He was among those who stood staunchly in the traditions of the Anglican divines of the seventeenth century, defending the apostolic character of the Church and its three-fold ministry, emphasizing the sacramental elements of church life, keenly aware of the unique witness of the Episcopal Church as opposed to Romanism on one hand and the Protestant denominations on the other, and jealous for the preservation of its historic Catholic heritage. "Evangelical Truth and Apostolic Order!" was Hobart's ringing watchword. Like Griswold with his remarks on "Low Papists," Hobart had much to say of those who disagreed with his position. "The Low Churchman," he wrote, "deprecates the distinguishing characteristics of the Church . . . is lukewarm or indifferent in advancing them." High churchmen, he claimed, were those "who insist on the ministrations and ordinances of the Church, as constituted by Christ and his apostles, because they are the means and pledges to the faithful of the salvation which is derived through the merits and intercession, and sanctifying grace of a divine Redeemer."

Hobart had his faults. His enormous output of tracts and pamphlets made no great contribution to theological learning; his impatience and quick temper sometimes made him a hard master of his clergy. Jealous for the prerogatives of his office, sensitive to criticism, Hobart was often abrupt and authoritarian. Yet his virtues outweighed these shortcomings. There was a touch of greatness in Hobart's episcopate that not only made itself felt in America, but also evoked the admiration of English churchmen as well.

For fourteen years Bishop Hobart tirelessly traveled the

---

[1] When Benjamn Moore died in 1816, Hobart succeeded him as both rector of Trinity Church and Bishop of New York.

length of his diocese, from Long Island to the Canadian border at the western corner of the state, reviving congregations, establishing missions and new parishes, raising funds to support the expansion, devoting his boundless energy to every project for the extension of the Church's educational and missionary task. Each year of his episcopate saw the steady advance of the Episcopal Church, particularly in the central and western portions of New York, and so remarkable was Hobart's work that only eight years after his death the first sub-division of his diocese took place in the creation of a new bishopric of Western New York. Today, six dioceses trace much of their strength to the sturdy churchmanship and aggressive evangelism of John Henry Hobart.

Easily the most colorful figure among this generation of new leaders was that of Philander Chase. Born in New Hampshire in 1775, a graduate of Dartmouth College who had been converted to the Episcopal Church by his study of the *Book of Common Prayer,* Chase was ordained in 1798. After a parochial ministry in a number of places—Chase was a restless soul—he boldly decided to head for the frontier. The stream of westward migration was approaching full flood, and Chase joined the throng of New Englanders who were moving into the wider spaces of Ohio. There in 1817, he became a freelance missionary, preaching, teaching, ministering the Sacraments, and forming little congregations of Episcopalians in the scattered settlements where he found them. Within a year he, with a few other brave clergy who had embarked upon similar pioneer work, had organized a diocese in Ohio. Elected its first bishop, Chase journeyed back East for consecration in 1819.

Philander Chase was a man of violent enthusiasm and, on

occasions, of stormy temper and contentious spirit. He was possessed of all the Evangelical fervor that Griswold displayed, yet combined, not with the latter's gentle persuasiveness, but rather with an authoritarian manner which exceeded that of Hobart. He would be sole master of every enterprise that engaged his diverse abilities—a tyranny, his opponents thought; a proper Scriptural patriarchal responsibility, he would have called it. Working without salary, supporting himself and his family on their farm, laboring to raise up clergy and educate them when Easterners turned a deaf ear to his appeals, using every unorthodox means to further the Church's mission, Chase was not popular with the bishops in the older seaboard dioceses. Every obstacle was put in the way of his famous trip to England, where nevertheless he triumphantly raised the money for his "school of the prophets" in the wilderness, Kenyon College.

In 1831 Bishop Chase's college and diocese rebelled against the man who did many things so well that he often forgot that others could do them at all. In self-righteous anger he resigned his bishopric, leaving behind him a diocese that had achieved security under his guiding hand. He moved into Michigan, turning his energies to the organization of the Church there. In 1835 he was drawn still further west, accepting a call as Bishop of Illinois and assuming once more the exhilarating burdens of a pioneer bishop, his dreams for the Church in the wilderness as fresh and inspiring as ever. Truly Chase was, as he was hailed in the House of Bishops that year, "a veteran soldier, a bishop of the Cross, whom hardships have never discouraged, whom no difficulties seem to daunt." Philander Chase was first and last a missionary, and on the foundations he laid beyond the Alleghenies the Episcopal Church moved slowly but surely into the Mid-West with the expanding American frontier.

It was not only in the rise of energetic leaders that the revival in these decades manifested its strength. A re-awakened awareness of the teaching obligation of the Church transformed its efforts in religious education. The traditional, and somewhat irregular, parochial training in the Cathechism was replaced by a vigorous Sunday School Movement, and throughout the Church the newly formed Sunday Schools and Bible Classes began their immense influence in rearing generations of Episcopalians in the religion of the Scriptures and the Prayer Book. On another educational level academies and colleges were founded under the auspices of the Church, in an era when all American denominations sought to meet the demand for higher education. Chase's Kenyon College in Ohio, Hobart's Geneva College (now Hobart) in New York State, and Washington College (now Trinity) in Connecticut all date from the early years of the nineteenth century. Moreover, these decades saw the foundation of seminaries for the better education of candidates for the ministry, then normally prepared for ordination by private study with learned clergymen. The General Theological Seminary was established in 1817, a few years before the Theological Seminary at Alexandria, Virginia, opened its doors.[2]

A deeper consciousness of the missionary task of the Church was one of the most important results of the revival. With the example before them of the expanding work of the two missionary societies of the Church of England—the Society for the Propagation of the Gospel and the

[2] The seminaries of the Episcopal Church are described in Chapter VII.

Church Missionary Society—the members of the Convention of 1821 formed *The Domestic and Foreign Missionary Society of the Protestant Episcopal Church.* For some years the Society labored valiantly against a lack of enthusiasm in some quarters and a widespread conviction that missions were the special concern of those interested. In 1835, however, a momentous change was made in the Society's constitution. Henceforth the ground of membership in the Society was to be membership in the Church itself. All Episcopalians were involved in the Church's evangelistic obligation. At the same time a "Board of Missions" was created for the more effective direction and control of the missionary enterprise. These steps bore immediate fruit. In the year after the Convention of 1835 the income of the Society was more than doubled, and a new sense of missionary responsibility spread rapidly throughout all the dioceses.

MISSIONARY EXPANSION

The sharpest missionary challenge to the Episcopal Church came from the American frontier. Already Philander Chase and his fellow workers had shown the way, and in 1835 the General Convention created the office of "missionary bishop," permitting the consecration of bishops, not simply for organized dioceses, but also to serve outside diocesan limits in the vast stretches of the West. Hitherto the inherited patterns of the Church's structure had been so rigidly conceived as actually to impede the work of evangelization on the frontier. Churchmen thought only in terms of a diocese as co-terminous with a state or territory of the Union. Each state or territory had qualified as a diocese when its resources were sufficient to permit and support such organization, while the national Church, scarcely more than a federation of such independent state-dioceses, had assumed little responsibility for the growing edge of the Church. But the consecration of Jackson Kemper in 1835 as a missionary bishop in the Northwest marked the beginning of a new era in expansion and growth.

The tardiness of the Church in overcoming its inertia and in modifying its structure kept Episcopal missionaries from accompanying the first bands of migrating Americans. Already the forest trails and mountain passes leading to the valleys of the Ohio and the Mississippi were jammed with a flood of pioneers. Thousands of families had poured into the Mid-West and were beginning to move still further, following the Oregon Trail, toiling over the Rocky Mountains, and finally conquering the last barrier in the overland route to the Pacific. Other American Churches had been quick to seize the oportunities for evangelism offered by this great movement. Presbyterians and Congregationalists made valiant efforts to minister to the migrating folk, though their influence was soon surpassed by that of the Baptists and the Methodists. Less conservative, more flexible in their organization—especially in their capacity to utilize the services of circuit-riding evangelists, lay preachers, and ministers who were not subjected to long and costly years of education—and more adaptable to the conditions of frontier life, the Baptists and the Methodists won thousands of adherents among the settlers, a fact which partly accounts for the large size of these denominations today.

If the expansion of the Episcopal Church was delayed, it was nevertheless, once started, an heroic story of devotion, self-sacrifice, and hardship—rewarded with perhaps surprising success. Jackson Kemper blazed an evangelistic trail through the settlements of the Mid-West from Missouri northwards into Wisconsin and Minnesota, followed by James Lloyd Breck and others. Everywhere parishes and missions came into being, new dioceses were gradually formed, schools established, and the foundations laid for the strength which the Episcopal Church shows in those areas today.

In the Southwest James Harvey Otey of Tennessee, a vigorous preacher and organizer, carried on a similar work, sharing the task of spreading the Church with Leonidas Polk, later Bishop of Louisiana, George Washington Freeman of Arkansas and the Indian Territory, and Alexander Gregg in Texas. In the far Northwest Thomas Fielding Scott led the way in the Oregon and Washington Territories; in the newly opened California, William Ingraham Kip began the establishment of missions and parishes along the Pacific coast.

Equally memorable with the names of these pioneer missionaries are those of the builders who followed them, bishops in whose long and faithful episcopates the work once started was expanded and strengthened: Joseph Cruikshank Talbot in the vast Diocese of the North-West, Henry Washington Lee in Iowa, Benjamin Bosworth Smith in Kentucky, Samuel McCoskry in Michigan, Henry Benjamin Whipple in Minnesota, Cicero Hawks in Missouri, George Upfold in Indiana, Benjamin Wister Morris in Oregon, and others too numerous to mention.

More than eighteen dioceses, many of them to be subdivided before the end of the nineteenth century, came into being west of the Alleghenies in these years before the Civil War when the Episcopal Church made its first great advances in the domestic mission field. In 1830 the communicant membership of the Church was approximately thirty-one thousand; in 1860 it was nearly five times that number, and a large proportion of these new communicants belonged to the sturdy and thriving congregations of the West.

While the greatest expansion of the Episcopal Church in foreign missions came during the two decades after the Civil War, these early years were those in which responsibility for overseas missionary work was clearly recognized. In 1830 a mission was started in Greece, shortly after the emancipation of the Greek people from Ottoman rule. The work was chiefly the forwarding of educational projects, though the General Convention considered the possibility of the evangelization of the Moslems in the Near East. In 1844 Horatio Southgate was consecrated bishop for "the Dominions and Dependencies of the Sultan of Turkey"—a quaint and somewhat grandiose designation. After five years' exploration of a task that proved thoroughly discouraging, he returned to become rector of the Church of the Advent in Boston.

Two missionaries sailed for China in 1835, and after nine years William Boone was made bishop in the Chinese mission. A little later the first missionaries entered Japan, among them two Episcopal clergymen. Although direct evangelism was impossible in that country until the edicts against Christianity had been withdrawn, the educational activities of these churchmen and others exercised a Christian influence that was to bear fruit in later years. Meanwhile Liberia had become the scene of the Church's work in 1835, and by 1850, when John Payne was made "Bishop of Cape Palmas and Parts Adjacent," the mission there was securely established.

From these beginnings grew the vast overseas enterprise of the Episcopal Church. Soon after the Civil War, missionary districts were organized in China and Japan, and work begun in Alaska. By the end of the nineteenth century, or a few years after, the independent Episcopal Churches in Brazil, Haiti, and Mexico were incorporated into the American Church as missionary districts, the congregations of the Church of England in the Hawaiian Islands had been transferred to the jurisdiction of the Episcopal Church, and districts had been formed in the former Spanish colonies of Cuba, Puerto Rico, and the Philippine Islands.[3]

STRIFE AND CONTROVERSY

The problem of slavery, involved as it was with economic interests and political differences over states' rights, divided Christians of many ecclesiastical allegiances in the mid years of the nineteenth century. Groups of Methodists and Baptists, for example, were separated from each other by the slavery question long before the Civil War. Episcopalians, dreading the menace of political division and endeavoring on each side to understand the position of their opponents, managed to preserve their unity until secession actually came. While in the North there were churchmen who shared the views of violent abolitionists and in the South those who echoed popular opinions concerning the inferiority of the Negro, on both sides there were still others who saw that the American race problem was one that would not yield easily to any immediate solution. Ultimately it was the secession of the southern states that forced a temporary division in the Episcopal Church.

The concept of the independence of a national Church, strong in the Anglican tradition, led to the formation of a separate autonomous Church in the Confederacy, in spiritual union with all other Anglican Churches but self-govern-

[3] A survey of the overseas missions of the Episcopal Church at the present time is contained in Chapter VIII.

ing in the new nation which Southerners sought to create. Accordingly, in 1861 the dioceses in the states which had withdrawn from the Union adopted a constitution, a body of canons, and a Prayer Book for *The Protestant Episcopal Church in the Confederate States of America.* Changes in the old formularies were few, virtually only those made necessary by the attempted political separation. In matters of doctrine, discipline, and worship the Confederate Church made no departure from its former traditions.

Just as the United States declined to recognize the validity of secession, so the Episcopal Church refused to regard the southern dioceses as withdrawn from the Church. General Convention in 1862 proclaimed its adherence to the cause of the Union, but wisely refrained from acknowledging the existence of schism. Each day of the Convention the roll call included the names of the dioceses whose bishops and deputies were absent. Through the years of bitter strife this attitude prevailed, strengthened by the ties of friendship and respect that still united the bishops on either side of the conflict. In 1865, six months after the surrender of General Lee, two bishops and a sprinkling of deputies from the South attended the General Convention in Philadelphia, harbingers of the return of the separated dioceses. In the same year the Council of the Confederate Church, recognizing that the circumstances in which separate organization was deemed necessary had disappeared, resolved that its dioceses were free to return to the Episcopal Church in the United States. The temporary division was over. The Church of the Confederacy ceased to exist.

At least two things were made plain in the experience of enforced separation. First, it was clearly evident that the maintenance of unity was largely owing to the episcopate.

Bishops, fully conscious of their responsibilities in the life of the whole Church, as well as in that of the local diocese, retained their sense of unity with one another as a corporate body. A striking example was thus given of the effectiveness of the episcopate as a ministry of unity. Second, the refusal to recognize schism in the Church and the ease with which its national structure was fully restored, revealed how far the Episcopal Church had advanced in the first half of the nineteenth century towards placing the welfare of the whole Church before the interests of particular dioceses. The earlier concept of a Church whose national being was simply that of an alliance of separate dioceses had been greatly altered in the years of recovery and expansion, and while some of the less admirable elements of "diocesanism" were still present, their strength was diminishing.

Controversy of one sort or another was a familiar feature of church life during the latter part of the last century. Most of these conflicts have now faded, or at least can be viewed in a dispassionate light. Detailed consideration of them is unnecessary; a few examples will suffice to illustrate the clash of opinion that arose over a number of issues, some out of developments of religious thought that affected every Church in the Anglican Communion, others shaped by the changing intellectual climate in which all Christian Churches found themselves a half-century or more ago. In the decades following the Civil War, for example, the impact of the Oxford Movement, first felt in America in the 'forties, created sharp antagonism between high and low churchmen.[4] Evangelicals were suspicious of the "Romanizing tendencies" of a movement that sought to restore to Anglicans the heritage of Catholic theology and devotion

[4] See *Chapters in Church History,* pages 230-235.

which was rightfully theirs. Moreover, these suspicions appeared justified by the conversion to the Roman Church from time to time of small numbers of extremists, perhaps the most conspicuous being that of Bishop Ives of North Carolina in 1852. By 1870 the tensions had created considerable partisan strife, and for a decade or more a heated controversy raged over the ritual and ceremonial practices that often accompanied a revival of emphasis upon the Catholic elements in the Church's life.

On the other side, orthodox clergy were gravely alarmed by attacks upon traditional theology, particularly that on the idea of baptismal regeneration, made by extreme low churchmen. In 1871 the deposition of a Chicago clergyman, Charles Cheney, by the Bishop of Illinois, for his unauthorized alterations in the Prayer Book services, provoked an outburst of conflict that in 1874 actually led to schism. George Cummins, Assistant Bishop of Kentucky, fearful of the influence of the high churchmen and aroused by the Cheney case, led a small group of dissidents out of the Episcopal Church, forming a body known as "The Reformed Episcopal Church." Their essential rejection was that of the comprehensiveness of Anglicanism, for in their re-fashioned formularies only the Protestant elements in the faith and practice of the Church were retained.

Across these partisan controversies cut another conflict, the disturbance created by the impact of advances in the physical sciences and the explorations of the new higher criticism of the Bible. The appearance of Darwin's *Origin of Species* in 1859, though preceded by the challenging conclusions of nineteenth-century geologists, provides a convenient point at which to date the doubts raised about some traditional religious beliefs by scientific pronouncements that appeared to deny a number of fundamental Christian convictions: belief in miracles, life after death, the doctrine of the Incarnation, the existence of a personal God, and others. The effect of the new scientific conclusions was to shake the faith of many people, some abandoning their religious allegiance in a mood of skepticism, others taking refuge in a reverent agnosticism. Almost at the same time English scholars, influenced by the European school of biblical criticism, began the publication of essays and commentaries in which the new light of historical criticism was turned upon the accepted interpretations of Scripture. To many pious churchmen the "licentious and rationalistic tendency" of these scholars was worse than the pronouncements of scientists.

Within the Church all parties were aroused by the necessity of defending Christianity, some at first simply denying the validity of the conclusions of scholars or opposing the traditional affirmations of orthodoxy to the discoveries of scientists. Others, drawn from the ranks of high and low churchmen alike, sought to defend the faith by restating its fundamental truths in the light of the results of scientific knowledge and biblical criticism. A liberal group, sometimes known as "Broad Churchmen," made the greatest effort to come to terms with contemporary thought, their ideas popularized by preachers like Phillips Brooks, rector of Trinity Church, Boston, and their intellectual influence exerted chiefly by members of the faculty of the Episcopal Theological School in Cambridge, Massachusetts.

From all these controversies the Episcopal Church emerged into the twentieth century stronger and more vigorous than ever before. The tensions of churchmanship had driven men to a deeper knowledge of the truly comprehensive nature of their Anglican heritage; the disturbances created by scientific discoveries had been met by a courageous exploration of the unity of truth as it was apprehended in every sphere of man's response to God; the end results of biblical criticism were revealed to be for the firmer grounding of the essentials of the Christian Gospel.

THE EPISCOPAL CHURCH TODAY

In a large measure the remaining chapters of this book constitute a discussion of the Episcopal Church today. These first few sections have presented a brief historical introduction to what follows: a detailed study of the nature and organization of the Episcopal Church, and a description of its activity in evangelism, social work, ecumenical relations, and other areas to which the energies of its clergy and laity are devoted. Occasionally, however, it is useful for a moment to stand back from the manifold busyness of the Church in all its activities and try to see more clearly where its influence is significant and where its weakness is most apparent.

With a little reflection and freedom from prejudice one may see evident weakness in the life and work of this Church as well as all others. For example, the program of the Episcopal Church on some levels, at least, is not sufficiently evangelistic. The national Church, enthusiastically supported by the dioceses and missionary districts, as well as by the indispensable assistance of the Woman's Auxiliary, is endeavoring to meet its missionary responsibilities on a scale never before attempted. But in the dioceses themselves the evangelistic outreach is often too feeble. Particularly is this true within the parishes. Most parishes consider their missionary duty well done if diocesan apportionments are faithfully met or even overpaid, thus enabling the diocese to maintain its own missions and assisted congregations and to fulfill in turn its obligations to the national Church. Unfortunately, there is little vivid consciousness of the personal challenge to evangelism that is the vocation of every Christian, and seldom is there a strong sense of the corporate responsibility for a parish to reproduce itself by establishing a mission in an area within or adjacent to its own parochial borders. Many parishes and missions, of course, have resources too meager for such an effort, but a surprising number may find those resources appearing in response to the will to meet the challenge. Here, certainly, is one of the greatest opportunities for the Church's growth and the conversion of men and women to Christ—by the local missionary concern of each well-founded parish to establish and nurture a new Episcopal congregation.

Furthermore, despite its long association with American life the Episcopal Church has not wholly succeeded in keeping pace with the changes that have affected the population of the United States in the last hundred years. The majority of Episcopalians are people of English stock. The Episcopal Church is not strong among the descendants of the many thousands of imigrants who poured into this country between 1850 and the first World War. Many of these new Americans, of course, brought with them a deep-rooted loyalty to their national or dominant Churches at home, notably the Irish Roman Catholics, the German and Scandinavian Lutherans, and the Eastern Orthodox peoples of the Balkan countries. Yet these allegiances have frequently been loosened, and many of the transplanted folk have joined either the large numbers of unchurched Americans or been temporarily won by the attractions of America's numerous revivalist sects. Social conservatism, an indifference to inequities in the economic order, and an acquiescence in identification with the educated and prosperous classes have frequently retarded the Episcopalian evangelistic outreach towards these peoples, particularly in the Eastern sections of the country. On the other hand, a Church that possesses far too few opportunities for ministry outside its ordered hierarchy of highly educated and expensively trained clergy, and that as yet has not fully exercised its capacities to supplement its Prayer Book with simple evangelical services and other forms of worship designed to reach the multitudes outside its traditions, is bound to be hampered in its efforts to enter as deeply as possible into contemporary American life. In recent years remarkable and encouraging efforts have been made to meet this challenge. The new rural work of the Town and Country Movement and the urban evangelism that has captured the zeal of many clergy and church workers in the crowded cities give promise of a broader and more effective ministry to Americans of all classes and races.

If these be at least two of the areas of weakness to which thoughtful Episcopalians are devoting attention today, there are on the other hand a number of aspects of church life in which the Episcopal Church reveals an unusual strength. The recent reawakening to the responsibilities of the Church's teaching ministry has resulted in a strong emphasis on Christian education on all levels. In nearly every parish and congregation an eager response to this effort is gradually producing a generation of Episcopalians better educated in matters concerning their faith and worship, and more keenly aware of the nature of the Church's mission than in the past. Even more encouraging has been the revival of an understanding of the Church as essentially the worshipping community of the People of God. Prayer Book revision in 1892, and again in 1928, gave new flexibility to the use of the services and greatly enriched them out of Christian spiritual experience, both ancient and contemporary. Liturgical study, nearly always the accompaniment of a deeper understanding of the centrality of worship in the Christian life, occupies the energies of many scholars and churchmen today, and it is not unlikely that a new revision of the Prayer Book services will appear before many years.

One of the notable achievements of the Episcopal Church in the last quarter-century has been its acceptance of a significant place in the ecumenical movements of modern Christendom. Not only have individual Episcopal bishops and leaders taken a prominent part in forwarding ecumenical co-operation and the study of approaches to church unity, but the Church itself has assumed increasing responsibility in such organizations as the National Council of the Churches of Christ and the World Council of Churches.

Finally, the American Episcopal Church today plays a role in the Anglican Communion of far greater importance than ever before. Its immense material resources, the vitality of its parochial life, its increasing intellectual contributions to Anglican thought, and the freedom in which it is enabled to lead the way in a number of courageous explorations of the full limits of the Anglican tradition—all give the Episcopal Church a new place of responsible leadership among the Anglican Churches throughout the world.

PART TWO

The Structure of the Episcopal Church

CHAPTER FOUR

The Constitution and Law of the Church

WE ARE increasingly aware today that to be a Christian means more than simply subscribing to a creed or accepting a particular standard of personal conduct. Our membership in Christ is a new orientation in faith, a personal commitment to Him. But no man can be a Christian by himself. Membership in Christ makes us members of each other in Him. We are, in the words of the Baptismal Service, "regenerate and grafted into the body of Christ's Church" and made living members of the same.[1] In other words, the Christian Gospel involves men in a new relationship to all the children of God. As Christians of the New Testament times realized, life as a follower of Christ means life in the Christian fellowship we call the Holy Catholic Church.[2]

This eternal fellowship has a visible existence on earth in the historic Church into the heritage of which we have entered. Here is the community of faith, reaching down

---

[1] *Book of Common Prayer,* page 280.

[2] See Volume I in this CHURCH'S TEACHING series, *The Holy Scriptures* (Greenwich: The Seabury Press, 1949), pages 160-163; and Volume III, *The Faith of the Church* (Greenwich: The Seabury Press, 1951), pages 126 ff. Also *Chapters in Church History,* page 27, and *The Worship of the Church,* pages 6-7.

through the centuries in unbroken testimony to His presence among men, bearing in its life the Gospel of redemption. Embracing men in this present life, this community has a given structure and shape which point men to the elements of the Gospel itself. The forms and institutions of the historic Church—the *Liturgy* of Christian worship, the *Law* that reflects God's design for the pattern of human life, the *Sacraments* of His grace, the *Scriptures* of His self-revelation, the testimony of the *Creed* to His mighty acts among men, the *Ministry* of Christ's own gift—all these are central to the life and growth of the Christian community of faith.

On one level, then, the Church touches us with the inward aspects of man's new orientation to Jesus Christ in faith and trust. At the opposite pole of our experience we know the Church in its mundane aspect, a conglomeration of buildings, endowments, organizations, and activities that sometimes appear quite irrelevant to its main purposes. But between these two is the level where they come together in the essential structure of Christian community life, the level where law and tradition, liturgy and sacrament, ministry and church order all bear to men elements within the Gospel itself. Other books in this series have dealt in detail with some of those elements in the life of the Episcopal Church. Here we are concerned particularly with the things of *church order,* the structural elements in the Church and the organization which has arisen out of them. We begin with the Constitution in which many principles of our church order are enshrined.

CONSTITUTIONAL REGULATIONS

The basic constitutional law of the Episcopal Church is contained in a set of several brief articles adopted by the

Convention of 1789 and amended from time to time by subsequent General Conventions. The majority of these articles relate to the government of the national Church and its dioceses. They regulate such matters as the composition and activity of General Convention, the erection of additional dioceses and missionary districts, the qualifications for episcopal office, the extent of the bishop's jurisdiction in its various forms, and the ecclesiastical courts through which discipline may be exercised over the clergy. The constitutional articles are the most important laws of the Church. Unlike those laws called *canons,* which may be altered at any session of General Convention, the provisions of the Constitution may be amended only by the action of two successive Conventions. Changes of a serious nature in the structure or order of the Church may not be made until there has been ample time for study and deliberation.[3]

In the main, the articles of the Constitution deal only with the essential structure of the Church's organization, leaving considerable freedom for amplification in the ordinary canon law of the national Church and the local regulations of each diocese. For example, the Constitution requires that there shall be a Standing Committee in every diocese, acting upon the bishop's request as his council of advice and empowered to assume temporary ecclesiastical authority during a vacancy in the episcopate. That is the extent of the constitutional provision, yet the additional powers and responsibilities given the Standing Committees by canon law are such as in most dioceses to associate a

[3] This same provision applies to changes in the *Book of Common Prayer.* Alterations or additions, except for the lections and psalms of Morning and Evening Prayer, may be made only if after being resolved in one meeting of General Convention and communicated to the dioceses during the triennium, they are adopted in the next succeeding Convention.

group of clergy and laymen with the bishop in many of the ordinary affairs of diocesan government. In that way the existence of the Standing Committee helps to create the constitutional character of the bishop's office in the American Episcopal Church in contrast to the older Anglican system in which the bishop was the autocratic ruler of his diocese.

Two of the constitutional articles deal with principles that possess more general interest than the purely administrative regulations. The first is Article VIII which sets out the solemn vow of conformity required to be taken by all ordained to the diaconate or the priesthood.[4] In addition to the promises made in the ordination services, the ordinand affirms "I do believe the Holy Scriptures of the Old and New Testaments to be the Word of God, and to contain all things necessary to salvation; and I do solemnly engage to conform to the Doctrine, Discipline, and Worship of the Protestant Episcopal Church in the United States of America." No clergyman takes upon himself a ministry of his own. He is admitted to a share of the ministry of Christ in His Church. In this solemn declaration he acknowledges the primary authority of Holy Scripture in all matters of saving doctrine, freely pledging his loyalty to that tradition of Christian faith and practice which is the heritage of this Church.[5] The declaration of conformity can never be made lightly for it lays upon the minister the grave moral obligation of obedient stewardship of those things with which he has been entrusted.

Similarly, Article X is of importance. It enjoins the use

---

[4] The declarations of those to be ordered deacons or priests are received by the bishop before the ordination takes place. A similar oath of conformity and obedience is made by the bishop during the service of his consecration.

[5] The authority of Holy Scripture is discussed in *The Faith of the Church*, pages 16-20.

of the official *Book of Common Prayer* in all the dioceses and missionary districts of the Church. The Constitution lays no restriction upon the right of bishops to issue special forms of worship under the Prayer Book rubrics "Concerning the Service of the Church." The effect of Article X is to give the force of constitutional law to the rubrical direction that the ordinary services of public worship in the Episcopal Church shall be those contained in the authorized standard *Book of Common Prayer.*

This constitutional regulation raises questions concerning the way in which Prayer Book services are conducted in our parishes, for few things are the source of more frequent comment or occasional distress than the variety that is encountered. Lack of rigid uniformity in this matter is not confined to the Episcopal Church, but is characteristic of the whole Anglican Communion. Services in one parish may be ceremoniously performed by the priest and his assistants, accompanied by elaborate choral settings for those portions of the services traditionally sung, while a minimum of ceremonial and only the music of hymns and anthems mark the worship of a neighboring church. Moreover, the usages of worship differ as widely as the manner of performing the services. Some ministers will wear the vestments long used in the western Catholic Church while celebrating the Eucharist; for others the simpler choir garb and stole will suffice for all sacramental services. Daily Communions will be the custom of one parish; less frequent celebrations will be the use in another. Outward acts of reverence at different points in the services will be the habit of one congregation, while the sign of the cross, genuflections, and other expressions of personal devotion will not be familiar in others.

The terms "high church" and "low church" are popularly

employed to describe these differences of ceremonial or externals, particularly when they confuse the uninstructed churchman or make it difficult for him to understand practices to which he is not accustomed. What is regrettable is the occasional opprobrious use of these words, for what is generally meant by each is a true expression of a part of our Anglican heritage.[6] To give these labels a partisan significance which assumes that one or the other involves disloyalty to our tradition is to threaten that comprehensive spirit which is central in the life of the Episcopal Church. The elaborations of worship familiar to the high churchman are no more of necessity leading him toward the authoritarian rigidity or dogmatic beliefs of Rome than the simplicity of the low churchman is inevitably divesting him of theological conviction or making him less of a loyal churchman.

The first point to note is that the Prayer Book, with its sparse rubrical directions and its reliance upon the force of custom, permits a wider latitude in the conduct of its authorized services than is generally understood. Tradition, not law, governs much of our ceremonial. We do things in the different ways that they have been done in Anglican Churches for centuries. No canon prescribes the vestments that shall be worn, the colors in which the Church proclaims the seasons of its year, the pectoral cross and ring that adorn the bishop, the use of candles on the altar, or a dozen other familiar usages. These are determined by custom and long use in the Church.[7] That is why changes gradually occur in the usages of worship. Tradition in any form is a living, growing expression of the spirit of a community, at once

---

[6] See *Chapters in Church History,* page 235.
[7] See *The Worship of the Church,* page 60.

guiding and molding its common life and at the same time itself slowly shaped by the experience of men.

The responsibility laid upon the individual by this variety is one of fuller understanding and appreciation of that to which he may not ordinarily be accustomed. Only then can he know the richness of his own tradition. Unfortunately, what we call the comprehensiveness of the Episcopal Church is sometimes merely a name for a kind of alliance in which parishes with different usages pursue their separate ways with little mutual appreciation of one another's spirituality. True Anglican comprehensiveness strikes deeper than that, and in these matters of worship it finds expression in a churchman's spirit of appreciation and understanding of uses and practices that the preferences of taste or the dictates of habit have not made his own.

The second point that raises questions is that the many ways of conducting Prayer Book services are sometimes accompanied by variations of an entirely different kind. Contrary to the law of the Church, unauthorized additions or changes are occasionally made in the prescribed rites of the *Book of Common Prayer*. Portions of services are variously omitted, altered, or rearranged, other prayers and devotions are introduced, or even substituted for the regular services, and the plain intent of some of the rubrics is ignored.[8] In a number of parishes some Prayer Book services are so entirely disused or the people so insufficiently instructed in their nature that considerable bewilderment is experienced upon encountering them elsewhere. This kind of irregularity is not the exclusive property of either high or low churchmen,

[8] A detailed account of this is contained in a recent publication of the official Liturgical Commission, *Prayer Book Studies: IV The Eucharistic Liturgy* (1953), pages 135-137.

as nearly all will admit. If prayers are used that are not "taken out of this book," as the rubric puts it, it makes little difference to the constitutional point what book they are taken from, though it may make a great deal of difference to the question of loyalty to the spirit of Anglican worship.

It is well to remember, as we seek to understand why these variations exist, that their extent is often absurdly exaggerated. Whatever alarm is aroused by a few cases of extreme disregard of the law, there is and always has been a reasonable standard of general uniformity in the Episcopal Church as a whole. Few clergy indulge their individual idiosyncrasies in conducting public worship to the point of deliberate lawlessness. The overwhelming majority conscientiously strive to be firmly loyal to their ordination vows. Why, then, should these irregularities exist? If the Church's law prescribes the Prayer Book services as they stand, why is that law not obeyed to the letter? This is the question that troubles a number of churchmen, and it must be answered as satisfactorily as possible.

In seeking the explanation for variations in our services, the first consideration is whether the legal regulation can always be obeyed "to the letter." If the clergy seek conscientiously and loyally to conform to the Church's law and still some deviations appear, it is possible that the very nature of the Church's worship makes its precise and rigid canonical regulation difficult. This is, in fact, the case. From time to time the needs of the human spirit are not adequately met in any existing liturgical forms. The mind of the Christian community is constantly shaped by the continuous experience of Christ's companionship, and just as constantly the patterns of worship in that community are cleansed and reformed, enriched and extended. Such has been the experience of the Christian Church from the beginning. Prayers and devotions came into popular use long before their formal authorization simply because people gave voice to the adoration, thanksgiving, and petition that was in their hearts. This is how a large number of collects and prayers found their way into the Prayer Book at each revision, not first because their beauty or antiquity appealed to liturgical experts, but because long use in some form had given them a place in the devotional life of the Church. Prayers for missions, for peace among the nations, for Christian service and social justice, the form for anointing the sick, commendatory intercessions for the dying, the provision of family prayers—all are examples of the gradual enrichment of our Prayer Book over four hundred years out of the developing spiritual perceptions of the Christian community.

Perhaps the most striking illustration of this inevitable process is that of explicit prayers for the dead. At the time of the Reformation these remembrances, together with requiem masses and other special devotions on behalf of the departed, were omitted from the revised Anglican services, chiefly because false doctrines and superstitious practices had been associated with them in the later Middle Ages. Yet in the 1928 revision of the American Prayer Book such intercessions appeared once more in the authorized services, and provision was made for a requiem celebration of the Holy Communion at the burial of the dead. Their public restoration was the result of their wide, though technically irregular, use in the Church. Men and women knew that death was neither the boundary of love nor a barrier to prayer. They remembered the welfare of those departed exactly as they had prayed for them in this present life. The fact that a generation or two ago it was a technical offense to utter in public services prayers that are now repeated day after day opens our understanding to one reason why the Church's worship cannot be rigidly controlled by the letter of any law.

There is, however, another reason why some alterations appear occasionally in our services. It springs from the very nature of our form of worship. The Episcopal Church uses an historic liturgy in its corporate worship. The Prayer Book rites are not a set of services devised or worked out from time to time by ecclesiastical authorities, nor are they even the invention of the Reformation divines four hundred years ago. On the contrary, these services are the plainest warrant of the antiquity of our Catholic heritage for they trace their lineage through the Reformation revision of medieval rites to the worship of the ancient and undivided Church.[9] This liturgy we use has always had, so to speak, a life of its own, gathering up the spiritual experience of each generation and transmitting its strength to those that follow. Through all the reforms and revisions that have occurred in nearly two thousand years, no break in the basic patterns of worship has marked the historic liturgies. For this reason Anglican revisions of the Prayer Book, like those of all Churches that use such a liturgy, often combine the results of contemporary spiritual perception with changes in the structure of services that bring them nearer the ancient patterns of worship in the universal Church. Some alterations in our services appear, therefore, out of the past life of the liturgy itself. They are no longer authorized, but because they were once part of our heritage of worship they are sometimes used.

This process is illustrated by two changes occasionally

---

[9] See *The Worship of the Church,* chapters iii-iv.

made in the service of Holy Communion. They have no authorization, and illustrate only the force of tradition. The *Gloria in Excelsis* is moved from its present position at the end of the service to the place where it anciently stood, after the *Kyrie Eleison* ("Lord have mercy upon us") near the beginning. That was its place in Archbishop Cranmer's first English Prayer Book of 1549. Similarly, the ancient salutation "The Lord be with you" is often restored to the beginning of the *Sursum Corda* ("Lift up your hearts"), and also placed at the opening of the whole service. Each time the people reply "And with thy spirit," a mutual salutation that has had a place in Christian worship as far back as we know.[10] We are not concerned here, of course, to defend such additions or alterations, or to decide whether or not they are desirable. They are, in fact, contrary to the letter of the law. They serve simply as illustrations of that tendency of the ancient patterns in the life of the liturgy to reassert themselves from time to time. Thus we understand better the reasons for some of the existing variations in Prayer Book services. These specific alterations are the result of the influence upon our worship exercised either by the Prayer Book of 1549, or the services used at present in other branches of the Anglican Communion, or the ancient structure of the Church's historic liturgy.

Such considerations may help us to understand why precise

---

[10] These particular changes have been suggested by the Liturgical Commission in its recent revision of the service of Holy Communion. See *Prayer Book Studies IV,* pages 168, 174, 238, 323-4, 331. The proposals of the Commission are "for the purpose of promoting study," and have been sanctioned by the House of Bishops only for "special use" with the authorization of the bishop of the diocese, "on a particular occasion." The resolution of the House of Bishops in 1953 stated that "no general authorization for continued use may be made of forms of service which are substitutes for those forms of service which are now in the *Book of Common Prayer,* nor may such substitute forms of service be used at times of regular public worship."

legislative action cannot either completely control the experiences of the Christian community at prayer, or wholly regulate the worship of a Church using an historic liturgy. Complete and rigid uniformity has seldom been known in any branch of the Catholic Church. When at times in history such uniformity has been briefly enforced by oppressive legislation, the result has been a kind of spiritual sterility from which worshippers sought release in numerous unregulated devotions that sprang up alongside the authorized rites.

Is the worship of the Episcopal Church, then, subject to no effective control? On the contrary, the existence of a reasonable uniformity and a wide conscientious concern with this matter show that it is subject to a very definite standard. The canon law of every Church of Catholic heritage has always fixed the norm and standard of its worship. For all Anglicans that standard is the *Book of Common Prayer,* each particular Church in the Anglican Communion having its own form in which the historic liturgy common to them all is enshrined. The Constitution sets this standard of worship in the life of the Episcopal Church, and necessarily it does so in the form of a requirement of church law. The function of the law is to guard and protect that tradition which is truly Anglican; it can neither prevent the natural growth of the Church's experience of worship nor always control deviations from its letter which spring from the very tradition the law protects.

We often speak, therefore, of the *spirit* of Anglican worship as commanding the loyalty of every Episcopalian. *It is this loyalty that is of supreme importance.* Deviations from the Prayer Book norm that give expression in prayer or worship to doctrines this Church does not hold, or introduce practices which have never been part of our spiritual tradition, are to be condemned as violations of the law both in letter and in spirit. The freedom and flexibility of our particular heritage are maintained only at the price of conscientious responsibility at this point. Evasion of this responsibility imperils the essential bond of unity all Anglicans find in their common possession of the Prayer Book liturgy and threatens the unique ethos of a Church that witnesses to the complementary character of those Christian apprehensions of truth which are sometimes narrowly divided by popular misuse of the words "Catholic" and "Protestant."

THE CANON LAW OF THE CHURCH

The brief articles of the Constitution are the basis of a much larger body of ecclesiastical law governing the life of the Episcopal Church. These regulations are called *canons,* a name given to the first laws enacted by councils of bishops in the Early Church. The word means "a straight measure" or "line"—a standard by which things may be judged—and it was applied to legislation of Church councils that aimed at formulating rules of right conduct or straightening out things amiss in the life of the Church.[11] Such regulations may be of two kinds: (1) *general canons,* enacted by General Convention and in force throughout all the dioceses and missionary districts of the Church; and (2) *diocesan canons,* passed by diocesan conventions and applicable within the several dioceses. The general canons are concerned with matters of importance in the life of the whole Church;

[11] Because they lived under a semimonastic "rule," the word *canon* became applied in the Middle Ages to the clergy of some collegiate and cathedral churches. Today it is still customary to call clergy associated with cathedrals by the title "Canon."

the diocesan canons pertain largely to local administrative affairs.

The majority of our general canons are neither new nor particularly the property of the Episcopal Church. Like their historic liturgy, all the Churches of the Anglican Communion have a heritage of church law, originally derived from the Church of England, which can be traced back through the Middle Ages to the earliest laws regulating the inner life of the ancient Catholic Church. A surprising number of canons, particularly those affecting the ministry, are modern forms of regulations first enacted in the third and fourth centuries. Yet the Church does not perpetuate legislation simply because it is rooted in antiquity. Canons are constantly repealed and amended to meet the changing historical situations in which the Church seeks to carry out its divinely appointed purpose. Some laws fall into disuse and gradually disappear. New regulations are formulated to meet issues presented by new historical conditions.

The general canon law of the Episcopal Church is readily divided into four sections, according to the subject matter of the canons. Two groups of canons, including over half the total number, consist of regulations governing the ministry of the Church. Another section is devoted to ecclesiastical organization and administration, while the remaining group deals briefly with some aspects of worship, supplementing the rubrics of the *Book of Common Prayer*.[12]

---

[12] The canon law is found in the official *Constitution and Canons for the Government of the Protestant Episcopal Church,* printed for the General Convention. This does not, of course, contain all ecclesiastical law operative in the life of the Episcopal Church. In addition, the constitution and canons of the several dioceses, such Prayer Book rubrics as have legal force, the civil laws of the various states relating to religious corporations, and such portions of the English canon law as may be shown to have at least the force of tradition in the Episcopal Church form parts of the total body of church law.

Much of this legislation is of little general interest and infrequent application. For example, one section of the canon law implements at length the constitutional provision of ecclesiastical courts for the trial of clergymen charged with offenses that might lead to their admonition, suspension, or deposition from the sacred ministry. These courts are the vestigial remnant of a far more elaborate juridical system that once extended to the clergy and laity alike. During the centuries of the Middle Ages, the courts of the Church exercised a coercive jurisdiction, supported by the power of the State, and the many matters that came within their competence touched the daily lives of all men and women. The ecclesiastical courts dealt not only with church affairs and with heresy and witchcraft, but also with matrimonial cases, certain breaches of contract and business matters, probate of wills and testamentary causes, scandal, drunkenness, and other moral offenses. All these involved Christian principles and required Christian discipline. With the rise of the modern secular State, however, the old alliance between the spiritual and temporal powers in medieval Christendom was terminated. The State assumed legal control over nearly all those affairs of its citizens once considered the concern of the Church. Moreover, in America the separation of Church and State and the wide acceptance of the principle of religious liberty deprived church courts of any coercive power. Today the right of a religious corporation to control its clergy or officers, fix the requirements for membership, conduct its worship and other activities, and manage its own internal affairs is, of course, acknowledged and protected in civil law, but the disciplinary weapons now possessed by church authorities are only those of excommunication and other spiritual censure. Ecclesiastical courts, therefore, have become internal tribunals, the function of which is restricted to infrequent trials of the clergy.

The Episcopal Church maintains the ancient principle of the indelibility of holy order—that is, a minister can never be deprived of the spiritual character of the office conferred upon him by God through the action of ordination.[13] But the right to exercise this ministry may for weighty cause be denied a man by the Church which once clothed him with that privilege and responsibility. In that case he may no longer celebrate the Sacraments or represent himself as a clergyman. Crime, immorality or other unbecoming conduct, disobedience to the Church's law in its various forms, neglect of the ministry, abandonment of this Church for another, or advisedly maintaining doctrines contrary to those of the Episcopal Church, are all offenses punishable by public censure or admonition, temporary suspension, or deposition from the sacred ministry. In different ways such acts constitute violations of the solemn vows taken at ordination. No blame, however, attaches to the clergyman who is led to renounce the ministry freely and for reasons that do not involve canonical offense. Circumstances may make the continuance of a man's work impossible, even after years of faithful service, and the honorable course is to seek release from the obligations of his ordination. In such cases the canons provide for the public certification that his deposition from the ministry is for causes which do not affect his moral character.

Unlike these disciplinary canons, the other set of regulations governing the ministry is in constant use. It consists chiefly of canons concerning the ordination or consecration of the three orders of ministers, together with a summary of

---

[13] Canon 65 provides for the *restoration* of the right to minister, not the *reordination* of a deposed clergyman.

the duties of each office. Reference to them is made later in the discussion of the nature of the ministry in the Episcopal Church.[14] Similarly, the administrative section of the Church's law, which includes canons governing the responsibilities of the officers of General Convention, prescribing the composition, powers, and duties of the National Council, regulating the financial affairs of the Church according to sound business methods, and generally dealing with ecclesiastical organization, is discussed in connection with a description of the administration of the Church's work.[15]

The fourth group of canons, containing those relating to worship, is relatively brief. Canon 22 creates the official Liturgical Commission to whose studies we have already referred in explaining the existence of variety in our public services. Another regulation authorizes certain hymns and anthems for use in church services.[16] Music is placed under the direction of the rector, "with such assistance as he may see fit to employ from persons skilled in music," and its character required to be seemly and appropriate. Other canons in this section define the standard *Book of Common Prayer* and require the authorization of its Custodian to appear on all editions or translations used in the Church, govern the consecration or abandonment of a church or chapel, and specify such translations of the Bible from which the lessons may be read at Morning or Evening Prayer.[17]

Canon 19 is of universal application. "All persons within

---

[14] See Chapter VII.

[15] See Chapters V and VI.

[16] Official publications are *The Hymnal 1940* and *The Choral Service*. The text of anthems is required by the Prayer Book rubric to be "in the words of Holy Scripture or of the Book of Common Prayer."

[17] The familiar King James Version is canonically the "Standard Bible" of the Episcopal Church. It may be used with or without the Marginal Readings of 1901. Three other translations are allowed: The English Revision of 1881, the American Revision of 1901, and the recent Revised Standard Version of 1952.

this Church," it reads, "shall celebrate and keep the Lord's Day, commonly called Sunday, by regular participation in the public worship of the Church . . ." This regulation enjoins obedience to the divine law in the Fourth Commandment "Remember that thou keep holy the Sabbath day." Our "bounden duty," as the Prayer Book puts it, is "to worship God every Sunday in his Church." [18] All Episcopalians are under obligation to affirm the unique membership of men with one another in Christ by regular participation in that corporate worship which is the chief activity of the Christian fellowship and the distinguishing mark of the Church as the mystical body of Christ.

The worship of God at its highest is a joyous and loving response to the initiative of God's love toward us. In it our lives are conformed more and more to the image and likeness of Jesus Christ our Saviour. Thus worship is the scene of love's strongest creative power—where we are "made one body with him, that he may dwell in us, and we in him." [19] One cannot legislate people into loving, but one can set before them their duty as Christians. The Church is wise enough to know that the path of duty is often the only way to spontaneous devotion. Indeed, in the Christian life faithful fulfillment of duty may often be the truest form of devotion.

THE CANONS CONCERNING HOLY MATRIMONY

Few canonical regulations of the Episcopal Church are of such immediate importance as Canons 17 and 18

---

[18] *Book of Common Prayer,* page 291.

[19] See the discussion in *The Worship of the Church,* pages 18-23.

governing the solemnization of Holy Matrimony, and containing the provisions for the annulment of marriage. These canons are binding upon all members of the Church; no Episcopal clergyman is allowed to solemnize any marriage except in accordance with them.

Part of this law is administrative. All marriages must be solemnized according to the laws of the State as well as those of the Church, in the presence of at least two witnesses. Three days' notice of the marriage must be given to the officiating minister, except when one party is a member of his congregation or other satisfactory evidence of responsibility is furnished. Even then the required notice may be waived only "for weighty cause, and such action shall be reported to the bishop." Both parties must receive personal instruction in the meaning of Christian marriage, and at least one of them shall have been baptized.

The doctrine of the Episcopal Church, summarized in the canon law, is that "marriage is a physical, spiritual, and mystical union of a man and woman created by their mutual consent of heart, mind, and will thereto, and is a Holy Estate instituted of God and is in intention lifelong." [20] This union is made "in the sight of God and in the face of this company" by mutual vows "till death us do part," and to it the Church brings the blessing of Almighty God.[21] In order that the persons to be married may affirm their understanding of the nature and purposes of Holy Matrimony, and engage themselves solemnly to seek their fulfillment, the canons require the following Declaration of Intention to be subscribed:

---

[20] Canon 18, Sec. 2 (b).

[21] See the service for the Solemnization of Matrimony, *Book of Common Prayer*, pp. 300-304.

We, —— and ——, desiring to receive the blessing of Holy Matrimony in the Church, do solemnly declare that we hold marriage to be a lifelong union of husband and wife as it is set forth in the Form of Solemnization of Holy Matrimony in the Book of Common Prayer. We believe it is for the purpose of mutual fellowship, encouragement, and understanding, for the procreation (if it may be) of children, and their physical and spiritual nurture, for the safeguarding and benefit of society. And we do engage ourselves, so far as in us lies, to make our utmost effort to establish this relationship and to seek God's help thereto.[22]

Such a marriage, freely and advisedly made by two persons without any impediment to their ability to enter upon this solemn contract, is a lifelong union.

The Church, however, has always recognized that there may be barriers to marriage in particular cases, that is, existing conditions which make it impossible for people freely to assume the full obligations and disciplines of Holy Matrimony. These are known as *canonical impediments* to marriage, and many of them obviously prevent the kind of union described in our doctrine of marriage. People may not marry within certain blood relationships—for example, sister and brother, uncle and niece. Marriages that are procured by force, fraud, or deception are not held to be valid. Children, or those under the age of puberty, are physically incompetent to contract marriage; insane persons are mentally incompetent to marry.

Other impediments recognized by canon law are less obvious but equally important. A couple may themselves create an impediment at the time they marry by entering into a private agreement inconsistent with the vows and purposes of Holy Matrimony. For example, a contract with

[22] Canon 17, Sec. 3.

each other to seek divorce if the marriage does not prove agreeable, or an understanding not to require mutual faithfulness, are agreements which limit their full consent "of heart, mind, and will" to the pledges between men and women whereby the Holy Estate of Christian marriage is created. Likewise, the canon law recognizes that the ability of a person to give full and competent consent to this union may be limited or made impossible by certain physical or psychological disorders.[23]

In a sense all impediments to Christian matrimony are simply barriers to the full, free, and competent *consent* "together in holy wedlock" by which this union is created. The parties entering upon Holy Matrimony are themselves the ministers of that sacramental action in the sight of God; the officiating priest solemnizes the marriage with the blessing of Almighty God upon those who pledge themselves to each other "to live together after God's ordinance."

We can now understand why the Church views a previous marriage, even though dissolved by civil authority, as presenting a barrier to second marriage except as the canons provide for the permission of the bishop to be given. No member of this Church may enter upon Holy Matrimony if the partner to a previous marriage is living, nor may an Episcopal clergyman solemnize the marriage of any person in these circumstances, until the bishop has given a favorable pastoral judgment in the matter. The bishop must be satisfied that the parties intend "a true Christian marriage," and that the judgment he gives conforms to the doctrine of this Church.

The canons permit an examination into the circumstances

[23] The full list of impediments is contained in Canon 17, Sec. 2 (b).

of the dissolution by civil authority of a previous marriage of any member of this Church in good standing, or that of any person a Church member wishes to marry. If such inquiry shows that any of the canonical impediments to Christian marriage exist or have existed in a union that was so dissolved, it may be declared that no marriage bond as recognized by this Church stands in the way of entrance upon Holy Matrimony. The civil validity of a former marriage, of course, is not affected or denied.

No canonical enactments can ever ensure the universal realization of the Christian ideal of Holy Matrimony, nor can legislation anticipate every hard case that may be presented for the Church's pastoral judgment. Ecclesiastical marriage laws have changed in the past, and they will undoubtedly continue to reflect the attempts of the Christian community to set forth and protect the full meaning of Christian marriage, and at the same time deal mercifully and redemptively with the human situation in a sinful world.

The pastoral aspects of the legislation on marriage are further emphasized by two regulations of Canon 16. In addition to the instruction required to be given by the minister before the solemnization of Holy Matrimony, the canons also provide for marriage counseling. Members of the Episcopal Church in marital difficulties are enjoined to seek the counsel of the clergy, whose duty it is to strive to prevent estrangement. Often patient and skillful pastoral care may assist people through the strains and tensions that sometimes imperil the marriage bond.

Furthermore, the Church's law makes provision for the reconciliation or admission to the Sacraments of those who have "married otherwise than as the word of God and the discipline of this Church allow."[24] The parish priest shall refer such cases to the bishop for a pastoral judgment, given under "the godly discipline both of justice and of mercy." This regulation may apply to the truly hard cases of men and women who married after civil divorce at a time when perhaps they were not, in the strict sense, Christian people. Never members of the Church, they may have been both ignorant of its doctrine of Holy Matrimony and unaware of the solemn obligations involved. The implication of the canon law is that such persons, eventually turning to the Church and seeking to build a Christian family life, need not be denied admission to the Sacraments because of their life under a different set of standards. These cases will not be infrequent in our secular society, and the Church's provision for reconciliation is wise and merciful. This canon, of course, is not restricted to such cases. It does not presuppose that all persons to whom it may apply are those who have never known or accepted the Christian disciplines. There may be other cases involving the restoration of men and women to communicant status. These, too, the bishop is empowered to consider, and he is charged with the responsibility of pastoral judgment.

LAW, TRADITION, AND CUSTOM

It is evident from this brief summary of the more important points in our Constitution and canon law that the Episcopal Church does not impose upon its people an elaborate set of minute ecclesiastical regulations. Our church law in the formal sense contains only the broadest kinds of

[24] The canons expressly provide that in respect to the Sacraments "no minister shall in any case refuse these ordinances to a penitent person in imminent danger of death." Canon 16, Sec. 3 (a).

legislative safeguards of the essential structure of church life. The reason for this is that the Episcopal Church stands within the freedom and flexibility of that Anglican tradition discussed in an earlier chapter. Any Christian tradition that is the living and continuing expression of the spirit of a community protects its integrity as much by the force of custom as by the prescript of legislation. Custom is sometimes the strongest element in life of the Churches of the Anglican Communion, not only in our ways and usages of worship, but also in many other areas of our corporate activity. The devotional practices and standards of Anglican piety, our ecclesiastical manners and behavior, our kinds of organizations, our theological outlook, and the very freedom and comprehensiveness of the Anglican spirit—all these derive their character more from the strength of custom than from the power of law. Again and again in the following pages dealing with further elements in the structure and organization of the Episcopal Church, we shall find custom and tradition to have an importance in our church life often greater than that of canonical regulations or law.

CHAPTER FIVE

National Organization and Administration

FOR the government of its life and the administration of its work, the Episcopal Church is organized on the national level by Constitution and canon law in a fashion that permits full scope to the democratic processes native to the American spirit and familiar in our political affairs. The highest legislative body of the Church is composed of representatives of the dioceses and missionary districts; the chief executive officers and administrative bodies are responsible to the elected deputies of the national Convention. Members of the Episcopal Church have a share in its government by voice or vote on the different levels of its organization. In this respect the polity of the Episcopal Church illustrates that flexibility with which our particular Catholic heritage permits the Church to enter fully the local life and culture of the American people and yet maintain unity with Churches of the Anglican Communion possessing other systems of organization and different national backgrounds. In part our principles of church organization were molded at the same time and under the same influences that brought the separate states into a single Republic after the Revolutionary War. In part, also, our organization is continuously affected by the American capacity for popular government and genius for devising administrative systems that work well and efficiently. Yet underneath both these influences the basic organizational structure of the Episcopal Church rests upon elements of ecclesiastical polity that have been part of the life of the Christian Church for centuries.

THE GENERAL CONVENTION

History bears repeated witness to the importance of ecclesiastical government through the activity of *synods,* that is, councils or conventions representative of the Church's responsible leadership. Ever since the first councils of the Early Church, periods of Church history marked by spiritual reinvigoration, renewed missionary zeal, or decisive Christian moral and social influence have also been times of constant synodical activity when bishops and clergy took common counsel for the more disciplined and effective discharge of their responsibilities.[1] This democratic form of synodical government is the constitutional heritage of the Anglican Churches, in contrast, for example, to the autocratic system by which the Church of Rome is governed. Influenced by the English *Convocation of the Clergy,* all the Churches of the Anglican Communion adhere to the ancient principle of church government by council or synod, each freely modifying or adapting this heritage to meet different local conditions.

Forced by historical circumstances to take the initiative in such modification when the American Revolution separated the colonial parishes from government by the mother Church, the Episcopal Church adapted the principle of synodical government under distinctive American influences.

---

[1] See *Chapters in Church History,* pages 36, 89-90, 103.

The framers of our Church's Constitution in 1789 were imbued with the democratic political ideals of the eighteenth century, and perhaps their most significant action was the admission of laymen to a direct voice and vote in the affairs of the Church through their membership in the highest legislative body. It was recognized that opportunity must be given to the members of the lay order for the exercise of their full responsibility in the life of the Church.

The national legislative synod of the Episcopal Church is the *General Convention,* a representative body that meets every three years, usually in September, at various cities throughout the United States. Its sessions last about two weeks. The ordinary constitutional duties of the Convention are chiefly the preparation of a program for the Church's work during the succeeding three years or *triennium,* together with the adoption of a budget to meet its expenses, and the enactment, repeal, or revision of canon laws. From time to time such special matters as changes in the Prayer Book, the admission of new dioceses, or the authorization of a revised hymnal may come before the Convention for appropriate action under the Constitution and canon law.

Often of significant importance is the action taken by the General Convention on reports made by official commissions that have been studying problems confronting the Church. Issues of Christian concern rising out of contemporary social or political conditions, relations with other Churches, new opportunities for missionary work created by the changing patterns of American society, and other similar matters are frequently presented for debate. Any ensuing action generally takes the form of a resolution in which the Convention seeks to express the mind of the Episcopal Church on the issue that has been raised.

In its triennial organization for this work the General Convention is, like our Congress, a bicameral legislative body, made up of a *House of Bishops,* composed of all bishops in the Church, both active and retired, and a *House of Deputies,* consisting of eight representatives (four priests and four laymen) from each diocese.[2] The two houses meet and deliberate separately; all acts of the Convention must pass both houses. Perhaps the greatest difficulty encountered by the General Convention today arises out of the size of its two houses. The bishops present may number more than a hundred and twenty-five, while over six hundred and fifty deputies sit in the other house.[3] While this extraordinary number of representatives reflects the constant growth in the number of dioceses during the last century, it results in a legislative body at once unwieldy and often insufficiently informed on many of the matters under debate. A vast amount of work is done in committee before reaching the floor of the Convention, a procedure necessary in the interests of efficiency but not helpful to the majority of deputies. In recent years proposals have been put forward to reduce the size of the House of Deputies, and one day such action may be taken. On the other hand, reduction in numbers will always diminish the representative character of the Convention without necessarily securing a better informed

[2] Dioceses have equal representation without respect to communicant strength. Missionary districts are entitled to representation by one priest and one layman, as is the Convocation of American Episcopal Churches in Europe.

[3] There are deputies from seventy-five dioceses and twenty-six missionary districts. In the House of Bishops, therefore, there may be over a hundred diocesan and missionary bishops. About a dozen dioceses regularly have suffragan bishops as well, and there are always seven or eight coadjutor bishops. Usually only a small number of the forty or fifty retired bishops attend Convention.

body of legislators. Any measure of democratic government, either in Church or State, carries with it the responsibility of intelligent and knowledgeable participation by those chosen to represent the people. The calling to serve a diocese as a deputy to General Convention is the highest deliberative and legislative responsibility the Church can confer upon its clerical and lay leaders. It imposes the duty of careful preliminary study of all issues that are to come before Convention and the will to approach them with Christian conviction and courage. As for the most part the issues are known and the deputies chosen well ahead of the triennial meeting, a preparatory program offered the deputies in each diocese would do much to lessen the difficulties created by the size of the Convention and the brevity of its sessions.

Procedure in the House of Deputies is normally conducted by the familiar parliamentary rules governing debate and legislative activity, though one constitutional provision guards against precipitate action on important issues. This is the procedure known as a "vote by orders," and it is at the same time a "vote by dioceses." On such crucial matters as a change in the Constitution of the Church or the revision of its *Book of Common Prayer,* or whenever requested by the representatives of any diocese, the clerical and lay deputies vote separately. Each diocese has one vote among its clerical deputies and one among its laymen. To pass, a measure must gain the concurrence of both orders and a majority of all votes cast in each. As there are four representatives from any diocese in each order polling themselves first to determine their decision, the vote of the four is announced as affirmative, negative, or divided. A vote equally divided is regarded as negative. Any matter of serious import, therefore, upon which a vote of this character is required or demanded ordinarily passes only if it commands a large measure of support.

At each meeting the House of Deputies elects its own President, a Secretary, and by concurrent action with the House of Bishops, a Treasurer of the Convention. Their duties are prescribed by canon law, as are those of other Convention officers.[4] The budget of General Convention, including the salary of the Presiding Bishop and the expenses of his office, and appropriations for the Convention's commissions through the triennium, is met by special assessment laid upon each diocese and missionary district, calculated on the basis of the number of clergy therein. The larger dioceses, therefore, bear the greater share of this central administrative expense.

Unlike the deputies whose term of office normally extends only during the Convention for which they are elected, the House of Bishops has a continuing life and meets usually at least once during the three years between General Conventions. Such meetings are not for the transaction of legislative business, but for common counsel on administrative problems, and for discussion and resolution on matters affecting the state of the Church or its witness to Christian principles in contemporary affairs. At these meetings, as well as at the sessions of a Convention, the bishops may issue an official *Pastoral Letter* required to be read in all congregations of the Episcopal Church. At such times also the House of Bishops may reorganize the Church's missionary districts or establish new areas of such work, and elect missionary bishops or transfer them from one district to another.

---

[4] Including the Registrar, the Recorder of Ordinations, the Custodian of the Prayer Book, and the Historiographer.

THE NATIONAL COUNCIL

Between the meetings of the General Convention the administration of its program for the Church's work during the triennium is entrusted to the direction of the *National Council,* an executive body whose thirty-one members are widely representative of the national Church. Sixteen of its number are elected by the General Convention—four bishops, four priests, and eight laymen.[5] Eight members are chosen by the provincial synods, one from each of the provinces into which the dioceses are grouped, and four women members of the Council are nominated by the Triennial of the Woman's Auxiliary. In addition, *ex officio* members include the Presiding Bishop as President of the Council, one or more Vice-Presidents, and the Treasurer of the Council.

The powers and duties of this central executive body are broadly stated in the canon law: "The Presiding Bishop and the National Council . . . shall have charge of the unification, development, and prosecution of the missionary, educational, and social work of the Church." The members of the National Council act under the canons as the board of directors of the corporation established in 1820-1821 and known as *The Domestic and Foreign Missionary Society of the Protestant Episcopal Church.* The responsibilities once exercised by the Society's "Board of Missions" became the central activity of the Council in the reorganization of the

---

[5] Their canonical term of office is six years, and elections are arranged so that half the members are chosen at one Convention, and half at the next. After serving a full term members of the Council elected by Convention are not eligible for reelection until three years have elapsed. The term of the provincial representatives and the women members is three years. They may serve a second term.

work of the national Church in 1919. Similarly, the functions of the old "General Board of Religious Education" and the "Joint Commission on Social Service" were assigned to the National Council at that time.

The National Council presents to each General Convention a three-year program for all aspects of the Church's work, together with a budget of its estimated cost. This may total nearly six million dollars annually, by far the greater part of which is raised by apportioning quotas to the dioceses and missionary districts of the Church. Three-quarters of the budget is for the support of missionary work, at home and abroad, and of the remainder the largest single sum in recent years has been that appropriated to the program of Christian education. Once adopted, after scrutiny and revision by the Convention's important *Committee on Program and Budget,* the National Council assumes full direction of the program of the general Church for the ensuing three years. Under the Council's authority new work may be initiated or developed as opportunity is presented, and the program outlined may be adapted, within limits set by the Convention, according to changing circumstances during the triennium.

Normally, the National Council meets quarterly at *Seabury House,* the National Conference Center of the Episcopal Church at Greenwich, Connecticut. At these meetings questions of strategy and policy are determined, responsibilities reviewed, and reports are heard from the officers of the various departments through which the work is done. The departments, with their directors, executive secretaries, and various assisting officers, constitute the permanent secretariat established in the offices of *Church Missions House* in New York City and *Tucker House* in Greenwich. They are the servants of the National Council and the agents of its decisions and actions. The existing departments, each of which may be organized into divisions representing different phases of its work, are those of Overseas Missions, the Home Department, Christian Education, Christian Social Relations, Promotion, and Finance.[6]

THE PRESIDING BISHOP

The chief executive officer of the General Convention—and thus of the national Church—is the *Presiding Bishop*.[7] He presides over meetings of the House of Bishops, and as President of the National Council he is the executive head of all the missionary, educational, and social work of the general Church. By canon law also he takes official order for the consecration of bishops elected by the dioceses, ordinarily acting as chief consecrator, and receives the resignations of all bishops. Over the missionary districts of the Church the Presiding Bishop exercises the jurisdiction possessed by the House of Bishops. Missionary bishops in the field report to him annually, and the care of a district devolves upon him in the case of the death or resignation of its bishop. The Presiding Bishop has jurisdiction over American Episcopal congregations in Europe, though he may assign direct episcopal oversight of them to another bishop.[8] The Presiding Bishop's office is the normal point of official contact between the Episcopal Church and other Churches

[6] The work of the Church through these departments is described in Chapters VIII-XII of Part III.

[7] His official residence is at *Dover House* in Greenwich and his office is at Church Missions House in New York.

[8] These congregations are not missions but churches serving Americans in European cities. Such organized parishes exist in Paris, Nice, Florence, Rome, Munich, Dresden, and Geneva, though the churches in the two German cities were destroyed in the last war.

or Provinces of the Anglican Communion; it is also the ordinary channel of our ecclesiastical relations with non-Anglican Churches.

While the Presiding Bishop is invested with the prestige that surrounds the Archbishops and Metropolitans in other Churches of the Anglican Communion, few of his canonical duties are those historically associated with the office of archbishop.[9] He exercises no direct pastoral oversight of a diocese of his own, nor does he possess visitatorial or juridical powers within the independent dioceses of the Episcopal Church. Both of these have been from time immemorial important functions of an archbishop in any branch of the Catholic Church. One cannot conceive the English Convocation enacting a canon changing or diminishing the kind of authority exercised by the Archbishops of Canterbury in succession since days of St. Augustine; but the General Convention can and does define or enlarge the authority of the Presiding Bishop. He is, in fact, not so much an archbishop as an executive bishop chosen to guide and direct the work the dioceses perform together as a national Church. But while the Constitution and canons may invest the Presiding Bishop with but few of the traditional archi-episcopal powers, the very broad range of his responsibilities makes his office more influential in both the spiritual and temporal affairs of the Church than that of many Anglican archbishops.

Few things illustrate more clearly the Episcopal Church's

---

[9] For the rise of archbishoprics in the Church see *Chapters in Church History*, pages 42-43. The Presiding Bishop of the Episcopal Church ranks in dignity with the Archbishops of Canterbury and York, the Primus of the Episcopal Church in Scotland, the Primate of Canada, the Metropolitan of the Church of India, Pakistan, Burma and Ceylon, the Presiding Bishop of the Nippon Sei Ko Kwai, and other heads of the different Churches and Provinces of the Anglican Communion.

adaptation of traditional institutions in a peculiarly American fashion than the history of the Presiding Bishop's office. Upon our first independence of the Church of England the presiding officer of the House of Bishops was the senior bishop in order of consecration. Except for a short period during which Bishops Seabury, White, and Provoost held the office in rotation, the rule of seniority was maintained for a hundred and twenty-five years. All during the nineteenth century, when the expansion of the Church through the vast areas of the West might have suggested the creation of archbishoprics or the establishment of several centers of authority, Episcopalians clung to their outworn and inefficient system. American distrust of central bureaucratic power was as strong then in the Church as it was in the State. The title "archbishop" had a foreign, undemocratic sound in the ears of American Protestant citizens, and history showed that ecclesiastical autocracy was often associated with archbishops. Neither the name nor the function was given the presiding officer of the House of Bishops.[10]

By 1919 the growth of the Church and the consequent increase in the Presiding Bishop's duties made it necessary to provide for leadership of a more energetic and less venerable character. The General Convention amended the Constitution to make the office an elective one, and for two decades a busy and active diocesan bishop was chosen to serve as Presiding Bishop of the national Church as well. Experience revealed the unworkable character of this arrangement. Any administrator among the bishops wise and

---

[10] The influence of the American scene is apparent when we observe the closer imitation of English uses in some parts of the British Commonwealth. The twenty-eight dioceses of the Church of England in Canada are grouped into four archbishoprics; the Church of England in Australia and Tasmania, with even fewer dioceses, has an equal number of metropolitans.

capable enough to shoulder executive responsibility on the national level was usually already fully occupied with the pastoral and administrative work of his own diocese. In 1943 the step was therefore taken by which the Presiding Bishop is required upon election to resign his diocesan jurisdiction in order that he may devote his whole ministry to the executive duties of his office.

Elected by the House of Bishops and confirmed in that election by the House of Deputies, a Presiding Bishop is as far as is possible the choice of the whole Church. He holds office until the November succeeding the General Convention which follows his sixty-eighth birthday (or which meets in his sixty-eighth year), and his pension assessment, like his salary, is one of the expenses of General Convention. These most recent changes in the nature of the Presiding Bishop's office have already given evidence both of new stability and the opportunity for the development of creative leadership in the administrative life of the Church. Not a little of the prestige and influence that has come to be associated with the modern office of Presiding Bishop is due to the capacities of the first two men to hold this executive position under the new canons, Henry St. George Tucker, formerly Bishop of Virginia, and Henry Knox Sherrill, formerly Bishop of Massachusetts.

THE COMMISSIONS OF GENERAL CONVENTION

Some aspects of the life and work of the Church require prolonged and expert study before recommendations are presented to the General Convention for its consideration and possible action. These matters are nearly always entrusted to the official *Joint Commissions* of the General

Convention. They are in effect special study groups, created for particular purposes and discharged when their work has been done. Their membership is not only "joint," that is, representative of both houses, but may also include members at large. Commissions meet as often as necessary for their deliberations, reporting to the Convention at the conclusion of the triennium.

At any one time a wide variety of topics is under study by commissions, often reflecting the matters of special concern to the Church at the moment. For example, one commission exists to study the operation of the present canons on Holy Matrimony and recommend amendments for their improvement, while another devotes its energies to a survey of the problems of evangelistic work in the great industrial areas where a challenging missionary opportunity has been newly recognized by many American Churches. Still others are appointed to make recommendations as widely different as those for the improvement of church music or more effective ways in which a firmer witness to Christian principles may be brought to bear upon our social and economic life.

Among the permanent commissions are two established by canon law, the *Standing Liturgical Commission* whose studies in preparation for possible Prayer Book revision command wide interest in the Church, and the *Standing Joint Commission on Theological Education,* to which the seminaries of the Church report annually in order that the specific needs and significant trends in theological education may be accurately placed before General Convention.

Two other commissions testify to the ecumenical interest of the Episcopal Church. The *Joint Commission on Ecumenical Relations* guides the participation of our Church in the activities of the National Council of Churches of Christ in the United States of America and the World Council of Churches, as well as generally seeking to strengthen our co-operation with other Christian bodies. The *Joint Commission on Approaches to Unity* is charged with the specific task of exploring by frank and earnest discussion with representatives of other Churches the ways of possible achievement of church unity.

One joint commission which has now disappeared left an abiding mark upon the spiritual life of the Church. In 1934 enthusiasm for the spiritual reinvigoration of the whole Episcopal Church launched a program known as the *Forward Movement,* and its guidance was entrusted to an official commission. The feature of the movement which proved most effective and made a lasting impact upon the life of the Church was the extensive publication of devotional literature in the form of tracts and pamphlets dealing with subjects of moral and spiritual concern to every communicant. This activity is still carried on by the *Forward Movement Publications,* under the general direction of the Presiding Bishop. *Forward Day-by-Day,* providing daily spiritual readings and devotions throughout the Church Year, is perhaps the best known and most widely used of these leaflets. Five times a year *Day-by-Day* appears and nearly a half-million copies of each issue are distributed all over the world.

Joint commissions are always the servants of the General Convention. They have no authority to commit the Church to particular opinions, though they may publish their findings for study, nor do they take any authorized action save that of making recommendations which may or may not be adopted by the Convention. Yet some of the most significant work for the Church is done in these commissions by men and women who give unsparingly their time and ability to the problems and issues assigned them.

THE WOMAN'S AUXILIARY

The *Woman's Auxiliary to the National Council* unites the women of the Church in a program that aims to stimulate the interest and enlist the participation of every woman in the whole program of the Church. The scope of the work is world-wide. While the Auxiliary shares in the work of each department of the National Council, its special emphasis is on missions, Christian education, and Christian social relations.

Women participate in these areas of work by an efficient organization modeled upon that of the Church's own organized life. Parochial groups of women are united on the diocesan level with officers chosen from the whole diocese, and these units are in turn represented by delegates to the *Triennial Meeting,* an assemblage which meets at the same time as the General Convention. In the Triennial the general program of Auxiliary work for the following three years is adopted. Working in close co-operation with the National Council, for election to which the Triennial nominates to the General Convention four women members, the Auxiliary makes a substantial contribution to the expenses of the Church's mission. The greater part of this contribution is through the *United Thank Offering,* an accumulation of special gifts from thousands of women in the Church during the triennium. Some idea of the extraordinary increase of this offering by Episcopal women may be gained from the fact that in 1889 the first United Thank Offering amounted to a little over two thousand dollars, while in 1952 the offering was close to two and a half million dollars.

General oversight of the whole program of the Auxiliary during the triennium is entrusted to an Executive Board.[11] Through its permanent secretariat in Church Missions House, the Board works closely with the departments of the National Council through which much of the women's share in the Church's program is implemented.

---

[11] Eight members of the Executive Board are elected by the Triennial; eight are chosen by the provinces. In addition, four others are members in the interests of national organizations whose work is coordinated with that of the Auxiliary by this representation: the *Episcopal Service for Youth,* the *Girls' Friendly Society,* the *Church Periodical Club,* and the *Daughters of the King*. The permanent Executive Secretary of the national Auxiliary is a member *ex-officio.*

CHAPTER SIX

The Dioceses of the Church

THE names of some Christian communions were originally adjectives describing the form of their ministry or indicating the kind of government considered essential to the good order of the Church. In the Presbyterian Church, for example, the central ministry is one of *presbyters,* a word meaning "elders." [1] While there is considerable variety in the functions of elders among Churches that adhere to this form of *polity* (the technical term for church government), it is generally true that the ministers of each local area form a presbytery by which new ministers are ordained and through which oversight of the parishes within the area is exercised. Similarly, the word "congregational" indicates the decisive part played by an individual congregation, both in conferring ministerial status upon its pastor and in governing the affairs of the independent local church. This polity is not only characteristic of the Congregational

[1] The word "presbyter" is used by the Episcopal Church as another name for its priests. Linguistically, Greek *presbyteros* became Latin *presbyter,* thence Anglo-Saxon *preost,* and English *priest.* Our usage is quite different from that of the Presbyterian Church. Where it is used in the canons, the word "presbyter" refers to the second order in the ancient three-fold Catholic ministry of bishops, priests, and deacons.

Church itself, but also of Protestant communions like the Baptists, Universalists, and others who have embraced the governmental principles of congregationalism. From the point of view of polity the Church of Rome might be described as "the *Papal* Church," emphasizing that its central governing authority is the Roman Papacy and that the Pope is the ultimate source of all ecclesiastical jurisdiction.

As its name indicates, the polity of the Episcopal Church is one where the ministers of ordination and chief governance are bishops. The word "episcopal" is derived from the term in the Greek New Testament meaning "overseer," and it is translated into English as "bishop." In other words, the title of our Church affirms that this communion is *Protestant,* because we agree with the Reformation protest against corruptions of the true Catholic and Apostolic faith, and at the same time *Episcopal* because we have received and continued the historic orders of the Christian ministry that were part of the life of the ancient Catholic Church. The ministry in all Churches of the Anglican Communion, like that in the Eastern Orthodox and Oriental Churches, the Old Catholic Church, and the Roman Catholic Church, though in the latter it is subordinated to the papal principle, is one in which bishops in the succession of the historic episcopate occupy an essential place. It is natural, therefore, that the chief unit of church life should still be the ancient *diocese,* an area consisting of the parishes and people under the care of the bishop.[2] The dioceses are not merely units of administrative convenience, but areas of the Christian community where the bishop is entrusted with the pastoral re-

[2] The name "diocese" was taken over by the Early Church from the administrative system of the Roman empire. There it referred to one of the divisions of civil organization.

sponsibilities of a Father-in-God to the people of Christ.

At the end of the American Revolution the first dioceses of the Episcopal Church were formed out of the colonial parishes in each of the new states. Since then, as the Church has grown in size and strength with the development of the country, the number of dioceses has increased to seventy-five, not counting the missionary districts. This increase was, of course, very gradual. New dioceses were formed in new states as they were admitted to the Union, and later the canons provided for their subdivision when the growth of the Church demanded it. Today a number of original state-dioceses are so divided. New York, for example, has six dioceses; Pennsylvania, five; and Texas, three dioceses, part of a fourth, and a missionary district. With very few exceptions, however, these divisions have been within state lines. In the Episcopal Church, only a small number of dioceses contain territory in more than one state.[3]

Despite this increase in the number of dioceses there has been little change in the constitutional pattern by which they form our national Church. At the time that the American Revolution forced an independent organization upon the Anglican colonial parishes, the first dioceses existed separately from each other before they agreed to the union in 1789 into a national Church. That union, like the original federation of our states, was one in which each diocese retained a large amount of autonomy, and today the dioceses still possess an independence far greater than that character-

[3] In most places this is in contrast to the Roman Catholic Church. Our associations with states have nearly always led to the names of our dioceses being drawn from the states, and even when subdivided the Episcopal dioceses usually have names like Western New York, Northern Indiana, Upper South Carolina, etc. Roman Catholic dioceses are more commonly named for their chief cities.

istic in most other Churches with episcopal polity. While in the early history of the Episcopal Church this may have stimulated its development, today it is not without some serious disadvantages. Diocesan participation in any national program or effort, for example, must be voluntarily given; it cannot be forced. Again, while the bishop's exercise of independent power within the diocese is restricted by the share in church government possessed by the Diocesan Convention or the Standing Committee, his independence in respect to the rest of the Church is almost complete. The smooth functioning of church-wide endeavors depends upon his wholehearted co-operation and participation, accepting for his diocese the share and responsibility assigned to it. Neither the General Convention nor the National Council, lacking control over the larger part of the Church's resources, can put men and money to work in missionary districts or other areas of crucial challenge without the voluntary co-operation of the dioceses. While there may be many good reasons for not changing the constitutional arrangements which have resulted in this diocesan independence, it must be recognized that at times it has seriously handicapped the effort of the Episcopal Church on the national level. Parochialism, or the absorption of the people of a parish with their own affairs to the exclusion of their responsibilities to the whole Church, is a common temptation every Christian community must face; there may be also an equally self-absorbing "diocesanism."

MISSIONS AND CONGREGATIONS

Often the most important evangelistic work in any diocese or missionary district is done in places where people meet as an *unorganized congregation.*[4] This is simply a group of families, living perhaps in a small town or rural area far from any established Episcopal church, who are nevertheless determined to maintain the life and ways of their Church. Their loyalty is kept strong by their experience of common worship. They meet regularly in one another's homes for "cottage services," the prayers sometimes taken by one of their number who has been made a lay reader, the Sacraments brought to them at other times by a priest who may travel many miles from the nearest parish to aid them. Such unorganized congregations exist in every diocese. Accurate statistics concerning their number are hard to obtain for they are not always reported among the ordinary parishes and missions. Some six hundred groups are known to be scattered among the dioceses in the United States, and there are probably many more. Wherever there are Episcopalians, an unorganized congregation may be formed, and to a large degree the promise of future growth in the Church lies in these congregations.

The unorganized congregation gives an excellent example of how much the Episcopal Church depends upon the initiative of its lay people. Frequently there are no resources to support a full-time minister, nor any clergyman to spare for the regular supervision of such a congregation. But that is only a temporary inconvenience. Every little band of Episcopalians can not only maintain and deepen its own corporate religious life, but even in doing so will inevitably exercise an evangelistic influence upon others. Services can be arranged and carried on by lay readers with occasional help

[4] Sometimes these are called "preaching stations," "mission stations," or other similar names. There is a wide diversity both in name and in the circumstances of their foundation.

from a visiting priest. Often the reality of Our Lord's presence comes with new meaning when "two or three are gathered together" in His Name, sustained by the familiar services of their *Book of Common Prayer*. There are always men and women ready to accept the responsibility of instructing the children of the group with the aid of such resources as a department of Christian education can provide. Few missionary efforts are more effective than the compelling enthusiasm of a congregation of people whose loyalty and devotion to their Church is proclaimed in this way. Their very continued corporate life is the means of their growth in strength and numbers.

Each diocese gives as much assistance as possible to its unorganized congregations. They are the parishes of the future. No diocese has unlimited resources of money and men, however, and often a priest cannot be found to bring the Sacraments to these congregations more frequently than once a month. Yet the ultimate resources of the group lie in the spiritual life of the people. It is the kind of personal commitment they make to Christ and His Church that matters. If that is wholehearted and without reserve, some of the joys and strength of the apostolic congregations of first-century Christianity will be felt by those families called to the vocation of living along the growing edge of the Church.

Between the unorganized congregation and the familiar independent parish church lies the *mission*. In many respects this is simply a parish that is financially unable to support itself and needs help from the diocese. The missionary budget of the diocese may provide a priest, pay some portion of the operating expenses of the mission, or give aid in other forms. As long as the mission is dependent upon the diocese, its measure of self-government is limited. Missions are under the direct supervision of the bishop, and he appoints their vicars or ministers-in-charge who exercise pastoral care of the people on his behalf.[5]

Missions vary a good deal in size and strength. In rural areas they frequently consist of small groups of people, perhaps only lately unorganized congregations, who may be worshipping in temporary church buildings and sharing the ministrations of a priest with one or two similar missions in that part of the diocese. Other missions are similar to long-established parishes in their activity and organization; only limited financial resources prevent self-support. Often in the large cities, "downtown parishes" that flourished a generation ago are now urban missions or parishes receiving diocesan aid. The original communicant families have moved to the suburbs, and with the changing patterns of city life the old church now serves a group of underprivileged people, often interracial in composition. Unable to carry on this essential work without help, the status of the former parish has become that of a diocesan mission.

It is difficult to exaggerate the importance of our mission-churches. There are in the United States (not counting the overseas missionary districts) approximately seventy-four hundred Episcopal churches. Nearly twenty-seven hundred of these are missions—over one-third of the total. Nothing could be a more vivid reminder of the missionary character of the Episcopal Church and the significance of these mis-

[5] In some dioceses the bishop places the missions under the general oversight of a priest known as an *Archdeacon*. A diocese may be divided into several "archdeaconries." In medieval times the archdeacon was one of the bishop's legal officers, encountered chiefly in the church courts. In the Episcopal Church he has become an assistant to the bishop with special responsibility for the missions of the diocese.

sions in its total life. Their support is the constant responsibility of every Episcopalian, for in every diocese the missions are a chief scene of the Church's advance.

In the missionary districts at home and abroad the National Council allots aid to the missions in accordance with the program and budget adopted by General Convention. Each independent diocese, however, supports its own missions, sometimes receiving aid for specialized missionary work, and every annual diocesan budget contains a large sum for this essential task. Some years ago, when American society was more stable than it is today, the general feeling was that missions would naturally grow in time to be self-supporting parishes. Diocesan aid, therefore, was sometimes distributed carefully and sparingly with the hope of stimulating efforts towards independence in the missions. Today this is no longer maintained everywhere as the best policy. It is clear that some missions can never become self-supporting. Much of the new urban work, for example, will always be the responsibility of the diocese. In the countryside, migration of people from rural areas to the cities often leaves the rural mission with little possibility of achieving self-support. Yet these same missions are constantly bringing the redemptive influence of the Church to bear upon ever-changing groups of people; they touch many who later migrate to urban parishes. The ultimate purpose of our missionary giving is not primarily to maintain institutions and organizations or to encourage their development. This may be an incidental necessity, but the central aim is the conversion of men and women to Jesus Christ. Proper stewardship may sometimes dictate the concentration of resources at one point or another, but the evangelistic task always remains paramount and the support of missions will be constantly the first obligation of the diocese.

THE PARISH CHURCH

The religious activities of most Episcopalians center in an established *parish church,* a unit of church life that has been familiar since the early Middle Ages. For many centuries the word "parish" meant a geographical area with definite bounds.[6] We think of the little village of rural England with its cluster of cottages around the common, above which soars the tower of the parish church. The borders of the parish might include, perhaps at some distance, a manor or two and a number of outlying farms, yet it is never very far to the boundary lines of adjoining parishes on every side. This geographical parish was transplanted to the American colonies by English settlers in the seventeenth century. Despite the religious differences between Puritan Massachusetts and Anglican Virginia, the parish in each was a territorial unit, and the name is still so used in some parts of the South today.

The modern parish of the Episcopal Church, however, has ceased to have any civic connotation, and it is not usually conceived of as a geographical area. When we speak of "our parish" today, we ordinarily mean the group of families and individuals who are associated with the church we attend. The parish, therefore, while still technically a geographical division, appears more commonly to be a community of people, drawn from a wide area and often with no ties of

---

[6] *Parochia* was a Graeco-Roman administrative term referring to a section or "quarter" of a city, generally outside the walls, where resident foreigners would live. It suggested to Christians the place of their "sojourning" in this world (*I Peter* 1:17), while their true home was in the city of God.

neighborhood, who worship and work together primarily as Episcopalians. This change has been made inevitable in a society where nearly half the people have no specific church allegiance, and the remainder are separated into a large number of denominations. But it has at least brought new emphasis to one fundamental truth—the parish is essentially a spiritual community, constantly drawing its strength from the presence of Christ in its corporate life, and always turning outward to bring His redemptive power to bear in the world around it.

In all the Episcopal parishes (including those in mission status) there are approximately two million nine hundred thousand baptized church members, of whom about one million eight hundred thousand are communicants.[7] The greatest numerical strength of the Church still lies in the eastern part of the country, and nearly half its baptized members live within the dioceses in New England, New York State, and thence southward through Virginia. These figures testify to the long association of the Episcopal Church with the urban centers and the older more populous sections of the East, but they do not indicate the movement which is at present under way. In recent years the increase of strength in other parts of the country has been rapid and encouraging, particularly in the Southwest, parts of the South, and in the Pacific areas. It is evident from the high percentages of growth in

[7] Among those Churches in the United States that report over a million adherents, the Episcopal Church ranks sixth—below the Roman Catholics, and the total numbers in the different groups of Baptists, Methodists, Lutherans, and Presbyterians; above the Disciples of Christ, Eastern Orthodox Christians of separate allegiances, Latter-Day Saints, Congregational-Christians, and members of the Churches of Christ. (See the tables in the Appendix.) Full statistical details are contained in the annual *Yearbook of American Churches,* published by the National Council of the Churches of Christ in the U.S.A.

these sections that the Church is now making a remarkable advance outside the eastern part of the United States.

The parish church may be viewed in a number of different aspects, and a brief consideration of some of them will suggest the character of the total life of a parochial community. First, the parish is organized as *a legal corporation,* very often known as "The Rector, Wardens, and Vestrymen of ——— Church." It is legally as well as canonically in union with the diocese where it is located. The body thus constituted holds and maintains the buildings, properties, and endowments. Subject to the state laws governing religious corporations, and the canon law of both Church and diocese, the wardens and vestrymen are the agents of the parishioners, elected by them in an annual parochial meeting. Through a treasurer or such other financial officers as may be employed, the vestry collects and expends the revenues of the parish in accordance with the canonical standards for the business affairs of the Church. In most places its members represent the parish in all matters concerning its clergymen. They are normally responsible for calling a new rector, unless diocesan canons or local laws make other provision; they must sign the testimonials of parochial candidates for Holy Orders.

Considerable variety exists among the dioceses in respect to the qualifications for office as a vestryman, or for voters in parish meetings. Generally speaking, vestrymen will be baptized members of the Church over twenty-one years of age. Communicant membership is sometimes required, and certainly in all cases desirable. Invariably, parishioners qualified to vote must be regular contributors and worshippers, over eighteen or twenty-one years old and either communicants or baptized persons as the local canons may dictate. In many dioceses both men and women are eligible to vote or to hold office. Terms of office vary considerably, but many parishes now have a system of rotation in office that constantly brings a different group of the laity into these posts of responsibility.

On the parish level the intelligent and active participation of lay people in the governance of the local church is essential to its fullest development. One form of lay ministry in the Episcopal Church is the faithful discharge of these obligations. Vestrymen are not simply trustees of parish finances, but parishioners who have been granted special opportunities for Christian leadership. Their stewardship of the temporalities of the church must be guided by an informed and enthusiastic devotion to its work; their responsibilities to the people of the parish may be carried out in many aspects of its life.

The parish may also be viewed as constituting *the community within which the cure of souls is entrusted to a priest of the Church.* At ordination to the priesthood he is charged as a messenger, watchman, and steward of the lord "to teach, and to premonish, to feed and provide for the Lord's family; to seek for Christ's sheep that are dispersed abroad, and for His children who are in the midst of this naughty world, that they may be saved through Christ for ever." [8] Among other vows, he solemnly promises to minister "the Doctrine and Sacraments, and the Discipline of Christ, as the Lord hath commanded, and as this Church hath received the same"; to be diligent in prayer and study; and to set forward peace and love among all Christian people. When he is

---

[8] See the service for "The Ordering of Priests" in the *Book of Common Prayer.*

instituted as *Rector* of the parish, the canons invest him with the control of the worship and the spiritual jurisdiction, and lay upon him a large number of specific administrative, educational, and pastoral duties.

While the bishop of a diocese appoints the ministers in charge of diocesan missions, the independent parish has the privilege of calling its own rector. According to the general canons, no vestry may elect a new rector until the bishop has been notified of the name of the clergyman proposed for election, and sufficient opportunity has been given for him to communicate with the vestry upon the matter. Normally the bishop recommends suitable priests for consideration; he knows both the needs of the parish in respect to the total strength of the diocese, and the abilities of particular clergymen better than is possible for the vestrymen. The election, however, is quite free. Notice of its completion is sent to the bishop, who, when satisfied that the man chosen is a duly qualified minister and has accepted the call, orders the pastoral relationship duly recorded.[9] While the provisions of diocesan canons or the state laws relating to religious corporations sometimes modify this practice, nearly always a rector so elected is permanently settled until he chooses to accept another call. He may not resign without the consent of the vestry, nor may he be removed except the bishop give his godly judgment thereto after a long canonical process governing the dissolution of the pastoral relation between the priest and his people.

Whatever ministerial assistance the rector may have is entirely under his direction. For various reasons parishes use such titles as *curate, associate rector,* or *assistant minister* to

---

[9] Some diocesan canons make the call of a rector a matter of close agreement between the bishop and the vestry at every point.

designate clergy associated with the rector in the pastoral care of the people. Such assistants are under the rector's authority, however, and are employed to help him fulfill the duties of his office.

The third aspect in which the parish church often appears is as *a convenient center for the activity of numerous parochial organizations.* In other words, the busy parish house with its offices and workrooms seems to reflect the most important concerns of the people. Meetings of the vestry, the Woman's Auxiliary and ladies' guilds, the Men's Club, the Young People's Fellowship, and branches of other national and diocesan organizations appear to be constant. Numerous committees assemble to plan the parish canvass, annual fairs and sales, suppers, silver teas, Sunday school picnics, and a dozen forms of promotional and philanthropic activity. Parish halls echo the whir of sewing machines, the click of needles, and the clatter of coffee cups. Stairways are cluttered with boxes of books and bales of clothing; guild rooms resound with speeches and addresses; gymnasiums are the scene of basketball games and scout drills. The sacristies smell faintly of the hot iron; the parish offices are filled with the staccato sound of typewriters and the rhythmic clank of mimeograph machines. One can hardly be blamed for assuming that all this bustle is more important than the quiet hush that descends when one enters the church next door.

There is no doubt that nearly every parish needs from time to time to submit its activities to careful and honest scrutiny. Frequently there is duplication of work and a waste of effort in superfluous organizations. But the scrutiny must be directed to more than mere loss of efficiency. It must search out purposes and motives as well. There is danger that organized groups may function merely to perpetuate themselves without reference to the Christian service they were once designed to render. Promotional activity for its own sake can be a deadly thing. It tends to satisfy people with successful achievement without raising the question of whether that achievement has anything to do with the primary redemptive and evangelistic purposes of the Church. Today there is a healthy and growing dissatisfaction with over-emphasis on promotion, but at the same time it is a mistake to dismiss all organized parochial activity of that sort as mere "parish-house religion." It should be subordinate to the primary function of the Christian parish, but it need not be irrelevant.

People in a parish find a valuable form of human community in their parochial organizations. They learn to work together, inspired by a common Christian profession, and are often made aware thereby of the needs of the Church beyond the parish and their own obligations to its wider task. At best this work can be made the means of a strong ministry of witness and service; every organization is a potential training cell of deeper devotion and self-sacrifice on the part of its members. The right relation between what goes on in the parish house and the fellowship in worship that centers in the church cannot be established by administrative measures. It issues from the right relation of these things in the minds and hearts of the people of the parish.

Finally, the parish may be seen as *the worshipping community*. Here it is essentially a community of faith, a microcosm of the whole Body of Christ, a fellowship of men and women with one another in Him, drawing their ultimate strength from His presence in their common life of prayer and sacrament. People have tender associations with their church. There they were baptized and first learned the secrets of man's inner life with God in prayer. There they found relief from the burdens of conscience in penitence and forgiveness. Before its altars they knelt to receive the Body and Blood of their Saviour, and took the solemn vows of Holy Matrimony. In the presence of God they offered their intercessions for their friends and families, their thanksgivings for the blessings of this life. There they remembered that in the midst of life we are in death, and from the church their loved ones were borne to the grave in sure and certain hope of the resurrection through our Lord Jesus Christ. But inseparable from these sacred moments of personal faith and awareness of God is the corporate experience of the whole parish in worship. In the Offices and Sacraments of the *Book of Common Prayer* men and women find their deepest community with God and with one another in Him. It is in our sacramental worship that we know we are made "one body with Him, that He may dwell in us and we in Him." This body is the parochial community of eternal significance.

THE BISHOP OF THE DIOCESE

Throughout the centuries of the Church's history the bishop has exercised his functions amid a variety of changing circumstances. In the Early Church he was the chief pastor of the people committed to his charge. Though he gradually delegated much of this responsibility to his priests, the bishop remained for a long time the normal celebrant of the Holy Communion in the Christian *parochia,* the chief minister of the sacramental life of the Christian community. In the Church of the late Roman Empire, however, the bishop's duties made him sometimes a theologian, sometimes a civil officer as well as an ecclesiastical administrator. Later the bishops in barbarian Europe were alternately missionaries and teachers, carrying the Gospel to barbarian tribes, civilizing their rude cultures with the Christian learning of antiquity. In turn medieval Europe saw another change. The feudal bishop was a powerful baron, often employed on business of state by the monarch and ruling his diocese from afar through his numerous officials. In eighteenth-century England the bishops appeared to be chiefly occupied with political affairs in the House of Lords; in the nineteenth century the members of the Anglican episcopate again recovered their intellectual and spiritual leadership of the Church.

To some extent these different circumstances affecting the bishop's functions have reflected the background and interests of different periods of history. Today this is still evident. The modern bishop in a populous diocese is involved in the exacting routine that governs the hours of a busy executive's life. The quiet peace of the ancient Cathedral close has given way to the efficient business atmosphere of the diocesan house; the books of study and contemplation are sometimes crowded by the files, typewriters, and dictating machines of modern administration. But these are only symbols, so to speak, of the outward circumstances in which the bishop exercises his functions today. They are no more truly part of his essential office than were the civic duties of ancient imperial bishops or the baronial responsibilities of medieval prelates. Underneath these external circumstances the true character of the episcopate has remained unchanged. The bishop is still the Father-in-God and counselor of his clergy, the leader and chief pastor of the people placed under his spiritual charge. If the bishop has never been able to devote his energies wholly to his spiritual responsibilities, it is perhaps only a sign that his ministry is always exercised in a world which the Church must enter at every point to bring into its society the redemptive activity of Jesus Christ.

Election was the ancient method of choosing bishops in the Church. This might be done by the people and clergy, or by other bishops, though in either case some participation was had by all. Today in the Episcopal Church these ancient customs are still maintained.[10] A bishop is chosen by the Diocesan Convention, according to the local canons governing episcopal elections, but before the Presiding Bishop may take order for his consecration the bishop-elect must receive the approval of the Church in the form of consents to his election by a majority of both the bishops and the Standing Committees of other dioceses. Bishops are ministers of the whole Church as well as of the locality where they have jurisdiction, and therefore must be acceptable to the Church at large.

Unless forced to resign for reasons of health or other circumstances, a bishop remains the chief pastor of a diocese until he is seventy-two years old, though he may choose to retire at sixty-eight. The canon law then requires that he resign his jurisdiction. He retains his voice and vote in the House of Bishops, and may continue to bear an active part in the life of the Church. The canonical provisions governing the duties of bishops are sparse. By church law he is required to visit the churches and congregations of his diocese regularly, administering Confirmation and inquiring concerning the life of the parish. He delivers pastoral charges to his clergy and people as necessary, presides over the Diocesan Convention and some other diocesan organizations,

---

[10] Except in the case of missionary bishops. The clergy and people of missionary districts have no part in the election of a bishop of the district.

and is responsible for the direct oversight of the missions of the diocese. He examines and ordains candidates for the ministry; he may give judgment in matrimonial causes or other matters brought to him under the canon law. His duties in respect to the national Church take him to the House of Bishops and may occupy him with numerous tasks on behalf of the Church's whole program. But these brief prescriptions of episcopal duties are greatly enlarged by numerous forms of activity dictated less by canon than by tradition and custom. The truth is that the bishop's responsibility in the Episcopal Church is determined not so much by precise regulation of his constitutional authority as by the demands of leadership in every phase of the Church's life. The spiritual, intellectual, and administrative capacities a man brings to this very exacting ministry are often the decisive elements in a great and notable episcopate.

Thus far we have been considering the bishop of a diocese, the *Diocesan,* as he is sometimes called. In many large dioceses, however, episcopal assistance is necessary if the bishop is adequately to provide pastoral oversight of all the parishes and missions. In that case the Convention of the diocese may elect an assistant bishop, known as a *Suffragan Bishop.* He is elected in the same manner as a Diocesan, but the suffragan bishop has no jurisdiction of his own. His authority is that of a bishop in the Church of God, and in the diocese he is an assistant who helps the Diocesan carry on his work. Most suffragans in fact, however, devote themselves to particular areas of diocesan work, often having oversight of missions and unorganized congregations. Thus the bishop of the diocese is relieved of one special part of his total task, though he nevertheless continues to be ultimately responsible for the whole life of the diocese. Upon the death or retirement of the Diocesan, the suffragan bishop may be elected to succeed him, or at any time he may be chosen Diocesan elsewhere, but suffragans do not succeed their Diocesans automatically.

Succession, however, is granted to a *Bishop Coadjutor,* that is, a bishop elected to assist the Diocesan, who at the time of his election is assigned a specific share of episcopal authority in the diocese. He may be given jurisdiction over the mission churches, the institutions, postulants and candidates for holy orders, or some other area of diocesan responsibility. Unlike a suffragan bishop, the coadjutor is not only an assistant; he actually shares part of the whole jurisdiction to which he will normally succeed. A coadjutor is usually chosen when the Diocesan is of advanced age and unable to carry on the work alone. His presence guarantees that there will be no break in the leadership of the diocese upon the death or retirement of its bishop. Because they have already accepted actual episcopal jurisdiction in a particular diocese, bishops coadjutor are not elected Diocesans elsewhere. It is not the custom of the Episcopal Church, unlike some other Churches of the Anglican Communion, to *translate* bishops who have jurisdiction, that is, to move them from one diocese to another. Consequently, only suffragan bishops or missionary bishops, neither of whom possess personal jurisdiction, are elected to episcopal offices in other dioceses or districts.

THE CATHEDRAL CHURCH

In most dioceses in the Episcopal Church there is one church closely associated with the bishop and which serves as a center of diocesan life. This is the *Cathedral.*[11] Usually

[11] The name comes from the word *cathedra,* meaning the chair or throne of the bishop. The Cathedral Church is the place where he is enthroned and maintains his seat as chief pastor of the diocese.

under the bishop's authority, its governing body is known as a "Chapter" rather than a vestry, and the members frequently include diocesan clergy as well as laymen representing what is often called "the Cathedral parish." Anciently the cathedrals had no parishioners. The duties of the *Dean, Canons,* and other clergy did not include pastoral care of a parochial community. While this is still the case in most English and European cathedrals, in the American Episcopal Church the traditional cathedral system has been radically altered.[12] Many of our cathedrals are simply large parishes that have agreed to such constitutional changes as will permit the bishop to exercise a greater control of the clergy, worship, and general activities. Others are cathedral foundations to which the worshipping congregation of a parish has been attached. In most places, therefore, the cathedral is not only a diocesan center but also a parish church where the dean and canons have a full pastoral ministry. Yet it remains preeminently the bishop's own church. He not only preaches the Word of God from its pulpit, but on special occasions he delivers the Church's message as it pertains to the life of his people. His prayers for all those committed to his charge are offered at its altar.

The cathedral serves the diocese in a number of ways, nearly all of which are possible because its resources are normally greater than those of any single parish church. One of its functions, for example, is to set a pattern of Anglican worship at its best. Cathedral services should be a model of beauty, reverence, and order, an inspiration to the parishes

---

[12] Two Episcopal cathedrals, however, are without parishioners and maintain much of the traditional cathedral atmosphere—the Cathedral of St. John the Divine in New York, and the Cathedral of St. Peter and St. Paul in Washington, D.C. In both, however, the clergy minister to those who seek help from members of the cathedral staff.

and missions, as well as an offering of the Christian sacrifice of worship that is relevant to men's needs because it is wholly devoted to the praise of Almighty God. At its services the parishes, clergy, and people of the diocese are remembered in regular intercession, and every Episcopalian in the diocese should feel the cathedral to be his spiritual home. Another of its functions is to provide a meeting-place where the diocesan family can come together for study and discussion as well as worship, its members seeking to know better both one another and their common tasks in Christ.

One of the oldest associations of cathedrals is with the educational life of the Church, and cathedral foundations today often include one or more schools. On the grounds of the Washington Cathedral, for example, there are both boys' and girls' schools, as well as the famous *College of Preachers,* an institution to which many of the clergy of the Episcopal Church are invited for short periods of special study of the art of preaching, one of the most valuable forms of post-ordination training. A similar college, called the *School of the Prophets* is associated with Grace Cathedral, San Francisco. While most cathedrals are not able to support such extensive institutions as these, every cathedral church can maintain an educational program. Diocesan schools of religion, frequent lecture courses and conferences, study groups for clergy and lay people—all these may be the means of presenting the Christian faith and life on different intellectual levels both to the people of the diocese and to non-Episcopalians who are attracted to the Church. Where the abilities of the staff permit, a cathedral properly extends this activity to programs of Christian social education and leadership in civic responsibilities, training in the spiritual life of prayer and devotion, the maintenance of counseling services, and a number of other forms of Christian ministry and witness that are beyond the reach of the ordinary parish.

THE ORGANIZATION AND WORK OF THE DIOCESE

The constitutional organization of a diocese of the Episcopal Church is similar to that of the national Church. Just as the dioceses and districts are represented in General Convention, so within each diocese the legislative synod is the annual *Diocesan Convention* (sometimes called the *Council, Synod,* or *Convocation*), consisting of all the clergy of the diocese and a number of lay delegates from each parish and mission. In some dioceses each church is entitled to an equal number of lay representatives; in others, representation is in proportion to the communicant strength of the parish. There are also different methods of voting. Delegates in some cases cast a single vote for the parish or mission they represent; in others they cast their votes as individuals. In every diocese, however, there are occasions when the diocesan canons permit or require a vote by orders. This in effect divides the Convention into two houses, clerical and lay, and a measure to be passed must receive the requisite number of votes in each order. All these matters are prescribed in diocesan canons, and the regulations vary sufficiently to make accurate generalizations impossible.

The Diocesan Convention is the scene of the legislative and deliberative activity of the diocese. One of its chief functions is the adoption of an annual budget in which provision is made for the maintenance of administrative work, the promotion of the missionary task within the diocese, and the acceptance of the diocesan share in the program of the national Church. The Convention also elects a bishop in the case of a vacancy in the episcopal office, chooses the deputies to General Convention and Provincial Synods, as well as such other officers as may be required by the canons. It grants assistance to new missions and admits parishes into union with the diocese, amends the diocesan constitution and enacts or repeals local canons, and receives the annual reports of the bishop and the departments and organizations of the diocese. These duties, however, do not exhaust the responsibilities of a Convention. Its annual meeting, presided over by the bishop, is often the yearly high point in the life of each diocese. In the Convention a strong sense of fellowship in the tasks of the Church is aroused by the participation of people from all parts of the diocese in framing their common program and accepting the challenges of advance work. In some dioceses the Woman's Auxiliary holds its diocesan meeting at the time of the Convention, and the services of corporate worship that bring together all the leaders of the diocese are strengthening and inspiring.

Diocesan officers, some elected by the Convention and some appointed by the bishop, consist of a *Secretary* of the Convention, a *Registrar,* whose duty it is to keep the archives of the diocese and the official records of its clergy, and a *Treasurer.* Each diocese also has a *Chancellor,* a lawyer who advises the bishop in legal matters, a group of *Examining Chaplains,* who examine all candidates for ordination, a *Standing Committee,* and such officers of a Diocesan Council or Executive Board as may be provided for in the constitution or canons. More highly organized dioceses may have other officials. Constitutionally, the members of the Standing Committee are the most important officers of a diocese, the only group qualified to act for the diocese as a whole. With few exceptions this body consists of three or four priests, normally the senior clergy of wide experience, and an equal number of communicant laymen. They act for the diocese in giving assent to episcopal elections in the Church; their recommendation is necessary at every stage in the preparation of a postulant of the diocese for priest's orders. They serve the bishop as a *Council of Advice,* thus being admitted to an important place in the governance of the diocese; if there be a vacancy in the episcopate they constitute the formal *Ecclesiastical Authority* until a new bishop has been secured.

In the ordinary work of the Church, however, the most important officers of the diocese are often the members of the Diocesan Council or Executive Board. This is a group of leaders, some in charge, under the bishop, of different phases of the diocesan program, some chosen at large. The Council functions on the diocesan level in much the same way as the National Council directs the program of the whole Church. Council members plan and co-ordinate the total program of evangelistic, educational, and social work; they are charged with the expenditure of such portions of the diocesan budget allotted to them. The departments of diocesan activity are represented on the Council—missions, Christian education, Christian social relations, promotion (the Field Department), and finance. When resources are sufficient there may be full-time executives in charge of these departments, as well as field secretaries and other trained workers. Most of the dioceses also number among their officers advisors for youth activities, chairmen of laymen's work, those in charge of summer conferences, members of boards entrusted with the oversight of schools, hospitals, convalescent homes, and other institutions of the diocese, and those responsible for diocesan publications and periodicals. At nearly every point in this program the diocesan officers of the Woman's Auxiliary play a vital part. Auxiliary members carry an important share of the Church's work in every diocese.

Everywhere there is ample opportunity for men and women to undertake work for the Church outside the immediate circle of parish life. The wide range of diocesan activities offers many different opportunities for the service that Episcopalians can give as members of a diocesan family. The parish or mission bears its part in the whole work not only by meeting its proportionate share of the expenses, but also by contributing the talents, abilities, and devotion of its people to the larger corporate life of the diocese.

THE MISSIONARY DISTRICT

The name given to an area of the Church's work which has not yet become an independent diocese is that of *Missionary District.*[13] In the United States there are twelve such districts, all located west of the Mississippi River; overseas mission fields contain a dozen more.[14] In these districts the national Church bears a large proportion of the burden of financial support, and the Home and Overseas Departments of the National Council share with the bishops in the field the chief responsibility for the advance and development of the work. Jurisdiction over such districts is possessed

---

[13] The brief discussion of missionary districts here is supplemented by the description of the mission fields in Chapters VIII and IX of Part III.

[14] In the United States are the missionary districts of *North Dakota, South Dakota, Salina* (in Kansas), *North Texas, Wyoming, Spokane* (in Washington), *Eastern Oregon, Idaho, Nevada, Utah, Arizona* and *San Joaquin* (in California). Overseas are the districts of the *Panama Canal Zone, Mexico, Puerto Rico, Cuba, Haiti, Brazil* (with three districts), the *Virgin Islands* (under the Bishop of Puerto Rico), the *Dominican Republic* (under the Bishop of Haïti), *Liberia, Alaska, Honolulu,* and *The Philippines.* See the maps in the Appendix.

by the House of Bishops on behalf of the whole Church whose missionary responsibility these territories are. Represented in General Convention by two deputies each, one priest and one layman, missionary districts have only a limited independence of the national Church, mainly in local affairs. Their councils and convocations function chiefly to promote evangelism in the area rather than to exercise the full self-government characteristic of a diocese. Missionary bishops are elected by the House of Bishops and may be moved from one missionary district to another if the House so decides. After the expiration of five years' service in the mission field such bishops are eligible for election as Diocesans, coadjutors, or suffragans.

Missionary districts vary enormously in size from the few scattered missions in the Dominican Republic, a district with no formal organization and administered by the neighboring Bishop of Haiti under the direction of the Presiding Bishop, to the District of Honolulu, organized as virtually an independent diocese and whose statistics reveal a greater communicant strength than that of some dioceses at home. Every now and then the advance of the Church's work in a missionary district is sufficient to admit of self-support, and the district is accordingly admitted to General Convention as a new diocese. In 1952, for example, the former missionary area of New Mexico and Southwest Texas became the seventy-fifth diocese of the Episcopal Church.

PROVINCIAL ORGANIZATION AND ACTIVITY

Anciently the Church was divided into *provinces,* each normally the sphere of an archbishop's jurisdiction and possessing some measure of autonomy and independence. In many Churches of the Anglican Communion these divisions still exist. The Church of England, for example, is divided into the two ancient provinces of Canterbury and York, each with its own archbishop and with parallel ecclesiastical organization. While the Episcopal Church uses the technical term "province" to describe different groups of dioceses within the national Church, our provinces are not separate and independent ecclesiastical jurisdictions. The diocese, not the province, is the basic constitutional unit; the Episcopal Church is really a single national province. The eight regional divisions are simply groupings of dioceses for greater convenience and closer co-operation in doing the work of the Church in different parts of the country.

Each province consists of the dioceses located in a given geographical area. The First Province is that of New England; the Second (including the missionary districts in the Atlantic area) and Third comprise the Middle Atlantic dioceses; the Province of Sewanee covers the southeastern states; the Fifth Province is that of the Mid-West; the Sixth and Seventh those of the Northwest and Southwest; and the Eighth Province is composed of the dioceses and missionary districts in the Pacific area. The organization of these provinces is modelled after that of the national Church. Representatives of the dioceses meet in a *Provincial Synod,* divided into a House of Bishops and a House of Clerical and Lay Deputies. Each province has its executive officers, a provincial council, and a number of departments through which the Church's program is assisted. Liaison with the general work of the Church is maintained through the presence on the National Council of a representative of each province, who may be a bishop, priest, or layman.

The legislative power of provincial synods is greatly restricted, on one hand by the independence of the dioceses and on the other by the Constitution of the national Church. The synods, therefore, are little more than official conferences by which the work of the Church in any given area may be increased in effectiveness and co-ordination. Yet the canons governing provincial organization are flexible enough to allow full development of provincial efforts to meet the special problems and opportunities presented to groups of dioceses in different parts of the country.

The chief fields of provincial activity are those of evangelism, youth work, Christian education, and college work. In the different provinces the intensity of the work varies with both the local needs and the resources with which the province is able to meet them. Some provinces do more extensive work than others, but all strive to develop provincial programs in these fields and render the utmost assistance to the dioceses and their parishes. In addition to this departmental activity there are provincial officers of the Woman's Auxiliary and other national organizations, a small number of provincial schools and institutions, and an important group of summer conferences operated by the provinces. Such annual gatherings as the Finger Lakes Conference of the Second Province, the Hood Conference of the Third Province, the Sewanee Summer Conference, and others play a strategic role in the Church's program of Christian education.

Provinces are differently situated in respect to the ways in which the work of the Church must be done. Rural work in New England, for example, presents aspects quite unlike those of the same work in the South or in the far West.

Again, the Indian work on the reservations of the western missionary districts has no counterpart in the East where there are special problems peculiar to the urban and industrial areas of the country. The existence of these differences makes the greatest value of provincial organization the fact that it permits close co-operation among dioceses that are challenged by similar opportunities. By contributing to the support of highly trained provincial leadership and special programs that few dioceses could maintain single-handed, the work is carried on with far greater effectiveness within each diocese of the province.

CHAPTER SEVEN

The Ministry of the Church

CHRISTIAN ministry of one kind or another is the vocation of all Christian people. The community of members of Christ is "a chosen generation, a royal priesthood, an holy nation, a peculiar people." So runs the description in I Peter 2:9, and one mark of that unique membership is the gift of a share in the priesthood of Christ in His Body the Church.[1] Every Christian is a priest to God for his brethren, and in this "priesthood of all believers" every Christian ministers to them of his own spiritual gifts, both within the fellowship of the Church and in his vocation or occupation in the world.[2] Thus we pray, in the second Good Friday collect, "for all estates of men in thy holy Church, that every member of the same, in his vocation and ministry, may truly and godly serve thee." [3]

Within this universal ministry of all Christians is the Church's ordained ministry of the clergy. These are those called of God, commissioned by Christ through their fellow churchmen, and ordained or consecrated in the apostolic

---

[1] See *The Faith of the Church,* pages 137-138.
[2] See *The Worship of the Church,* pages 205-207.
[3] *Book of Common Prayer,* page 156.

succession to perform special functions necessary for the continuation of the Church's life and the fulfillment of its redemptive task. The official ministry of the Episcopal Church, as we have already seen, is the historic and Catholic three-fold order of *Bishops, Priests,* and *Deacons.* The spiritual powers and responsibilities of each order are clearly set forth in the Prayer Book and its Ordinal; their administrative functions and duties are prescribed in the Constitution and canon law.

The bishop is a chief pastor. Consecrated by other bishops with whom he shares oversight of the welfare of the whole Church and the advance of its mission, his particular charge is the spiritual government of the diocese which has chosen him for this office. He administers Confirmation; he alone can confer Holy Orders upon others. Because today a bishop can seldom minister personally and directly to his flock, as bishops anciently did, his first concern is for his clergy to whose pastoral care he entrusts his people. The usual parochial minister is the priest. While the preaching of the Word of God and the administration of the Church's Sacraments have been for centuries the central functions of the priest's order, the full scope of these duties embraces every Christian educational, pastoral, and spiritual activity. The deacon generally acts as an assistant minister, helping the priest in the parish or ministering under the bishop's supervision in a mission or unorganized congregation of the diocese. The sacramental functions of his order are limited. He cannot celebrate the Holy Communion, pronounce Absolution, give the solemn blessing of the Church, or perform other acts of the priesthood.

But no such brief description of the official duties of the ministry can convey the challenging nature of this calling or the total demands it makes upon a man's life and character. Pastoral care requires a patient, outreaching love for the children of God everywhere, without respect of persons or concern for oneself. Spiritual leadership rests upon a faithful and humble devotion to God's truth and a capacity to bring it intelligently and fearlessly to bear upon the situations that confront men in the world. No vocation demands a higher standard of personal integrity than the priesthood, for the judgments that help a man to grow are seldom imposed upon the priest by others; they are the acts of God and he must find them for himself in the quality of his inner life. In the striking phrase that roused people to their full capacity for heroism in the last war, the Christian ministry asks of a man "blood, sweat, and tears." Perhaps that is why it has called out of every generation a share of its finest manhood. The blood is that of a life spent for others; the sweat that of long study, vigilant prayer, and constant labor in circumstances often discouraging and unrewarding; the tears those of compassion in which the priest lives the sorrows, temptations, and troubles of those he seeks to bring closer to Christ. For these things only the grace of God is sufficient, but that same grace brings an inward joy and a sense of purpose which transcend all else in the Christian ministry.

PREPARATION FOR THE MINISTRY

Men are not ordained to the ministry easily or quickly. The standards of learning and theological preparation for this exacting vocation are precisely specified by the canons of the Church. Before ordination a candidate must satisfy the *Examining Chaplains,* a group of learned clergy in his diocese, that he has sufficiently studied the major disciplines of theology, as well as having had a thorough introduction to the practical aspects of pastoral work. The ideal incorporated in the canon law is that preparation for the ministry combines three things—spiritual growth and development which will affect the quality of a man's pastoral care; academic theological study that will shape his preaching and teaching; and professional training equipping him for the responsibilities of leadership in the parish. Actually these cannot be so neatly separated one from the other. All three affect every part of a man's ministry, and necessarily he embarks upon them simultaneously.

Normally the scene of this preparation is one of the theological seminaries of the Episcopal Church. When a young man has been graduated from college, or has the equivalent of a college education, with the approval of his rector he takes the first step towards future ordination. Presenting the required testimonials of health and character, he is admitted *Postulant* by his bishop, unless that step has already been taken, and enters a seminary for its three-year course. Postulancy is a period of trial on both sides, so to speak. A number of men, uncertain of vocation but conscientiously drawn to make at least a beginning, find inward assurance of a call to the priesthood during their postulancy. Others may come to realize that the ministry is not the vocation which God has given them. The Church at the same time tests a man's devotion, integrity, and potential abilities, for ordinarily not until he has been a postulant for a year is he admitted to the decisive status of *Candidate for Holy Orders*. At the conclusion of a postulant's first seminary year, testimonials of his character, scholastic record, and personal qualifications for the ministry are laid before the Standing Committee of his diocese. All those who should know best both the virtues and faults of a postulant—the rector and vestry of his parish, the faculty members in his seminary, and the bishop himself—are involved in this moment of considered judgment for the sake of the man and the Church. Favorable action by the Standing Committee recommends to the bishop his admission to candidacy, a status in which he normally remains until the end of his seminary course.

The care taken in the Church to ensure what the Prayer Book calls "a due supply of persons fitted to serve God in the ministry" is not terminated by admission to candidacy. Graduation from a seminary or the reception of a bachelor's degree in divinity does not automatically qualify a man for ordination. When the Examining Chaplains are satisfied with his academic preparation, the Standing Committee must again act to recommend him to be ordained, first to the diaconate, and after a period of six months to a year or more, to the priesthood. Each recommendation requires appropriate testimonials, those for the first ordination including another certificate of mental and physical health as well as a final judgment from the seminary in respect to personal qualifications.

Such are the normal regulations governing preparation for the ministry. The Church, however, recognizes that the call of God may come to a man after he has already entered some business or profession. In that case the canons provide for special preparation in which account is taken of both a man's age and experience. Some of these candidates study for ordination under the supervision of clergy in their dioceses; others spend at least a year at a seminary undertaking a special course. It is not uncommon today to encounter in our seminaries former lawyers, businessmen, engineers, college professors, and former ministers of other Churches, all preparing to begin life afresh in the Holy Orders, often at the cost of great personal sacrifice to them and their families.

THE THEOLOGICAL SEMINARIES

Our theological seminaries are, unhappily, too little known to the great mass of Church people. The average communicant is likely to have only the vaguest idea of how and where his rector prepared for ordination, and sometimes he thinks of this chiefly as "studying the Bible." The seminaries are theological graduate schools, the counterpart of law or medical schools, where a man is trained in the major disciplines of theological study: the Scriptures and their interpretation, the doctrines that govern Christian faith and life, and the history of the Church. In addition, a whole range of allied studies form a part of the curriculum: worship, missions, the history and philosophy of religion, apologetics, ethics, and numerous elective courses in different aspects of the major subjects. These academic studies are accompanied by an introduction to the practical and professional work of the ministry through training in preaching, Christian education, rural and urban sociology, pastoral care, and parochial administration. Furthermore, today nearly all our seminarians give their summers to supervised field training and experience in hospitals, missions, and programs of practical work. The seminary does not equip a man fully to meet every possible contingency that may arise in his ministry. No institution can do that. It seeks, however, to assist him in forging a living tool out of his own vocation by which the work of Christ in his Church may be done faithfully and effectively.

There are eleven theological seminaries of the Episcopal

Church.[4] In them the majority of candidates for Holy Orders receive their theological education and professional training.[5] The seminaries vary in size, more than a hundred students being a large institution; and in location, being situated variously in metropolitan areas, university centers, or small towns of the countryside. More important, they differ from one another in the traditions that give each school its distinctive character. For the most part these differences of spirit and outlook are signs of vigor in the life of the seminaries. An institution whose vitality is sustained by the impact of generations of men would be colorless indeed if it had not acquired a distinctive ethos that is reflected in its common life and helps to mold the minds of its graduates. Furthermore, the variety and flexibility of the Anglican tradition itself finds natural expression in the differences that characterize the seminaries.

The oldest of the seminaries is the *General Theological Seminary* in New York, founded in 1817 as an institution which should "have the united support of the whole Church of these United States, and should be under the superintendence and control of the General Convention." The establishment of this center for "general" theological education

---

[4] There are three other seminaries located in overseas missionary districts: *St. Andrew's Theological Seminary* in the Philippines; the *Séminaire Théologal de l'Eglise Episcopale d'Haiti* in Haiti; and the *Seminário Teológico da Igreja Episcopal Brasileria* at Porto Alegre, Brazil. Staffed partly by American clergy, these schools prepare men for the native ministry in each mission field.

[5] Occasionally candidates receive their theological training at other than Episcopal institutions. The Union Theological Seminary in New York, the Yale Divinity School, the Harvard Divinity School, and the University of Chicago all have a number of graduates in the Episcopal ministry, as do some other Protestant schools. Often a man attending one of these institutions transfers to a Church seminary for at least a year's study before ordination. Some clergy have done the major part of their theological study abroad, generally in the colleges of Oxford or Cambridge.

soon diminished the previous practice of reading privately for orders. Proposals then current for the creation of diocesan seminaries to train men locally were largely set aside.[6] By the circumstances of its foundation the General Seminary became the official seminary of the Church, though it received no support from church funds and the "superintendence and control" was seldom very onerous. Today, when the canons provide for the recognition of a number of institutions as "theological seminaries of this Church," the chief distinguishing mark of General Seminary's official character is the election of a majority of its governing board of trustees by the General Convention.

Within a few years of its foundation General Seminary exercised a powerful influence throughout the Church. Among its vigorous supporters was the energetic and conservative John Henry Hobart, intensely loyal to the Prayer Book and concerned to emphasize the unique character of the Episcopal Church among the non-Roman Churches in America. Something of this devotion to the historic Catholic heritage of Anglicanism at its best was implanted in the growing traditions of the General Seminary. Through the years the seminary has occupied a notable position in the intellectual life of the Episcopal Church, numbering among its faculty members many of the finest Anglican scholars in this country. Today, with its large faculty, numerous resources, and strategic situation among the unique facilities

---

[6] Under the urgency of training the large number of men who offered themselves for the ministry when a serious shortage of clergy existed at the end of the last war, the practice of studying privately for orders received new impetus in some dioceses. One long inactive diocesan seminary, originally chartered in 1834 as the *Theological Seminary of the Episcopal Church in Kentucky,* reopened in Lexington, Kentucky, to train men for the needs of the ministry in that area. Since its reopening this seminary has broadened its aims, and today its resources and facilities are steadily expanding.

of New York City, the General Seminary fulfills not only its original purpose, but also enrolls an increasing number of clergy for advanced theological study.

The youngest of the seminaries is the *Episcopal Theological Seminary of the Southwest,* located at Austin, Texas, adjacent to the University of Texas and its affiliated institutions. Situated in an area far from the older seminaries, this school meets a long need for a center of theological training in the Southwest, and reflects the vigorous advance of the Episcopal Church in that part of the country during the last few decades. Each year the Seminary of the Southwest grows stronger in resources, personnel, and reputation; its future is filled with great promise of service to the Church.

The ministry of the Church in the South has long been associated with two older seminaries in that region whose graduates have dispersed as well throughout all the dioceses and missionary districts in the United States and overseas. The *School of Theology* of the University of the South, a Church college in Tennessee owned by the dioceses of the southern provinces, was established in 1878. Commonly known as "Sewanee," the seminary is attached to the university as its theological graduate school. In a long and notable history of service to both Church and community in the southern states, the university and its seminary have provided distinguished Christian leadership among clergy and laymen alike.

The *Protestant Episcopal Theological Seminary in Virginia* at Alexandria, largest of the southern schools and the rival of the General Seminary in the size of its undergraduate body, was founded under Evangelical auspices and opened in 1823 as a result of combined action by the Virginia diocesan convention and a group organized to promote theological education, known as "The Society for the Education of Pious Young Men for the Ministry." Almost at once the seminary began its notable association with the mission fields of the Church to which the ardent Evangelical spirit characteristic of the institution carried many of its graduates. Virginia men were responsible for the foundation and first beginnings of missionary work in many of our present overseas districts. Today the Virginia Seminary, which has recently completed a highly successful building program, occupies an influential place in the life of the Church. The warm fellowship of its community life and the earnest Evangelical piety of its tradition combine to maintain at the school much of the original spirit of its founders.

One of the commanding figures in the development of theological education in the Episcopal Church was Alonzo Potter, a brilliant graduate of Union College who had the distinction of being confirmed by Bishop White and being ordained by Bishop Hobart. Himself Bishop of Pennsylvania during the Civil War years, and his younger brother and son successively Bishops of New York, the Potters were among the great pastors and administrators of the nineteenth century. In 1861, concerned by the inability of northern students to attend the Virginia Seminary during the war, Alonzo Potter founded the *Divinity School of the Protestant Episcopal Church in Philadelphia* and launched it upon its long career of service to the Church. The Philadelphia seminary has made significant contributions to theological education. From time to time its faculty has contained some of the most distinguished scholars of the Episcopal Church; it has pioneered in such experiments as the requirement of clinical training for all students and the theological education of ordinands and women workers in the same institution.

Two seminaries are located in New England, the older being the *Berkeley Divinity School,* founded in 1854 by Bishop Williams at Middletown, Connecticut, and subsequently moved to New Haven where it enjoys the advantages of affiliation with Yale University and its divinity school. For a long time chiefly associated with Connecticut and the neighboring dioceses, today Berkeley's influence is greatly extended. Its students are drawn from many areas and its graduates are widely distributed throughout the Church, while recent expansion has converted a traditionally small school into one of the larger Episcopal seminaries. Yet Berkeley is still loyal to the conservative ideals of Connecticut churchmanship and invigorated by the sturdy spirit which has characterized that outlook since the days of Bishop Seabury.

In 1867 the other New England seminary was founded by a group of distinguished Bostonians in Cambridge, Massachusetts, where the *Episcopal Theological School* in close proximity to Harvard University has the use of its wide academic resources in an affiliation similar to that of Berkeley with Yale. One unique feature has characterized the Episcopal Theological School from the beginning. With a board of trustees composed entirely of interested laymen, the seminary was spared the restraints of ecclesiastical control and free to explore fearlessly the intellectual gains of nineteenth-century Liberalism. The spirit of the school was marked by a vigorous Evangelicalism of the type represented in the teaching and preaching of Phillips Brooks, open on all sides to new apprehensions of Christian truth. Perhaps the greatest contribution of this seminary to the scholarship of the Church was its staunch espousal of the new science of biblical criticism in a day when what is now universally accepted was then regarded as a dangerous if not heretical pursuit. This high standard of intellectual integrity and ready welcome to truth from all quarters has often attracted to this seminary men of widely different schools of thought. Today the influence of its tradition is strong in both the leadership and the academic life of the whole Church.

On the west coast is the *Church Divinity School of the Pacific,* founded by Bishop Nichols of California in 1893, and in 1930 moved to its present location at Berkeley. There it enjoys the use of the resources of the University of California and the Pacific School of Religion. Long a small institution, the Church Divinity School was never adequate to serve the growing needs of the far western provinces. Recent reinvigoration, however, has greatly increased its size and strength and given it a place of critical importance in the life of the Episcopal Church. A large, strong theological school in the West will be the inevitable accompaniment of the steady growth of the Church in that area.

There are three other seminaries, all in midwestern states. In 1824 the irascible and intrepid Philander Chase, one of the most remarkable missionaries to carry the Episcopal Church into the frontier country, founded the first seminary of the Church west of the Alleghenies. English benefactors gave liberally to the foundation, and their names are perpetuated today in the names of the college, seminary, and town. Located in 1828 at Gambier, Ohio, within a few years the seminary of Kenyon College was separated from the undergraduate department and became known as *Bexley Hall, The Divinity School of Kenyon College.* One of the earliest distinctions of the Hall was the large number of graduates who went out into the missionary work of the surrounding areas as the West was opened up. Today Bexley, offering the intimate fellowship of a smaller seminary, continues its association with Kenyon as the theological graduate school of that college.

The foundation of *Nashotah House* was associated with the notable missionary bishop, Jackson Kemper. Consecrated in 1835, Kemper began his pioneer work, as we have seen in an earlier chapter, in the vast area of the Missouri and Indiana Territories, a supervision shortly enlarged to include Wisconsin and Iowa. The best memorial of Kemper's work is a sentence in the resolution passed by the Board of Missions upon his retirement—"six dioceses where he began with none, and 172 clergymen where he was first sustained by only two." Behind that factual statement of incredible achievement is a story of sacrifice and courage, of repeated heartache and new resolution that is scarcely matched in the missionary annals of our Church.

Many of Kemper's new clergy came from the seminary on the shores of Nashotah Lake. Originally intended to be a community of missionary priests entrusted to the care of James Lloyd Breck and William Adams, who had responded to Kemper's appeal at the General Seminary, Nashotah House soon became a theological training center. By the middle of the nineteenth century its life was intimately connected with the new dioceses forming in Kemper's old single jurisdiction. Beginning with a tradition of American high churchmanship and later markedly affected by the influences of the Oxford Movement, Nashotah House has always sought to give full expression to the Catholic heritage of Anglicanism. Its influence today provides more than a little of that emphasis which is an essential part of the unique ethos of the Episcopal Church.

The third midwestern seminary unites the traditions of two older institutions. The indefatigable missionary labors of Breck took him through the great Northwest Territory, and at Faribault, Minnesota, in 1858 he established the mission and school from which developed the Seabury Divinity School. A quarter of a century later, William Edward McLaren, Bishop of Chicago, founded the Western Theological Seminary in that city. In 1933 these two seminaries were united in the *Seabury-Western Theological Seminary* in Evanston, Illinois. The wisdom of the merger has been amply attested by the growth and development of Seabury-Western. It has been the heir of the strength in the traditions of both older schools. Strategically situated close to Northwestern University and other educational institutions, Seabury-Western offers its students not only the intellectual opportunities of Evanston, but also the advantages of training in the great metropolitan area of Chicago.

No such brief review can do justice to the distinctive character of each of our seminaries, but one thing is true of them all. In the corporate religious life that centers in the chapel of every school, men find that spiritual maturity which must accompany all academic and professional training for the ministry. After all, the priest is first and last a man of God. Growth in the things of the spirit is the constant aim of every seminary community.

VOCATIONS WITHIN THE MINISTRY

We ordinarily think of the clergyman as a parish priest, the rector or minister-in-charge of the local congregation. He is responsible for its evangelistic, social, and educational activities as well as for the pastoral care of its people. The great majority of men ordained to the ministry serve in this capacity, and despite the changes appearing in modern society, the ancient place of the parish as the local unit of the Church's life is still central in our thinking.

There are, however, a number of special vocations within the ministry, some as old as the Church itself, others formed out of the recognition of new opportunities presented by new times. All involve a ministry of pastoral care, but its exercise is within the particular circumstances of specialized work for the advancement of the Church's task. Some men, for example, are called to the Church's oldest ministry, that of the *missionary*. While in one sense all Christians are missionaries, there is a unique evangelistic challenge offered by pagan lands. To plant the Church of Christ where it never has been requires a measure of special training and demands a high degree of self-sacrifice. As long as the Church seeks to carry out God's purpose for men there will be missionaries among those called to its ministry. Today in modern industrial society this vocation has been broadened. The ministry in urban and industrial centers, frequently with thousands of unchurched people, has assumed many of the characteristics of true missionary work. An increasing number of *urban priests,* as they are called, are devoting themselves to the evangelistic and pastoral opportunities offered among the industrial workers and in the crowded cities. Similarly, changing patterns in American society have created special problems for the Church in the remote rural areas of the country. A particular vocation to rural work shapes itself in the minds of many men preparing for ordination.

The ministry of *teachers,* as ancient and necessary in the life of the Church as that of missionaries, has expanded far beyond the faculties of theological seminaries, Church colleges and schools. Often there is opportunity for a priest to join a college or university staff as a teacher of history, philosophy, or some other subject normally regarded as purely secular. There he may bring to bear not only Christian conviction and example, but also the intellectual influence of one whose interpretation of human knowledge and events is governed by the Christian revelation.

Chaplaincies of one kind or another are a growing form of particular ministry. Army, Navy, and Air Force chaplains carry the ministrations of the Church to men in their country's service, while chaplains in schools, colleges, hospitals, prisons, and other institutions exercise a ministry of care and counseling not normally within reach of the parish priest. Like other forms of specialized ministry, these posts give scope for the dedication of men's particular abilities and talents to the service of God.

The canons of the Episcopal Church provide for the exercise of one special vocation that is less well-known than others. This is the so-called *perpetual diaconate,* the ministry of a man who is ordained deacon without necessarily advancing to the priesthood. Remaining part of the time in secular employment, he may devote himself to assisting in a parish or assuming temporary charge of a mission or unorganized congregation. This limited ministry gives a man, to whom a full-time ministry may be impossible for reasons of age or lack of university education, opportunity to serve both the needs of the Church and his own inward calling.[7]

[7] The canons require the full preparation if such men desire advancement to the priesthood.

RELIGIOUS ORDERS

One special vocation is shared by men, some ordained and some laymen, and by women. Throughout the Christian ages the call to a life of prayer, study, and service, lived with others under the religious vows of poverty, chastity, and obedience, has been a constant form of ministry. As early as the third century men discovered that in a life of self-renunciation, dedicated to the glory of God and the service of mankind that His vision inspires, there is a witness to Christian absolutes which will always be present in the Church's life. The community of those wholly given to the things of God is a constant reminder that the Christian life on every level should be one of brotherhood, self-sacrifice, and service, empowered by the hidden companionship of Christ in prayer.

The power of this ideal inspired men and women through the centuries to embrace what came to be called "the religious life." In the Church of the Roman Empire the compelling witness of the monks strengthened the whole Christian body against the temptation of compromise with the secular ways and values of the imperial world. In the dark days when barbarism threatened to engulf the culture of the West, the flame of learning and virtue was kept alight in the monasteries, those same religious communities from whose missionary spirit the Christian faith spread to evangelize the world about them. In the high Middle Ages, year in and year out, the worship of men and women in the cloister reminded their brethren in the field and workshop, the cottage and castle, that the first loyalty of a Christian society was to Almighty God.[8]

---

[8] See *Chapters in Church History*, pages 63-66, 109-110.

For nearly a thousand years the religious communities served the growth of Western civilization well. Within their gates were schools, hospitals, sanctuaries of rest and refreshment, libraries and treasuries, training grounds for statesmen and ecclesiastics, centers of the development of arts and crafts, agricultural skills and new forms of husbandry—all the work of generations of men and women who gave themselves first to the religious life. But the monasteries were subject to the same alternating periods of greatness and decline that mark the history of many Christian institutions. Decay and revival, suppression and reform—these are familiar words in the story of conventual life through the years.

The gravest crisis in monastic history occurred during the sixteenth-century Reformation. The continental Protestant reformers repudiated the principle of the religious life, challenging the popular medieval notion that monasticism was a "higher way" of Christian living. They insisted that the virtues and ideals of religious brotherhood should be part of all Christian family and community life. In place of the discipline of poverty assumed by a few, they recalled every Christian to the responsibility of stewardship. Strict adherence to the law in God's Word and the sacred duty of marital and familial devotion were set above the old vows of obedience and chastity.

Free from the passions of controversy, we can see now, as the Church did in its early centuries, that these things are not mutually exclusive. In the sixteenth century, however, monasticism was so far decayed and so closely associated with both the religious and economic evils of the old order, that where the papal system was swept away its religious houses were secularized or destroyed. As on the continent, so in

England, organized religious orders disappeared with the repudiation of the papal jurisdiction at this time. Perhaps in England their disappearance was less because Englishmen denied the principle of the religious life, than because the monastic institution itself, too long and too deeply involved in the whole medieval order, could not find a basis upon which to survive the social, economic, and religious changes that were creating the modern world.

Yet the ancient principle of this Christian vocation reasserted itself in Anglicanism about a hundred years ago. Its revival bore testimony to the fact that the Catholic life was not confined to the Roman Church, but in its broadest aspects formed a part of the Anglican heritage. Slowly but surely religious orders for both men and women have grown throughout the Anglican Communion, and in 1930 the Lambeth Conference expressed its gratitude for the contribution made to a deeper spiritual life in the Church and for the notable services in the mission field by those "who have given their lives in complete sacrifice as a supreme act of worship of God and for His immediate service." [9]

In the Episcopal Church the canon law governing the ministry in its various forms recognizes the vocation of men and women to the religious life and provides for the regulation of such communities. There are fifteen orders for women in our Church. Their diversified activities record the sacrifices and accomplishments of scores of women who have found a ministry for Christ and His Church in the special vocation to which they have been called. Homes for aged women, girls, and children, rest and retreat houses, hospitals and convalescent centers are operated by a number of communities, including the *All Saints Sisters of the Poor* in

[9] *Report of the Lambeth Conference, 1930,* pages 62, 184.

Maryland, the *Community of St. Saviour* in California, the *Community of St. John Baptist,* the *Sisterhood of the Holy Nativity,* and the *Society of St. Margaret,* sisters of the latter being also at work in the missionary district of Haiti. Christian education has always been of primary interest to the religious orders, and sisters of nearly all our communities find opportunities to teach. Several orders maintain day or boarding schools. The *Order of St. Helena* at Versailles, Kentucky, operates the Margaret Hall School; St. John Baptist School in New Jersey is owned by the community of that name. St. Mary's School at Peekskill, New York, Kemper Hall in Kenosha, Wisconsin, and St. Mary's School in Sewanee, Tennessee, are operated by the *Community of St. Mary,* an order whose total work includes nearly all the different activities of the sisterhoods and ranges as far afield as the missionary district of The Philippines.[10]

Brief mention of three of the eleven religious orders for men in the Episcopal Church will illustrate the kinds of activity in which all of them engage. The *Mission Priests of St. John the Evangelist,* commonly known from the English foundation as "Cowley Fathers," have their monastery in Cambridge, Massachusetts, with branch houses in Boston, Chicago, and Oyama in Japan. While the order is in charge of several parishes and missions, its priests are chiefly known for spiritual direction, the conduct of retreats, and the preaching of parochial missions widely throughout the Church. The *Order of the Holy Cross,* an American foundation and one of the larger men's communities, is best known to many Episcopalians for two strikingly diverse achieve-

[10] For a list of other women's orders and their work, as well as a brief description of all the orders for men, see *The Episcopal Church Annual* (New York: Morehouse-Gorham), a handbook of information and statistical data.

ments—the foundation of Kent School in Connecticut and the famous mission at Bolahun in the interior of Liberia. There a remarkable work is done among the tribesmen in forty evangelistic centers and schools for over five hundred boys and girls. Normally four or five priests of the order are stationed in the African mission, assisted by a half-dozen nuns of the English community of the Sisters of the Holy Name who have oversight of the work with native girls. From its monastery at West Park, New York, the order also operates a school for boys in the mountains of Tennessee and maintains a western house in California. Of a slightly different type is the *Order of St. Benedict,* a community still closely associated with Nashdom Abbey in England where its American founders first entered the religious life. The rule of prayer and study at St. Gregory's Priory in Three Rivers, Michigan, reflects the ancient Benedictine Rule that has had a central place in western Christian monasticism for centuries. While the priests of the order exercise a ministry of preaching and spiritual direction, this is always secondary to the activity of the community itself in the corporate worship of God.

Inevitably a description of the religious orders in the Episcopal Church emphasizes their works, charitable and philanthropic, educational and missionary. These are the services inspired by that vision of God to which the life of a religious community is directed. Then, too, Americans are practical folk; we like to know what people *do.* But it must not be forgotten that the essential character of this life of self-dedication cannot be measured by what is seen or done. The primary activity of the religious orders will always be setting forth that from which all Christian service ultimately springs—the glory of God and the praise of His Holy Name.

THE MINISTRY OF WOMEN

In the Episcopal Church, in addition to their participation in the work of the Woman's Auxiliary, women have been brought into service in a large number of administrative posts and policy-making bodies. Diocesan canons, for example, permit women to serve on parochial vestries and as delegates to diocesan conventions in nearly half the dioceses and missionary districts. Women carry a responsible burden of the work in diocesan councils and departments, and on the national level they are represented in the National Council and on several commissions of General Convention. Only for election to the House of Deputies of the Convention itself are they ineligible. The Constitution prescribes that each diocese be represented by four *laymen,* a word that has been traditionally interpreted to restrict this office to men. Because it appears difficult to find a Christian basis for distinction in principle between men and women as lay persons, in 1952 an attempt was made to amend the Constitution to permit women to serve as deputies. Significantly enough, the action was defeated, not by the clergy but by the vote of laymen.

Other opportunities for women workers in the Church, in addition to new administrative responsibilities, have increased steadily in the last few decades. Evangelists, doctors, nurses, and teachers have long performed invaluable services in the missionary districts, and today there are always places in hospitals, schools, and mission stations for women who give themselves to these forms of Christian ministry. The most recent expansion of women's work, however, is associated with developments in the fields of Christian education, social service, and college work. At least half of all the women workers in the Church are engaged in these activities, the greater number serving as parochial directors of religious education. A third of the dioceses employ supervisors of diocesan educational programs, and an increasing number of Episcopal student centers at women's colleges, coeducational universities, or nearby parishes are seeking women trained for the special opportunities offered there for evangelism, education, and personal counseling. The present difficulty here is chiefly with problems of recruitment. The Church on the parish level has insufficiently presented its women with these forms of service as Christian vocations. Relatively few women are aware of the increasing opportunities for such work, or the challenge that it presents for a career of special ministry.

Facilities for proper training of professional workers who will serve in the fields of education or social work, either at home or in the missionary districts, are at present provided in two institutions, *St. Margaret's House* at Berkeley, California, and *Windham House* in New York City (now combined with the former St. Mary's House of Philadelphia). In each house college graduates are equipped with the necessary theological preparation for their work, as well as with graduate professional degrees taken respectively at the University of California and Columbia University or through the institutions affiliated with each. Appropriate preparation for work in the Episcopal Church is received by the California students in the Church Divinity School of the Pacific, while Windham House students take special courses at the General Theological Seminary. Institutions of the character of St. Margaret's House and Windham House ensure proper spiritual and intellectual preparation, offer supervised experience in field work, and provide a corporate life during the period of training for women's work.

The question is sometimes raised of the ordination of women to the regular ministry. During the last twenty-five years the admission of women to the ordained ministry has received frequent discussion in some Churches of the Anglican Communion. Arguments for their ordination are ordinarily grounded upon contemporary participation of women on an equal basis with men in nearly all forms of professional responsibility and leadership in the secular world.

Reasons against this departure from the ancient custom of Catholic Christendom are sometimes difficult to discuss objectively and without prejudice. It has been pointed out, for example, that many of the activities of women Protestant ministers are already open to Episcopalian women, either as deaconesses, missionary workers, members of religious orders, or in the other professional positions open to Church workers. A more common objection, and one that usually provokes some debate, is that women are temperamentally unfitted for the strains of the pastoral office. Again, many would maintain that the office of priesthood, in its capacity as spiritual fatherhood, is essentially a man's vocation. More cogent than any of these arguments, perhaps, is the point that the requirements of marriage and motherhood, which could hardly be denied ordained women, preclude that self-abandonment to the priestly ministry that has always sharply distinguished it from other professional activities.

Whatever be the effect of such argument, the ordination of women to the ministry has no precedent in the ancient Catholic tradition which is a central part of the Anglican heritage. As one of the branches of the Anglican Communion, the Episcopal Church could not readily depart from this common tradition without wide agreement upon this innovation among fellow Anglicans, nor would it be likely that such a step could be taken without careful consideration of the views in other Catholic Churches which have inherited similar traditions.[11] The Lambeth Conference of 1930, after an extended discussion of the ministry of women, resolved that "The Order of *Deaconess* is for women the one and only Order of the ministry which we can recommend our branch of the Catholic Church to recognize and use." [12] The bishops assembled at the Conference urged more adequate provision for the participation of women in the administrative responsibilities of the Church's life.

THE ORDER OF DEACONESS

The traditional means of the ministerial activity of women, apart from the religious orders, has been through the office of *Deaconess*. This revival of a primitive office in the Church's life came towards the end of the nineteenth century when associations of women for the purpose of serving the Church had become numerous. In 1889 canonical recognition and regulation of such vocations was made in the provisions of canon law governing the ministry of deaconesses.

A candidate must be unmarried or widowed, at least twenty-five years of age, and vouched for in testimonials of character, fitness, and health not unlike those required of

[11] See the report of a commission appointed by the Presiding Bishop to inform the United Church Women of the National Council of Churches concerning the status and services of women in the Episcopal Church. The commission included lay and clerical members in addition to representation of the National Executive Board of the Woman's Auxiliary.

[12] *Report of the Lambeth Conference, 1930,* page 60. The statement was reaffirmed by the Lambeth Conference of 1948. *Report, 1948,* page 52.

men ordained to Holy Orders. Her preparation, in addition to at least a high school education, must have included a study of the basic theological subjects and the principles of social work. Generally preparation extends over a two-year period, and unless a candidate has had suitable previous experience a term of field work under competent supervision is a necessary part of her training. The *Central House for Deaconesses,* opened in 1953 at the McLaren Foundation in Sycamore, Illinois, is now a testing and training center for deaconess candidates.

Admitted for the work of this ministerial office by the bishop in a solemn ceremony,[13] a deaconess is subject to episcopal jurisdiction in the same manner as the clergy. She is an assistant in the parish, mission, or institution where appointed, with special care of the Church's work among women and children. A deaconess may have a responsible share in parochial or diocesan programs of social work and Christian education, a pastoral ministry to the sick and underprivileged; and with the approval of the bishop, she may read Morning and Evening Prayer and deliver addresses at such services. In the absence of a clergyman she may also baptize children. These latter functions reflect the valuable work of deaconesses in the Church's missionary districts where often without their ministrations mission stations could not have been kept open.

Today there are slightly over a hundred deaconesses in the Episcopal Church, about a third of whom have retired

---

[13] While the Prayer Book contains no form for the admission of deaconesses, Canon 51, Sec. 9 requires the use of a religious service prescribed either by General Convention or by the bishop of the diocese. The *Book of Offices,* compiled by the Liturgical Commission and commended for use by General Convention, contains a "Form for the Setting Apart of Deaconesses." *Book of Offices,* 2nd Edition, 1949 (New York: The Church Pension Fund), pages 13-18.

from active service. This represents a sharp decline in recent years from the number formerly at work at any given time. In part this is due to the opening of a greater variety of work for women in the Church, and in part it may be due to the exacting standards of discipline and personal devotion required of a deaconess in her individual ministry. The deaconess' life often appears a lonely one and many women, drawn to a religious vocation, prefer the corporate fellowship offered in the communities of sisters. Yet all ministry has aspects of human loneliness when the only sustaining companionship is that of our Lord, and the Church has not yet brought out of its life any office for women that will take the place of the deaconess order.

THE MINISTRY OF LAYMEN

Ample description has already been given of the wide administrative and governmental responsibilities placed on the laymen of the Episcopal Church at every level from leadership in unorganized congregations to participation in the legislative work of General Convention. These obligations are the potential ministry of every communicant layman. Yet often people forget the vocational aspects of this work. They think of "ministry" only as that which is concerned with the Church's pastoral, liturgical, or evangelistic activity. Even in this more technical sense, however, Episcopal laymen are not merely the object of the ministrations of the clergy; they may have this kind of ministry as well. Two national organizations direct the energies of laymen into these channels. One is the *Presiding Bishop's Committee for Laymen's Work,* chiefly a co-ordinating and recruiting agency by which the total program for laymen is assisted. The other is the widespread *Brotherhood of St. Andrew* whose rules of prayer and service are directed towards leading men and boys into the fullest participation in the Church's worship and mission.

The canons provide for a liturgical ministry for laymen in the office of *Lay Reader,* a modern counterpart of some of the minor ministries that anciently existed in the Church. Lay readers are licensed annually by the bishop for work in the diocese, either assisting a parish priest or taking services during a vacancy in a parish or mission. They are given the privilege of reading the offices of Morning and Evening Prayer, the service of the Burial of the Dead, the Epistle in the Holy Communion, and of reading approved sermons to the congregations.[14] Here is a ministry for active and devoted laymen that fills a constant need in every diocese. There are over seven thousand lay readers, and many missions are served from time to time by the labors of faithful men who fill their Sundays with this work. Not only are the missions kept open, but the life of worship and evangelism continues to grow under such ministrations. Similarly, many parishes in which the rector is single-handed are enabled by the co-operation of a group of lay readers to have the offices of Morning and Evening Prayer offered daily.

If such a ministry is chiefly liturgical, that of the members of the *Church Army* is primarily evangelistic. This is an organization of lay missionaries and evangelists, including women as well as men, whose training center is located at the *Parishfield Community* in Michigan. Whenever possible the Church Army is ready to provide bishops with full-time workers in mission fields and other areas where lay leadership may be effectively used. The Parishfield Community,

---

[14] Canon 50 gives precise directions concerning the portions of Prayer Book services permitted to be read by lay readers.

with which the Church Army is associated, is itself one of the most interesting and important experiments in evangelism in the Church. There a group of Christian families have established a center of spiritual renewal. They are regularly visited by groups from parishes, colleges, industrial associations, and other forms of community in which the need for Christian reorientation has been felt.

THE CARE OF THE CLERGY

In the budget of every Episcopal parish there is an item labelled "Pension Fund," representing a payment made regularly by the vestry to *The Church Pension Fund,* an organization incorporated in the State of New York, whose trustees are elected by the General Convention in accordance with canon law. This corporation administers the national pension system for the care of retired or disabled clergy, their widows, and minor children.

Nearly a half-century ago, a vigorous movement was launched to provide adequately for retired clergy, most of whom after years of faithful service at small salaries faced the bleak prospect of retirement into semi-poverty or worse. Alleviation was then possible only by a grant from one of the numerous societies for clergy relief. In other words, men who had given a lifetime to the Church became in the end objects of charity on the part of those whose concern had been aroused. The energetic and extraordinarily successful work of a group of men headed by William Lawrence, then Bishop of Massachusetts, ended this deplorable situation. The movement led by Bishop Lawrence—indeed, few would qualify the statement that he managed it almost single-handed—resulted in the establishment of a sound national pension system in 1917.

Lawrence's cherished principle was, as he once put it, that "every parish should year by year pay as assessments a certain added percentage of their rector's salary, which, forwarded to the Church Pension Fund, would be put at interest, and on the basis of actuarial tables, be sufficient to see him and his widow through to the end of their lives; in other words it was part of his life salary, but a deferred salary, held for later years, when it would be paid out to him in proportion to the salaries of his life: those who had received larger salaries would have larger pensions." It is clear that Bishop Lawrence's idea was not that the Church should take over a charitable responsibility of supporting its clergy when age or disability terminated their service, but rather that the Church Pension Fund, acting as trustee for those portions of clergy salaries gradually accumulated in the Fund over the years, would be able to return to retired clergy over sixty-eight years of age and no longer exercising an active ministry a stipend which was rightfully theirs by virtue of the amount of the salaries they had received during the years of active service. There is no accounting between resources and liabilities in the Fund at the individual level; the balance is maintained only at the group level. The contributions from all the parishes and missions form a common pool out of which all pensions are paid. Thus the individual clergyman receives his pension out of a common fund and not out of accumulated moneys related to the assessments paid by the parishes he has served. Each parish, therefore, may be said to pay a part of each pension that is granted in this group plan.

While the Church Pension Fund is established by canon law, its administration is in the hands of the trustees who are empowered to determine the pensions and premiums, beyond the established minimum, in accordance with sound actuarial practice and the insurance laws of the State of New York. Parishes currently pay annually a sum equal to fifteen percent of the rector's salary. This permits the retirement of most clergymen at the age of sixty-eight with pensions roughly equivalent to one-half their average salaries over the years of their ministry. Widows receive half that amount, and there are other allowances for minor children or in the case of a clergyman totally and permanently disabled. Because the pension represents a sum considered to have been earned, it is paid to the beneficiary regardless of other sources of income possessed by him.

Figures often change and may not be accurate for a particular year, but usually at any given time the Church Pension Fund is paying pensions to more than nine hundred retired, and about one hundred and twenty-five disabled clergy, with an average annual allowance of about fifteen hundred dollars. Some fifteen hundred widows receive an average of seven hundred and fifty dollars each, and over one hundred and fifty minor orphaned children are paid an average of four hundred dollars each. This represents a measure of care for the clergy of which the Church may justly be proud.

PART THREE

The Activity of the Episcopal Church

CHAPTER EIGHT

Overseas Missions

CONSIDERATION of the activity of the Episcopal Church appropriately begins with its missionary effort. The National Council, organized to direct and implement the Church's evangelistic task, as well as its work in the fields of Christian education, social relations, promotion, and advancement, is heir to the responsibilities exercised by the former "Board of Missions" for *The Domestic and Foreign Missionary Society of the Protestant Episcopal Church.*[1] Three-quarters of the national budget is devoted to missionary work, at home or abroad, and it is with this central activity that our discussion of the work of the Church naturally begins.

Primary in all Christian activity is the evangelistic outreach—the conversion of men and women to Jesus Christ and their saving incorporation into His Body, the Church. That is the final end of all our efforts. "Go ye therefore, and teach all nations, baptizing them in the name of the Father, and of the Son, and of the Holy Ghost: Teaching them to observe all things whatsoever I have commanded you: and, lo, I am with you alway, even unto the end of the world." [2] The divine command sets before us the paramount Christian obligation. Every Christian, in the full sense of that

---

[1] See Chapter V.
[2] Matthew 28: 19-20.

word, is a missionary, seeking to reach the children of God everywhere with the redeeming Gospel of Him who is the Father of us all, who gave His only-begotten Son that we might know the fulness of human life here and hereafter.

The universal claims of Christianity and the consequent case for Christian missions may be presented in a number of ways, all relevant to aspects of man's personal and social life.[3] But in the end the goal of all Christian evangelism is the establishment, under the power of the Holy Spirit, of the supremacy of Jesus Christ in the hearts of men and over the affairs of their common life. It was that which carried St. Paul around a hostile Mediterranean world, that took St. Boniface into the perilous forests of Germany, and which impelled the monks of Iona to brave the wild seas and unfriendly shores of northern Europe. It was that for which the Jesuit Fathers suffered torture at the hands of the North American Indians, and for which hundreds of devoted men and women cheerfully embraced the loneliness and hardships of life on the tropical islands of the South Seas or in some remote hinterland of continental Asia or Africa. Church history in its most dramatic aspect is missionary history, the saga of redemption in every land and clime through a Gospel given by those who have received it.

In this continuing Christian effort the Episcopal Church has its own share and responsibility. One aspect of the Church's missionary enterprise—that of work beyond the borders of the United States—is brought under the direction of the *Overseas Department* of the National Council. To this Department is entrusted the tasks of preparing a pro-

[3] See James Thayer Addison's *Our Expanding Church* (New York: The National Council, 1944), pages 3-18; 99-122; and the arresting suggestions made by Charles Duell Kean in *The Christian Gospel and the Parish Church* (Greenwich: The Seabury Press, 1953).

gram and a budget, and of formulating strategy and policy for our work around the world. The selection, preparation, and care of missionary personnel, both lay and clerical, is undertaken by the Department, as well as the oversight of all overseas mission fields. While the following brief description of each of our missionary areas is far from an adequate summary, yet from it we may gain some idea of the scope of the overseas work of the Episcopal Church.

THE ALASKAN OPPORTUNITY

Few places in the world possess the fascination exercised by the immense territory of Alaska, an undeveloped empire approximately one-fifth the size of the United States. Amid its mountains and forests, stretching from the far Northwest into the Arctic polar regions, lies the last wilderness frontier under the American flag. There is, perhaps, just enough of the frontiersman left in the average American to respond to the beckoning attractions of a vast land whose full exploration still lies in the future. Less than a hundred years ago Alaska was derisively labeled "Seward's Folly," for in 1867 few shared the enthusiasm of the Secretary of State, William H. Seward, for its purchase from Imperial Russia. Today none would acclaim the acquisition of this North American territory from Russian hands as other than an act of far-sighted statesmanship. The discovery of the extent of its rich natural resources, the opening of the country by highway and air traffic, its strategic importance to our national defense, and the rapid population increase in recent years have all aroused new interest in Alaska.

Geographical location and immense size make Alaska a land of sharp contrasts. The southern coastal region with its four-hundred-mile strip reaching down towards the United States is the most populous area. There are situated the oldest cities and ports, and the centers of industry—fishing, mining, lumbering, and the pulp mills. There, too, are the majority of the American settlers. Behind the coastal area lies the vast wilderness of the interior, hundreds of miles of forested land, the home of the semi-nomadic Alaskan Indians. The interior is traversed by the valleys of the Yukon River system and broken by mountain ranges that rise to North America's highest peak, Mt. McKinley. To the far north lies the third contrasting sector of the country, the bleak and desolate Arctic tundra, the land of Eskimo villages and settlements.

Christianity first came to Alaska with the missions of the Russian Orthodox Church at the end of the eighteenth century, and by 1867 there were two dozen Russian clergy in the coastal settlements. By that time Church of England missionaries from western Canada had penetrated the interior to reach the Indians along the Yukon. The interest of the Episcopal Church was aroused soon after the American purchase, but it was not until 1887 that the first permanent mission was started at Anvik by John Chapman, a young graduate of the General Theological Seminary who volunteered for work in Alaska. Chapman was soon followed by others, and in 1892 the *Missionary District of Alaska* was organized. Three years later the famous Peter Trimble Rowe was consecrated its first bishop, beginning an indefatigable missionary ministry that extended over forty years.

Today the work of the Episcopal Church in Alaska is done in two dozen parishes and missions, with many outstations, and in the well-known Hudson Stuck Memorial Hospital. About twenty clergymen are assisted by an equal or greater number of American and native lay workers. Towards this effort the Church at home contributes about a hundred and ten thousand dollars annually, chiefly in the form of allowances and salaries of missionaries, while the Alaskans themselves raise about one-fourth of the total budget of the District. Though the Episcopal Church shows its greatest strength in Fairbanks, Anchorage, Seward, and the coastal towns, our missionary effort is increasingly strong in the remote settlement of the interior and, to the north, in the Artic region. Consequently, many of the missions carry on a remarkable work with the Indians, or, as is the case in the Point Hope area, with the Eskimos.

The District reports nearly three thousand communicants and about twice as many baptized members of the Episcopal Church, a small number if it is remembered that there are two or three parishes in New York City with more communicants each than in all Alaska. But what matters is the proportion of church members in the population, not the total number alone. In the United States one out of every ninety-two persons is a communicant of the Episcopal Church; in Alaska, one out of every fifty people—a much higher ratio than at home, and a striking witness to the growth of the mission in the territory.

Alaska is a land of the future, but our missionary opportunity is greatest at the present moment. By deepening and strengthening the Christian effort on all sides today, the Church will be strong and influential in the days of Alaska's full development.

THE PACIFIC ISLANDS

Out in the Pacific, southwestwards from Alaska, are the American Hawaiian Islands, far better known to thousands of tourists and travelers than Alaska. They are the center of the far-flung *Missionary District of Honolulu,* a jurisdiction now embracing the Hawaiian Islands, American Samoa, Guam, Midway and Wake Islands, and Okinawa. Here is one of the most flourishing and rapidly expanding areas of the Church's missionary work. Financial support from home, while approximately the same in amount as is given to Alaska, is in almost exactly the reverse proportion. The Church through the National Council supports about one-quarter of the work of the District; the people of the islands meet three-quarters of their budget themselves. Honolulu is closer to the status of an independent diocese than any other overseas missionary district in the Episcopal Church.

The Anglican Church first touched the "Sandwich Islands," as the Hawaiian archipelago was originally called, with English traders, explorers, and their chaplains in the late eighteenth century, but no organized work was then done among the natives. When the royal family of the Hawaiian Kingdom appealed to Queen Victoria for Anglican clergy in 1850, however, the response was immediate. Missions and schools were founded by Thomas Staley, the first Anglican bishop, who numbered among his co-workers some sisters of the first Anglican religious community founded since the Reformation, the Society of the Holy Trinity. The celebrated Mother Lydia Sellon herself, friend of Edward Bouverie Pusey and founder of the order, spent some time in the Hawaiian mission.

By 1898, when the islands were annexed by the United States after a revolution had overturned the native monarchy, the work of the English Church was firmly established. With the coming of American rule, the Church of England transferred its jurisdiction to the Episcopal Church, and in 1902 our first missionary bishop replaced his English predecessor. The last half century has been a period of rapid growth of the Church under American leadership, building securely upon the sure foundations laid by devoted English missionaries in the earlier years.

The statistics of the Hawaiian mission reveal a surprisingly strong church life. There are approximately fifteen thousand baptized members of the Episcopal Church, over nine thousand of whom are communicants. More than a dozen of our independent dioceses at home report less communicant strength than Honolulu. About forty clergy are actively at work in the fifty parishes and missions of the District, with six or seven trained women workers assisting them. Two of the largest and oldest Church schools are located in Honolulu, both founded in 1867: the famous Iolani School with its eight hundred boys, and St. Andrew's Priory with five hundred girls, the latter started by the English nuns and now in charge of the American Sisters of the Community of the Transfiguration.

Two features of the missionary work in the District of Honolulu are especially noteworthy. The first is the interracial character of church life. The population of the islands is a unique mixture of races—so much so that within the memory of some missionaries, Episcopalians used their Prayer Book in five languages: English, Hawaiian, Chinese, Japanese, and Korean. Add to these a large Filipino population and a not inconsiderable group of Puerto Ricans, and the result is a racial diversity that is difficult to duplicate elsewhere in the world. Yet among these peoples there is little or no racial prejudice or discrimination, and an intermingling in the Christian community that witnesses to the common brotherhood of all men.

The other striking aspect of the opportunity presented to the Church in the Hawaiian Islands is the large number of non-Christian peoples—about a quarter of a million, chiefly Orientals. The territory is a land not only of American churches and schools, but of Buddhist and Shinto temples as well. These thousands of non-Christians on our doorstep, so to speak, offer a missionary challenge that can be adequately met only by a steadfast willingness to advance the Gospel of Christ and His Church with all our strength and resources.

THE CHURCH IN THE FAR EAST

The Bishop of Honolulu is over two thousand miles from his farthest point of visitation, American Samoa, where episcopal acts are often performed for him by the Anglican Bishop in Polynesia, himself in charge of an equally far-flung missionary diocese of the Church of the Province of New Zealand. There in the broad expanse of the Pacific Ocean these sister Churches of the Anglican Communion touch each other. Spreading thence through the island-studded seas, halfway around the world where west becomes east, are the Polynesian and Melanesian missions of the New Zealand Church, the Borneo diocese of the Church of England, and the American *Missionary District of the Philippines,* known locally as the Philippine Episcopal Church.

The Philippine archipelago contains literally thousands of islands and volcanic islets which for nearly four centuries formed part of the vast Spanish Empire built up in the sixteenth century. The Filipinos, like all the natives in the Spanish overseas possessions, were speedily converted to Roman Catholicism, though it is little exaggeration to say that their religious beliefs and practices were deeply tinged with pagan superstition, and their Christian adherence often merely nominal. In 1898 the guns of Admiral Dewey's cruisers in Manila Bay brought the islands into American possession, a prize of the Spanish-American War. The recent grant of independence, however, has now made the Philippine Republic a free nation.

The Episcopal Church came to Manila as an organized mission in 1902, under the leadership of a devoted and far-sighted missionary bishop, Charles Henry Brent. His initial evangelistic policy was simple and effective. The Episcopal Church would seek to reach, not primarily the Roman Catholic Filipinos, but the numerous pagan peoples of the islands, untouched by the Roman Church—the fierce Igorots of northern Luzon, the Mohammedan Moros and other non-Christian peoples on Mindanao, and the thousands of Chinese in and around Manila. In time, of course, Filipinos were attracted by the earnest and sacrificial work of the missionaries, but still today the Philippine Episcopal Church is closely identified with the groups first reached by Bishop Brent.

The vitality of the Philippine mission was amply demonstrated during and after the second World War. Through its terrible years clergy and mission workers were interned, congregations scattered, and the destruction of churches, mission buildings, schools, and hospitals was all but complete. Yet the Church has recovered with renewed vigor. Today churches and schools are crowded, congregations have more than doubled, and an ambitious program of reconstruction and expansion is well under way. The new diocesan center in Manila, for example, will comprise the Cathedral, the buildings of St. Andrew's Seminary, a new St. Luke's Hospital and Nurses' Training School, as well as offices and residences for the district and institutional staff.

In number of communicants—over fifteen thousand, with twice as many baptized members—the Philippine Church is the largest of our missionary districts. There are more than eighty missions and outstations, served by forty priests, many of whom are natives, trained at St. Andrew's Theological Seminary in Manila. Three large hospitals and two dozen schools are maintained by the Church, and to the total work of the mission in the Philippines the National Council appropriates nearly three hundred thousand dollars annually, the largest single missionary expenditure in the budget. Even this cannot meet the expanding opportunities in the Philippine mission. Increased appropriations are simply signs of the Church's advance. If the need is great in this field today, it only means that the chance to create a stronghold of Christian evangelization in the Far East has never been more promising.

The unique situation in the Philippines is the relation between the Episcopal Church and the native *Iglesia Filipina Independiente,* the Philippine Independent Church, a body of some two million Catholic Christians who broke away from control by the Spanish Romanist hierarchy in the last decade of the nineteenth century and formed a national Church. For nearly fifty years this group maintained all the traditional elements of Catholic church life, except that their bishops were chosen and commissioned without episcopal consecration. The original schism was led by priests; no Roman Catholic bishop joined the native Church. In

1948, however, after prolonged negotiations in which The Rt. Rev. Norman S. Binsted of the missionary district took a leading part, the House of Bishops of the Episcopal Church granted the request of the Filipinos for the gift of orders within the historic apostolic succession. Three of our bishops consecrated Monsignor Isabelo de los Reyes, the Obispo Maximo, and two other prelates of the Philippine Independent Church, as bishops in the apostolic succession. As a result of this bold and almost unprecedented step, the closest co-operation exists today between the two Churches. They are still separate bodies, but already their possible union is foreshadowed. The day may come when their combined strength will manifest itself in a powerful native Philippine witness to true Catholic Christianity.

CHINA AND JAPAN

The familiar Anglican Churches of the Far East are China's *Chung Hua Sheng Kung Hui* and the *Nippon Sei Ko Kwai* in Japan.[4] Each is a separate and autonomous Church of the Anglican Communion, though both had their beginnings in the missionary activity of the English, Canadian, and American Churches.

The first Episcopal missionaries went to China in 1835, and for seventy-five years the Church grew slowly and steadily among the Chinese people. In 1912 the three missionary districts supported by the Episcopal Church—Shanghai, Hankow, and Anking—became simultaneously dioceses in the newly organized national Chinese Church, together with those districts where English and Canadian missionaries pursued the same task of Christian evangelization and

[4] The names are translated as *Holy Catholic Church in China* and *Holy Catholic Church in Japan.*

education. A quarter-century later, at the outbreak of the second World War, the Chung Hua Sheng Kung Hui had become a vigorous indigenous Church, with a large part of its leadership in the hands of Chinese bishops and clergy. Nevertheless the Episcopal Church still maintained its responsibility for the original three districts, our American staff at times numbering as many as one hundred and fifty workers, with annual appropriations from the National Council amounting to more than a half million dollars. A long list of flourishing mission centers, schools, universities, and hospitals testified to the strong Christian influence the Church brought to bear upon the Chinese through evangelism, education, and numerous forms of social service.

The history of our work in Japan is very similar. Episcopal missionaries entered Japan in 1859, six years after Commodore Perry's squadron opened the door which the Japanese had closed to the Western nations. Though for some time direct evangelism was forbidden by the Japanese government, the early missionaries brought a vital Christian influence to bear in the rapidly changing patterns of Japanese cultural life. It was not long before conversions were made, and when the edicts against Christianity were rescinded the Church made steady advances on all sides. In 1887 the missionary areas supported by the Church of England, the Canadian Church, and the Episcopal Church were united into the independent Anglican province of the Nippon Sei Ko Kwai, and in 1923 Tokyo and Osaka became self-supporting dioceses under Japanese bishops. As in China, we continued to assume responsibility for the work in three dioceses, our missionary districts of Kyoto, North Kwanto, and Tohoku. Many such well-known Christian institutions as St. Paul's University, St. Margaret's and St. Agnes' Schools,

St. Luke's Medical Center, and St. Barnabas' Hospital owe their foundation and development to the devotion and support of Episcopalians.

Through the years Japanese leadership came so rapidly to the fore that by 1940, when the Imperial government forbade foreigners to hold any ecclesiastical positions of executive responsibility, the Japanese bishops and clergy were able to carry on without the help of American or English missionaries. Few things so dramatically illustrate the strength of the Japanese Church as its ability to survive the sudden withdrawal of all leading foreign personnel and overseas financial assistance.

The second World War and its aftermath radically affected the condition of the Chinese and Japanese Churches, as well as our whole Christian missionary effort in the Far East. Communist domination has closed China entirely to the Christian mission from outside. In 1951 all Episcopal workers were withdrawn from China, together with other Anglican missionaries, and little is known today of the fate of the Chung Hua Sheng Kung Hui behind the Far Eastern iron curtain. There is no doubt that the sacrifices and sufferings of individual Christians have been great, nor is there any denying the fact that the immediate future is dark and uncertain. Increased Communist power in the East means more intense hostility to Christianity and further jeopardy to the results of a century of missionary activity. Among the many millions in China's population, Christians were but a small minority, those of our own Church numbering perhaps scarcely more than seventy-five thousand. While the influence of Christians in China was disproportionately strong in the days of her freedom, owing in part to the impact of the missionaries upon the educated and governing classes, that situation is undoubtedly reversed under a Communist government. Yet there can be no ground for ultimate despair. The Chinese Church still lives. One inescapable lesson of history is that Christianity has powers of survival beyond those of any earthly political regime. The day will come when the Church will again proclaim the Lord Christ beyond the horizons of the China Sea, along the banks of the Yangtze, and in the shadow of the Great Wall. Our task now is one of constant readiness, with both men and resources, and with the courage to offer them when the day of opportunity dawns.

In Japan, on the other hand, the immediate opportunity is critical and urgent. The Nippon Sei Ko Kwai emerged from the war, weakened by loss of numbers and widespread destruction of church property, but nonetheless with undiminished resolution for the future. Under the able leadership of Michael Hinsuke Yashiro, the Presiding Bishop in the post-war years, recovery and reconstruction has been phenomenally rapid. Today, as perhaps never before, Christian spiritual influence is strong in Japan. Our first opportunity is that of assisting the Japanese Church in making that influence decisive in the life of the nation.

The major missionary effort of the Episcopal Church in Japan is no longer to provide leadership or establish missionary districts. The native bishops and clergy do not need that kind of assistance. Our part is to help them with missionaries and workers who will become temporarily members of the Nippon Sei Ko Kwai, to send them teachers and scholars for the universities and the seminary until such time as the Japanese Church can again bring men adequately trained for special Christian vocations out of its own life, and, perhaps above all, to grant them generously of our greater financial resources. In other words, we have that responsibility which one member of the Anglican fellowship of Churches always bears towards a sister Church in need. Consequently, today our missionary budget for overseas work includes more than two hundred thousand dollars for Japan. Next to that given to the Philippine mission, this is the largest expenditure in any overseas area, a sign that the Church is alive to the critical importance of Christian witness in the Far East.

CENTRAL AMERICA

Turning from the Pacific overseas missions to the Atlantic, we enter Latin America. South of the United States in the neighboring Mexican Republic is the *Missionary District of Mexico,* a missionary field with a Mexican bishop, two dozen Mexican clergy, and about three thousand communicants. The work of the District is heavily subsidized from the United States, for the Mexican Episcopalians, struggling against government restrictions, Romanist hostility, and the handicap of inadequate resources are unable to provide any large measure of self-support.

The origins of the efforts of the Episcopal Church in Mexico lie tangled in a story that is partly the saga of a courageous search for spiritual freedom, and partly a record of lost opportunities. As in the Philippine Islands, the end of oppressive Spanish rule in Latin Mexico ultimately launched a movement among some Roman Catholic clergy and their people for a national Catholic Church. There is a striking parallel on one side with the Philippine Independent Church; on the other, with the Church of England in the sixteenth century, for *La Sociedad Catolicá Apostolicá Mexicana* sought to establish a Church both Catholic and reformed.

In 1874, however, our House of Bishops refused the requests of nationalist Mexican clergy that one of their number be consecrated to the episcopate in order to maintain the ministerial succession necessary to a fully Catholic church life. Instead, an American bishop journeyed to Mexico to ordain their candidates for the diaconate and the priesthood; no further step, it was felt, could be taken. Moreover, five years later when a bishop was actually consecrated for the Mexicans, he was an American, not a native, and unfortunately resigned his post within a very few years. Nearly twenty years after these first attempts by the Mexicans to secure an episcopate, the House of Bishops still deemed it unwise to accede to requests to consecrate a Mexican priest. There was, perhaps, more excuse for the refusal at this time. Through the years the independent Mexican Church—by that time known as *La Iglesia de Jesus*—had declined in numbers, strength, and stability.

By 1904 the situation was altered by the presence in Mexico of a large number of American and British residents who desired the services of the Church. A missionary district was organized and a bishop sent. Two years later he received the remnant of *La Iglesia de Jesus* into the District, and with it a significant area of Mexican work. Today the Mexican bishop, native clergy and people we assist are the spiritual descendants of those who originally attempted to form a national and non-Roman Catholic Church.

Further south in Central America lies the *Missionary District of Panama Canal Zone,* a jurisdiction embracing not only the American Zone, but also missions and outstations in the adjacent Republics of Panama, Colombia, Costa Rica, and Nicaragua. Though missionary beginnings had been made in Panama as early as 1850, it was not until 1904, when the construction of the Canal was undertaken, that the Church began to occupy a significant place in the religious life of the isthmus. At that time the presence of so many Americans, as well as the transportation there of thousands of British West Indian laborers—all traditionally Anglicans—confronted the Episcopal Church with an evangelistic and pastoral obligation that could not be ignored.

The District was formally organized in 1919, including southern Panama, Colombia, and the Zone. In 1947 oversight of the missions in Costa Rica, Nicaragua, and northern Panama was transferred from the Bishop of British Honduras to the Episcopal Bishop of Panama, an example of strategic missionary co-operation between our Church and the sister Anglican Church of the Province of the West Indies. Today the work in the District is varied in character, reaching American and British residents, West Indian Negroes, Spanish Americans, and primitive native Indian tribesmen. The relatively large number of communicants—about seven thousand—indicates the strength and importance of this missionary field.

THE CHURCH IN THE CARIBBEAN

The Episcopal Church supports five missionary districts on the islands of the West Indies in the Caribbean Sea, the *Districts of Cuba, Puerto Rico,* and the *Dominican Republic,* in all of which the work is predominantly among people of Spanish background; the *District of Haiti,* where the citizens of the Negro Republic combine their primitive native traditions with French culture and language; and that of the American *Virgin Islands,* on which are four or five large English-speaking congregations of West Indian Negroes, at one time part of the British Diocese of Antigua.[5]

Missionary activity among the folk of both Spanish and Negro descent in Cuba and Puerto Rico began, as in the Philippines, soon after the conclusion of the Spanish-American War. Both districts were constituted in 1901, bishops being sent to them shortly afterwards. On the islands the veneer of nominal Roman Catholic allegiance characteristic of Spanish imperial Catholicism had been almost universal for centuries, and the advance of missions from other Churches was discouragingly slow. Yet the Christian effort they made was sorely needed. Conditions of acute over-population and its resulting economic distress, the poverty, ignorance, and disease among the depressed classes, the failure of traditional Spanish Romanism to reach large numbers of people with any compelling effectiveness—all created opportunities for launching a program of Christian education and community service simultaneously with the task of direct evangelism. Schools, hospitals, clinics, and social service centers are familiar adjuncts to our mission churches in the West Indies.

Today, after more than a half century of sustained and devoted missionary effort, both of these districts are still very largely supported from home. In the case of Cuba, more than seventy-five per cent of the necessary money comes from the National Council's budget; in Puerto Rico, more than eighty per cent. Their combined communicant strength is approxi-

[5] Neither the District of the Virgin Islands nor that of the Dominican Republic has its own bishop. The Bishop of Puerto Rico at present exercises jurisdiction over the parishes on the Virgin Islands, and the Bishop of Haiti takes charge of the Dominican missions in the eastern half of the same island.

mately fourteen to sixteen thousand if the smaller and newer mission in the Dominican Republic is added, or about one in every seven hundred people in these Spanish-speaking areas. Compared with statistics in other missionary fields, that is an exceedingly small ratio, but no enterprise of Christian evangelism can be properly evaluated in terms of numbers of adherents. Probably the work of the Episcopal Church in the formerly Spanish islands will always need to be heavily subsidized. Nevertheless, its Christian witness to the full personal and social implications of the Gospel cannot be abandoned.

The situation among the Negroes of the French or Creole-speaking Republic of Haiti, however, is entirely different. While our measure of financial support is high, there the Episcopal Church maintains its second largest missionary district, with over fourteen thousand communicants and more than three times that number of baptized persons. Significantly too, nearly all of its thirty clergy and hundred or more lay workers are native Haitians. Among the eighty-odd churches and mission stations are a number of well-established parishes of considerable size and influence.

The Haitian Church has a unique history. In 1861 an American Negro priest of the Episcopal Church, James Theodore Holly, settled in Haiti with a number of emigrants from the United States, seizing the opportunity to develop a self-governing and independent native Church in the Republic. His energy and zeal was rewarded with an increasing number of adherents, and in 1874 they appealed to the House of Bishops, as did the Mexicans, for a bishop. The request from Haiti was granted. Holly, elected by his fellow churchmen, was consecrated bishop for what was known as *L'Église Orthodox Apostolique Haitienne.* For nearly forty years Holly labored successfully against all difficulties and discouragements. Haiti, a backward and undeveloped land, with its dense population of peoples then at least not only ignorant but enthralled in large numbers by the primitive superstitions of voodoo, was not an easy missionary field for Christian workers. Yet Holly's missions and parish schools slowly but firmly took hold, and upon his death in 1911 the Church in Haiti was, by common agreement, taken over as an Episcopal missionary district. Today little missionary work is as rewarding as that done among the Haitians. Everywhere Holly's original foundations have been expanded, and the evangelistic advance is steady and encouraging. The almost completely native character of the Haitian Church is both the heritage of its unique past and the basis of its future promise.

THE EPISCOPAL CHURCH IN BRAZIL

Among the South Americans of Portuguese descent in the Republic of Brazil is the *Igreja Episcopal Brasileira,* a national Brazilian Church whose three dioceses of Central, Southern, and Southwestern Brazil are missionary districts of our Church. The Brazilian Church is in the first and tentative stages of a movement towards an autonomous and self-governing Anglican Church, a situation in some ways similar to that in China or Japan a half century or more ago.

Though the first Episcopal missionaries were sent to Brazil in the middle of the last century, it was not until the arrival of Lucien Lee Kinsolving and James Morris that the work became permanent. Their labors, and those of the steady stream of missionaries and lay workers—nearly all associated with the Virginia Seminary—who joined them, met with a ready response from the Brazilians. By 1907, a missionary district had been organized with Kinsolving as its first bishop, and for the last fifty years the growth of the Church has been rapid. In 1949 the Brazilian mission was divided into three Districts, marking the beginning of a national organization that may some day be that of an independent Church of the Anglican Communion.

One of the interesting features of the work in Brazil is the evangelization of peoples of different nations and races who have been welcomed as immigrants by the Brazilians. The Episcopal Church, for example, has no less than seven Japanese clergy in Brazil, ministering to their compatriots who work as fruit growers or laborers on the large coffee plantations.

The communicant membership of the Episcopal Church in Brazil is about eighty-five hundred, a figure that places Brazil seventh in communicant size among all our missionary districts, domestic or foreign. Appropriations from the National Council total over a hundred and sixty thousand dollars annually, devoted to salaries, allowances, and administrative expenses. The Brazilian Church operates a large number of schools, best known among which are St. Margaret's School for girls in Pelotas, and the Southern Cross School at Port Alegre. Like the Districts of Haiti and the Philippine Islands, Brazil has its own theological seminary, a vital factor in the training of Brazilians for leadership in their own Church. The future of the Brazilian mission is bright with promise and well-founded hope. The friendly Brazilians have proved earnest adherents of the Church, and the steady advances in the past will undoubtedly continue in the future.

THE LIBERIAN MISSION

Across the Atlantic from Brazil lies the *Missionary District of Liberia,* comprising the territory of the Negro Republic located under the western bulge of the African continent. In the British Colonies adjacent to the District are the English dioceses of the Church of the Province of West Africa, one of the most recently formed self-governing Churches of the Anglican Communion.

For more than a century Liberia has been a free and independent nation; its first settlements established early in the nineteenth century by freed slaves returning to their homeland under the auspices of the American Colonization Society. Recognized as a sovereign state, the Republic of Liberia was proclaimed in 1847, and its government has always been on the closest terms with those of the great western democracies, the United States and Great Britain.

The story of the foundation and development of the little Republic amid the hardships and hazards of the steaming African jungle is an heroic one. Even today, after a hundred years of civilizing efforts, the social, educational, and economic responsibilities of the relatively few thousands of English-speaking Negroes who form the governing class are sufficient to daunt men of less courage than the Liberians. Their country is peopled with over a million and a half primitive African tribesmen, inhabiting the forests and the stretches of back country; their resources are few; their land yields but slowly to agricultural and economic development.

Our mission in Liberia is as old as the settlements. The Church went with the early colonists, and its firm foundation is associated with the labors of John Payne, a young graduate of the Virginia Seminary who became the first bishop in the

District in 1851. As in Haiti, from the beginning, Negro clergy and lay workers have played a vital role in the evangelization of their brethren. Today, after a century and more of missionary effort, the Church has nearly five thousand communicants in Liberia, chiefly in the areas of Cape Mount, Monrovia, Lower Buchanan, Cape Palmas, and other coastal towns. The Christian enterprise is not easy in this corner of Africa. Mohammedanism has made large inroads among many of the tribesmen, while the primitive native religions are still deeply rooted in others. In the more settled and civilized coastal areas, the secularism characteristic of so much of modern cosmopolitan society is strongly present. Support from home is necessarily in high proportion in Liberia. It sustains the Church's programs in the educational field, including many parochial day schools, a high school at Robertsport, and Cuttington College and Divinity School at Suakoko; in social and medical services; and in the development of modern husbandry and farming which is an essential factor in the advance of the country and its people.

Back in Liberia's hinterland, at Bolahun, is the remarkable mission conducted by the monks of the American Order of the Holy Cross, with the assistance of members of the English Sisterhood of the Holy Name. Bolahun, with its church, schools, and hospital, its many evangelistic outstations, and its hundreds of communicants among the primitive peoples of the area, is a center from which the Christian faith radiates to the native tribesmen throughout a large section of the interior.

The African natives who kneel in adoration of Jesus in the clearings in the humid jungle near Bolahun would seem to have little in common with the Alaskan Eskimos who sing

His praises along the frigid Artic shores at Point Hope. But the one thing they have in common—the Lord Christ—makes them fellow members of His Church, children of the One God and Father of us all. From Alaska westwards across the Pacific, through the Far East, and from the Atlantic shores to the Continent of Africa, the Episcopal Church has gone, encircling the globe in obedience to our Lord's command, and bearing witness to both the true catholicity and the redemptive power of the Christian faith among all mankind.

CHAPTER NINE

Missionary Work at Home

IN CONTRAST to the overseas work of the Episcopal Church, now chiefly directed and maintained, as we have seen, by the National Council through the Overseas Department, evangelism at home is carried on by a large number of groups, organizations, and agencies. Provinces, dioceses, parishes, regional branches of the Woman's Auxiliary and other societies, all conduct or support various kinds of domestic missionary programs. On the national level oversight of this work is entrusted by the National Council to the *Home Department,* and through its Divisions and co-operating agencies the national Church carries on such domestic missionary work as is considered to be the responsibility of all Episcopalians. In any discussion of the functions of the Home Department, however, it must be remembered that in the total effort of the Episcopal Church in this broad field of home missions, by far the larger share is still carried on locally, that is, by the dioceses themselves. Over five million dollars a year, or approximately four times the whole budget administered by Home Department, is raised within the dioceses and missionary districts for the furtherance of their own missionary projects. No summary, therefore, of the Department's activity can do justice to the total extent and variety of the domestic missionary work of the whole Episcopal Church.

The Home Department of the National Council is organized into four Divisions, each with its executive secretary, staff of assistants, and field workers. A brief review of the responsibilities of these Divisions will indicate the wide scope of work that is regarded as part of the national Church's domestic mission.

THE DIVISION OF DOMESTIC MISSIONS

The primary administrative responsibility of the Home Department, exercised through the *Division of Domestic Missions,* is that of support and assistance to the missionary districts of the Church that lie within the borders of continental United States. Like the overseas districts, these areas are not self-supporting, and a large portion of their maintenance is provided by the Church through the National Council.[1] Over a half-million dollars, or considerably more than a third of the normal budget of the Home Department, is expended annually in the twelve missionary districts: *Arizona, Eastern Oregon, Idaho, Nevada, North Dakota, North Texas, Salina, San Joaquin, South Dakota, Spokane, Utah,* and *Wyoming.*[2] These districts vary greatly in size and strength, South Dakota and Spokane being among the largest with more than eleven thousand and eighty-five hundred communicants respectively; Utah, Salina, and Nevada being the smallest, having less than three thousand each. The average domestic missionary district is considerably smaller in numbers of church people than its counterpart overseas, largely because the missionary districts at home are

---

[1] See the discussion of missionary districts and missionary bishops, page 138.

[2] The Home Department also makes grants to "Aided Dioceses," generally to assist in meeting the costs of special missionary projects within the borders of these dioceses that are of concern to the whole Church—for example, the Church's work among Indians and Negroes.

located in the more sparsely settled areas of the United States. As has been already pointed out, the ratio statistic is the only one of significant importance in estimating the strength of the Church. In this respect the missionary districts vary widely, some having a proportion of Episcopalians in their total population which is higher than the national average; others, a proportion considerably lower. But in nearly all the districts the rate of the Church's growth is encouragingly steady, and often missionary districts report an annual increase in communicant strength greater than that of many independent dioceses.

From the strategic point of view little work can claim priority over that in the missionary districts. Here the Church pushes forward at its growing edge, along the front line of evangelism, reaching out to thousands of unchurched people, meeting the rapid shifts in America's population, and extending its message and influence as far as possible. Meanwhile, each missionary district itself moves gradually towards self-support. In 1937, for example, Oklahoma became an independent diocese; in 1952 the former missionary district of New Mexico and Southwest Texas was admitted to diocesan status. A number of others now approach independence, though there will probably always be districts where local conditions make the achievement of diocesan status extremely remote, if not impossible. Such areas will continue to command the interest and support of the national Church.

THE CHURCH ON THE RESERVATION

Within many of the missionary districts—and some dioceses as well—there lies a particular challenge to the Church's mission: the evangelism and Christian care of the

American Indian. Approximately four hundred thousand Indians still dwell in our land, two-thirds of whom live on the western Indian Reservations.[3] Today the Indian is free to come and go as he will, thanks to the modern enlightened policy of the United States Indian Service. This government bureau exists to administer such Indian lands and property as the federal government holds in trust for the tribes, to provide educational, medical, and social services, and to help train the Indian to take his place in America's economic order and general way of life.

The Indian's adjustment is not easy. He finds life hard. The lands of the reservations are frequently poor farming areas. Opportunities for making a living at other work are scarce on or near the reservations. Incentive is still low among the Indians; disease rates are high. Furthermore, when he leaves the reservation the Indian not infrequently encounters forms of social and racial prejudice of which Americans are becoming increasingly ashamed.

The Episcopal Church has had a long history of contact with the Indians. Shortly after his consecration in 1811, Bishop Hobart started a program of evangelism among the Oneida Indians in New York State, and when the Oneidas were deported to Wisconsin in 1823 the Church went with them. There they later became the particular object of Jackson Kemper's ministrations. As the missionaries followed the expanding frontier in the mid years of the nineteenth century, more and more interest was aroused in Indian missions. James Breck started work with the Chippewas in Minnesota, and shortly afterwards William Hobart Hare

[3] The United States Indian Service estimates that there are over sixty thousand Indian families on the reservations, and that there are sufficient number of Americans with a high proportion of Indian blood to total four hundred thousand.

began his famous ministry among the Sioux and the Dakotas as missionary bishop in the Niobrara jurisdiction of Nebraska and South Dakota. For thirty-six years Bishop Hare labored with the Indians of that region, and the extraordinary success of the Episcopal Church there is a glowing testimony to his long years of devoted work. Today in the Niobrara Deanery, under the supervision of the missionary district of South Dakota, there are over ten thousand Indian church members, a large number of Church schools and homes, and more than ninety chapels on the reservations. This region is served by many Indian clergy and workers, and its importance is such that the Home Department allocates to it nearly ninety thousand dollars annually from the budget for domestic missions.

While no other single area of Indian work is of this extent, surprisingly large numbers of Indians are reached by the Church. In many places in the country there are missions maintained within the dioceses without assistance from the National Council. In other dioceses aid is given to enable a wider program of evangelism and more special services to the Indians than would be otherwise possible. Among these, the Diocese of Fond du Lac still includes the Oneida mission; Minnesota conducts a notable mission among settlements of Dakotas and Chippewas; New Mexico and Southwest Texas ministers to a large group of Navajos. In the missionary districts, apart from South Dakota, there is a famous Navajo mission at Fort Defiance, Arizona, and an equally well known work among the Arapahoe Indians at Ethete, Wyoming; Idaho, Utah, Nevada, and North Dakota all conduct vigorous programs with the Indians. In all, eighteen different tribes of American Indians are in some way touched by the Church. Where the missions have achieved remarkable success, notably among the Dakotas and the Chippewas, Indian leadership in church life has been strong, and the future promise is very great. Yet this field offers an imperative challenge to the Church as the Indian, increasing in numbers, seeks to find that fullness of life and opportunity which is rightfully his.

THE INTER-RACIAL FELLOWSHIP

Nearly eighty thousand Negroes belong to the Episcopal Church. About two hundred and fifty of our clergy are drawn from this race. The largest single congregation —St. Philip's Church in New York City—is a parish almost entirely Negro in membership. In recent years Negro leadership, both administrative and pastoral, has come to play an essential part in the Church's life and is no longer restricted to work with Negro communicants. But the Episcopal Church has not yet begun to do the work among the Negro people in America that is our evangelistic responsibility. Too few of our parishes, for example, are bi-racial; too many of our people are unconsciously affected by prejudices and forms of discrimination that are sometimes apparent in secular society. On this matter, however, the Episcopal Church takes a firm stand with the other Churches of the Anglican Communion. Urging members of the Church "to continue to witness strongly and wisely against all forms of discrimination," the findings unanimously adopted at the Anglican Congress of 1954 assert that "in the work of the Church we should welcome people of any race at any service conducted by a priest or layman of any ethnic origin, and bring them into the full fellowship of the congregation and its organization." [4]

---

[4] *Report of the Anglican Congress 1954,* page 201.

Much of the work the Church does with Negro people is that done with all men and women—in the ordinary parishes and missions, some all-Negro, some bi-racial, throughout the dioceses and missionary districts. But because of the heavy concentration of the Negro population in certain sections of the country, notably the southern rural areas and the northern industrial and urban centers, creating a specialized opportunity in some dioceses, and because of the inseparable connection between the activities of the Church and the difficulties attending the adjustment of the races, the Home Department maintains an administrative secretariat for Negro work to assist the whole Church both in ministering to Negroes and in realizing its full potential as a Christian community of all men, regardless of race or color.

The Department's plans and programs for work among Negroes are formulated with the counsel of a *Bi-racial Subcommittee,* composed of representative churchmen from North and South, clerical and lay, and National Council officers from the departments entrusted with the oversight of rural evangelism, Christian social relations, and other fields closely touching the Negro work. With their co-operation plans are made for the strengthening and expansion of existing programs. Conferences are promoted among workers in the Negro field throughout the Church; studies are made of particular areas where new evangelistic efforts may be launched, or old work better done. A recruiting program is carried on to help increase the present number of able Negro clergy, who are now trained in all the seminaries of the Church.

The Home Department, in this field as others, offers its resources and knowledge to the dioceses in order to help make more effective their own work among Negro people.

Such appropriations for diocesan assistance as are made by the National Council through the Church, totaling about thirty thousand dollars a year, are grants of aid to assist in maintaining schools, missions, clergy, and other workers. By far the largest support given by the national Church is to the work done through the *American Church Institute for Negroes,* a Church corporation responsible to the National Council and the General Convention, and chartered in 1906 "to promote the education of the Negroes in the Southern States." The officers of the Institute and the National Council work closely together, the Director of the Home Department being the president of the Institute's Board. Nearly two hundred thousand dollars is annually appropriated from the budget of the National Church to further the activity of the Institute in one hospital and six colleges and schools in southern dioceses. St. Augustine's College at Raleigh, North Carolina, St. Paul's Polytechnic Institute at Lawrenceville, Virginia, Voorhees School and Junior College in South Carolina, and Okalona High School and Junior College in Mississippi are among the well established educational institutions where the Institute brings Christian influence and the Church's assistance to bear. Over six thousand young men and women receive their academic education and vocational training in these schools in which the Institute does its splendid work. Its record of achievement in helping to build Christian character and Church loyalties among new generations of Negro leaders is one of the notable aspects of our entire work with the Negro people.

THE CHURCH ON THE CAMPUS

Turning to another area of the Church's mission at home, it is evident that there are few communities presenting a more arresting challenge, both spiritual and intellectual, than the hundreds of universities and colleges in the United States. In the majority of these institutions young men and women are made part of a community life which for more than two generations has been predominantly secular in its orientation. During the past few decades the average American college student found little to help hold him to his religious loyalties when he moved onto the campus for the final period in his formal education. As a result, thousands of potential leaders in business, the professions, and other areas of our national life were separated from the Church during their college years, a separation which often proved permanent.

The opportunity presented by this situation, however, is more than simply that of extending effective pastoral ministrations to Episcopalian young people away from home. That is only one of many aspects of the task. The challenge on its widest scale is to a specialized form of missionary work: the evangelization of the college community itself. Here is a ministry that engages not only the clergy and professional college workers, but also every committed Christian churchman on the campus. The proclamation that Christ is the Way, the Truth, and the Life comes with special meaning in the intellectual atmosphere of a university. It is Christ the Truth in whom man's search for wisdom and enlightenment truly ends; it is only in Christ the Way and the Life that man finds the right use of the powers and insights God gives him. In other words, in the college scene the conversion of individuals is inseparable from the attempt to give a Christian orientation to the life and thought of the whole academic community. If this is to be done effectively, the revelance of theological truth to the truth that is pursued in the sciences, liberal arts, and social studies must be made plain. With that goal, what we call "college work" becomes a distinct and specialized aspect of the Church's mission.

On the national scale the formation and general oversight of a program for this work is the responsibility of the Home Department's *Division of College Work*. Its plans are framed by the members of the *National Commission on College Work,* a group widely representative of Church and college interests throughout the country. Formulating general policies to guide the work of the Division, this Commission authorizes specific programs and allocates the funds available for their furtherance. The National Council appropriates approximately a hundred thousand dollars a year for the activities of the Division of College Work, about half of which is used to help pay the salaries of college workers.

A parallel organization, represented on the Commission and co-operating with the efforts of the official College Work Division, is the independent *Church Society for College Work,* giving opportunity for a large number of interested Episcopalians to share in the support of this part of the Church's mission. The Society performs a variety of functions. Its grants assist in placing clergy and workers in college communities; its educational and vocational conferences promote this work and recruit men to it, as well as to the Church's ministry in general. The Society also sponsors a fellowship of prayer for the welfare of college work and all who are engaged in it.

Definite aims and convictions guide the efforts of the College Work Division. Summarized in a few sentences, they are these: First, every college campus is viewed as an appropriate mission field of the Episcopal Church. The primary task is precisely the same as that confronting us in Liberia, Alaska, on the Indian Reservations, in the rural field, or elsewhere along the Church's missionary frontier—the evangelization of men and women in the circumstances where they are found. On every campus this effort to reach both Episcopalians and the unchurched does not stop with the students organized by parish clergy or college chaplains into *Canterbury Clubs;* faculty and college staff members as well are related to the total *Canterbury Program,* as the work of the Episcopal Church is called. There is also a parallel program designed to interest faculty members in theology, to lead them to a better knowledge of the religious perspectives of their own academic discipline, and to help them make more effective their Christian witness and influence in the college community.[5] Finally, the whole effort is towards a parish-centered evangelism. The aim is to relate the members of the college or university to the Christian life and activity of the nearest Episcopal parish church. In the normal worshipping and working unit of church life the men and women of the college group take their place with others.

The Division of College Work conducts its programs in close co-operation with other departments of the National Council, and particularly with the Youth Division of the Department of Christian Education. Moreover, it maintains liaison with the World Student Christian Federation, an agency of inter-church co-operation which seeks "to lead

[5] One of the outstanding services in the Faculty Program is the publication by the National Council of pamphlets called *Faculty Papers,* a series of essays designed to stimulate a wider interest in Christian intellectual activity. *Faculty Notes,* a brief review, is also circulated under the auspices of the College Work Division.

students to accept the Christian faith in God, Father, Son, and Holy Spirit, according to the Scriptures; and to live as true disciples of Jesus Christ."

At the present time the Episcopal Church maintains at least some semblance of interest in nearly seven hundred universities and colleges in the United States. In many of these lack of resources permits little more than a concern on the part of the nearest Episcopal parish priest. In others, parishes adjacent to the campus have assistant clergy or women workers whose ministry is fully given to the Canterbury Program. At a few colleges or universities there are special foundations providing for chaplains to Episcopal students, such as the Rhinelander Foundation at Harvard or the Proctor Foundation at Princeton.

The maintenance of all this work, of course, is not wholly the responsibility of the College Work Division. Much of it is supported by the regional departments or commissions existing in each of the eight provinces of the Church. Provincial activity has always been particularly strong in this aspect of the Church's domestic mission. Furthermore, today individual dioceses are assuming a larger share of participation in the opportunities offered by the colleges within their borders. The whole program, therefore, is one widely spread through the different centers of church activity, and one of the chief functions of the national Division is the guidance, strengthening, and support of work undertaken on the provincial, diocesan, and parochial levels.

No discussion of the Church on the campus is complete without mention of the universities and colleges that are intimately connected with the Church, either as distinctively Episcopal institutions or as those which have had a traditional association with the Episcopal Church. They are actually few in number: *Bard College* (formerly St. Stephen's) in New York State—now only remoted related to the Church; *Carleton College,* the "Church college of Minnesota"; *Columbia University,* where the Colonial Church atmosphere of the former King's College has now become little more than an association in which the official university chapel is Episcopalian; *St. Augustine's College* in North Carolina, an affiliate of the American Church Institute for Negroes and open to its assistance and influence; *Kenyon College* in Ohio; *Hobart College* (with William Smith College for women) in New York State; *Trinity College* in Connecticut; and the *University of the South* in Tennessee. One or two others might be included, but it is often difficult to determine exactly the point at which association with the Church is significant enough to warrant any designation as a "Church college."

The Episcopal Church never succeeded in establishing very many colleges across the country in the same fashion as have the larger Protestant denominations. In the early and middle years of the nineteenth century Lutheran, Baptist, and Methodist colleges sprang up on all sides, many of which have been maintained down to the present day. Our own efforts in this direction were weak and the colleges actually founded nearly all disappeared after a brief and melancholy existence. Nor have subsequent modern attempts to establish Episcopal colleges been notably successful—on the contrary, most of them have been resounding failures. Perhaps this has not been wholly disastrous. While the few existing excellent Church colleges perform an immensely valuable and necessary function, the attempt to duplicate them on a large scale would inevitably lessen the support and interest given to the task of reaching into the secular institutions with the challenge of Christianity. The Church cannot withdraw itself from involvement in American life, and in the end the missionary opportunity in the American secular colleges cannot be ignored. Here the Church concentrates its efforts to bring Christian orientation and commitment into the life of the campus community.

THE ARMED FORCES DIVISION

One aspect of the Home Department's activity is brought under the oversight of the *Armed Forces Division.* During and since the last war an unprecedented number of men and women have been part of the nation's military, air, and naval forces. Today there are still thousands serving in the defense effort of the United States, and apparently these numbers will remain high for some years to come. Spiritual ministrations to the churchmen among them and evangelistic outreach towards others are urgent and primary responsibilities in the Church's mission.

The Armed Forces Division is charged with the task of recruiting and assisting Episcopal chaplains in the Army, Navy, and Air Force, in the National Guard, and in the hospitals of the Veterans Administration. Every clergyman seeking appointment as a chaplain must have the endorsement of the Division. After he has been commissioned, the Division assists him with discretionary fund grants, field altars, vestments, and religious literature for distribution among the service personnel he seeks to reach. In some cases the Division shares in the payment of clergy pension premiums. Often in areas of military or naval installations where there is no Episcopal chaplain, grants are made to the dioceses or missionary districts to help provide the expenses of priestly ministrations to the men and women located there.

The budget appropriation for the Armed Forces Division is a variable one, chiefly depending on the number of Episcopal chaplains. The assistance in payment of pension premiums, provision of copies of the *Armed Forces Prayer Book* and other literature, and the appropriations made to dioceses to help provide services and pastoral care for men and women in the armed forces are generally the largest amounts in the budget.

Two problems have offered perennial difficulties in the concern of the Episcopal Church with its chaplains in the nation's forces. The first is the number of our clergy serving the Church and the nation in this ministry. Because of the fairly rapid changes any figures are likely to be inaccurate after a short time, but in 1954, in round numbers, there were about fifty Episcopal chaplains in the Army, thirty in the Navy, twenty in the Air Force, and twenty in the institutions of the Veterans Administration—a total of approximately one hundred and twenty out of seven thousand three hundred Episcopal clergymen. The quota of chaplains allotted by the government to the Episcopal Church is rarely filled; nearly always there is both room and pressing need for thirty or forty more priests who will offer themselves for this vital work of the Church.

The second problem is that of the pastoral care of the chaplains themselves. Removed from the fellowship of diocesan clergy, generally struggling single-handed with a task that demands heroic dedication and offers limitless opportunity, our chaplains need every assistance and support that can help sustain them in their work. The executive secretary of the Armed Forces Division—himself a priest—is constantly in the field, traveling among the chaplains, bringing them aid, encouragement, and counsel. But necessarily he must spend a large amount of time and energy in the administrative work of the Division, nor can he provide for the chaplains the same pastoral or sacramental ministrations that are the functions of a bishop. He cannot, for example, bring the rite of Confirmation to the men and women whom the chaplains reach. Increasing assistance in meeting these needs, however, is given by Anglican bishops all over the world in whose jurisdictions installations of the armed forces are located. Moreover, several of our own bishops are charged from time to time with the special responsibility of visiting the chaplains' posts, bringing to them such care and ministrations as the Church at home can provide.

TOWN AND COUNTRY WORK

One of the most important fields of evangelistic work is the Church's mission in the rural areas of the United States. Over fifty million Americans live in villages or hamlets, in rural town-centers, on ranches or farms, in mining and lumbering camps, all within "Rural America." Moreover, today these vast stretches of the country have lost the static atmosphere of the past. New and mechanized means of transportation, agriculture, and industry have transformed the old stable patterns of rural life and stimulated the growth of town-centers which serve wide areas of farm and ranch lands. The stability of the rural population has been shaken; migrant workers in large numbers are a familiar part of the modern countryside.[6]

[6] There is an admirable analysis of rural America and its challenge to the Church in E. Dargan Butt's *Preach There Also* (Evanston: The Seabury-Western Theological Seminary, 1954).

The opportunity presented to the Churches by this changing situation is one almost limitless in its scope, and on all sides today there is a growing and encouraging response. In many places the old, inefficient, and diffuse activity once conducted by small village churches with inadequate resources and little knowledge of the special problems of rural life is now giving place to a new approach to rural evangelism. The Roman Catholic Church has been extraordinarily successful in its recent activity in country areas; the National Council of the Churches of Christ has explored resources and fashioned programs to assist the reawakened Protestant efforts in these regions. The Episcopal Church, long associated with the heavily populated urban centers of America, has been slower to reach effectively into the town and country areas. But in recent years, and notably in the last decade, our vision has broadened and our resources for implementing the Church's mission in this field have developed rapidly. Today, where new programs for our Church's rural work are in effect an astonishing measure of success attests the vital place the Episcopal Church can occupy in rural America.

The rural regions still constitute the backbone of the nation. Their people provide a large part of the population of our cities, and on the evangelization of these areas depends in large measure the Church's effective fulfillment of its redemptive mission. While the immediate responsibility for this work falls upon the dioceses and missionary districts, the national Church since 1949 has provided an agency of assistance on both the practical and the policy-making level in the *Town and Country Division* of the Home Department. "To develop, administer, and execute a national plan for rural work which will assist each diocese, missionary district, and local field" in extending and strengthening the work of the Church in town and country areas, in bringing Christian witness and influence to bear on all phases of rural community life, in providing pastoral care and the Sacraments for Episcopalians and evangelizing the unchurched, in maintaining continuous Christian education, and in co-operating with other Churches and agencies striving to improve rural welfare—these are the purposes and aims of the Division.

One of its principal activities is the field training of clergy and seminary students in preparation for a ministry in the rural areas. This program is designed to supplement the basic theological education and professional training received at the seminaries by the experience of rural field work under expert supervision. Summer courses for students are held at the *National Town-Country Church Institute* at Parkville, Missouri, where the Roanridge Farm and a Demonstration Homestead bring to the special training offered by the Institute the practical experience of actual rural life and work. Supervised field work in various dioceses and districts follows the study program each summer, and at the conclusion of the period there is a final session of evaluation and interpretation at Parkville.

The success of the Roanridge experiment has led to the establishment of other field training projects for students and seminarians, some sponsored by the Town and Country Division, others under diocesan or provincial auspices with the co-operation of the Division. Among such are the *Southern Rural Church Institute* at Valle Crucis, North Carolina, the *Southwest Rural Church Institute* in Texas, the *Intercultural Rural Church Institute* in Arizona, and the *Parish Training Programs* of the Provinces of New England and

Washington. In a number of other places similar programs are in process of development, exploring the opportunities for the more effective training of clergy and workers in the rural field.

The Town and Country Division carries its educational efforts beyond the direct training of seminarians or workers. Conferences are sponsored regularly throughout the country for clergy actually engaged in rural work; grants are made for graduate study in rural sociology and allied subjects; close contact is maintained with the Department of Christian Education, especially in the Church School-by-Mail; seminaries are assisted in providing special lectureships on rural evangelism; literature, motion pictures, and filmstrips are made available to acquaint church people with the problems and opportunities of this work.

In all phases of its activity the Division has the counsel and assistance of an independent agency, the *Rural Workers' Fellowship of the Episcopal Church,* a society that exists to promote the interest of the whole Church in the ministry and mission to rural America, to increase the fellowship among rural workers, and to aid the National Council in the program of its Town and Country Division. For over a quarter of a century the Fellowship has labored to these ends, and no small part of our reawakened sense of responsibility to rural evangelism is owing to its continued efforts.[7]

Working closely with the Division of Town and Country, as well as with other offices in the Home and Overseas Departments, is the National Council's *Unit of Research and Field Study,* organized in 1950 to give bishops and diocesan

---

[7] *Cross Roads,* the quarterly journal of the Rural Workers' Fellowship, is one of the most valuable aids in presenting the aims and objectives of the Fellowship and stimulating an interest in its work.

departments technical guidance, personal supervision, and professional evaluation in surveying the activity of the Church within the particular dioceses. Surveys are made upon request, aiming at providing leaders in the diocese with an expert interpretation of the Church's task in any local area and suggestions for improving the effectiveness of its work. With such surveys the Division co-operates, often temporarily supporting a "demonstration field" in which evangelism is begun and extended in a particular area to show both methods and goals of the rural mission. In this, as in all other activities, the Division seeks constantly to strengthen and foster the growth of departments of Town and Country work in the provinces and in the dioceses. The final responsibility for the Church's rural work must be met in the local areas. All the programs and resources of an active national Division can be ultimately effective only as they are appropriated by the dioceses and districts in which the rural missions and parishes lie, and where the thousands of unchurched people live.

CHAPTER TEN

Christian Education

FEW THINGS have stirred the Episcopal Church so deeply in the last decade as its vigorous awakening on all levels of church life to the responsibilities of Christian education. On every side in recent years dioceses, parishes, and missions, and many organizations within the Church, have embarked upon new and revitalized programs of religious education for all age groups. Church conferences, diocesan teacher training institutes, parish adult study programs and lectures, summer study groups, and other agencies for the better education of Episcopalians in the knowledge and immediate relevance of the resources of their spiritual heritage have not only been redoubled in numbers, but have also attracted the enthusiastic participation of thousands of church people.

This awakening has produced an amazing output of popular books and pamphlets designed to assist the ordinary churchman to a better understanding of the implications of his Christian commitment. Perhaps most notable among these, at least for their wide and unprecedented sale among Episcopalians, have been the volumes of THE CHURCH'S TEACHING, a series of books on the Bible, Church history, the Church's faith, worship, and life, produced since 1949 and used everywhere throughout the Church for adult reading and study groups, with confirmation classes of men and women, and as general resource books in the development of other materials of Christian education.[1] Moreover, long dissatisfaction with inadequate teaching materials for Church school classes and meager resources for adult study has resulted in the production of new and far better materials on every age level. Today an increasing number of courses is available for Episcopal Sunday schools, vacation Church school classes, or for use in the sacred studies classes of private and parochial schools. The first of the new courses authorized by the General Convention, known as *The Seabury Series,* made their appearance in 1955. In use at that time in many parishes and missions were some of the new lessons of *The Episcopal Church Fellowship Series,* planned and published by the Morehouse-Gorham Company, and the older but still popular *Cloister Series* and *Pastoral Series.* Also used in many parts of the country were the H. M. Jacobs' *Episcopal Church Series,* the *St. James Lessons,* and the materials of *The Pittsburgh Plan.*[2]

The immediate responsibility for Christian education rests with the parish or mission. There is the normal setting in which the Christian faith and life is lived; there is the redemptive community of the Christian fellowship in which Christian education is an integral part of the total apprehension and proclamation of the Gospel by living members of the Body of Christ. To assist the parish in reaching its goals effectively, and to unify parochial educational programs with those of the larger Church family, each diocese maintains a department of Christian education, today often

---

[1] This book is Volume VI in THE CHURCH'S TEACHING. The other volumes have been referred to in preceding chapters.

[2] Some of these unofficial materials received the endorsement of the National Council's Department of Christian Education in its suggested *Interim Church School Study Courses* for use until such time as the courses in the new official curriculum became available.

under the supervision of a full-time priest or highly trained director of religious education, and often one of the most active areas of diocesan work. Diocesan departments provide teacher training courses or institutes, plan and arrange summer conferences, camps, and vacation Church schools, and make available to parishes and missions the new materials and resources for Christian education that are being steadily produced—in all ways assuming a co-ordinating leadership in facing the problems and grasping the opportunities before the Church in this field. The departments in the dioceses and missionary districts are essential links between the educational programs and aims of the national Church and the parishes and congregations where those aims are realized in terms of deeper discipleship in the lives of church people.

THE NATIONAL DEPARTMENT

The chief responsibility for developing and co-ordinating the whole effort of the Episcopal Church in Christian education lies with the National Council's *Department of Christian Education.* Drastically reorganized after the General Convention of 1946, when the Church commissioned a wide expansion of its activities, the Department's programs stretch over every field of the Church's educational task: the formulation of principles by which activity in this effort may be guided, and aims to which it may be effectively directed; the development and production of courses for Church schools and study materials for adults; assistance and advice to diocesan departments in implementing their work; field training of leaders and teachers; and the constant alert investigation of ways and means to strengthen the Church's educational program everywhere.

Today the Department of Christian Education includes no

less than six Divisions of work, maintains its own offices at Tucker House in Greenwich, Connecticut, in close proximity to the offices of its publisher, The Seabury Press, employs a large number of executive officers, editors, authors and consultants, research assistants, secretaries, and field workers, and is supported by an appropriation of over three hundred thousand dollars annually from the budget of the National Church.

CHILDREN, YOUTH, AND ADULTS

The *Children's Division* of the Department of Christian Education is primarily concerned with the religious education of Church children and all who share in that responsibility—particularly, of course, parents and teachers. The Division recommends materials suitable for use in Episcopal Sunday schools; study courses are made available for vacation Church schools, an increasing summer activity in many dioceses and districts; texts are suggested for use in weekday instruction, where time released by public school authorities allows weekday religious education; and constant stimulation is given the expanding program of Church school-by-mail, a project by which Christian training is given thousands of isolated children in the rural areas of many dioceses and missionary districts.

This Division also undertakes the promotion of two special offerings of the Church's children: the *Children's Missionary Offering,* normally totalling over a half-million dollars annually; and the *Birthday Thank Offering,* a more modest venture designated from time to time for the support of special projects in the Church's work.

Today the youth work of the Episcopal Church is guided and correlated within the Department by the *Division of*

Youth. This Division was established to strengthen and extend the total experience of young people within the life of the parish and to help make more effective their Christian witness and work in the wider community in which they live. Working closely with youth advisors in each diocese and using the provincial and diocesan youth conferences as special agencies for leadership training, the Division seeks the better co-ordination of the programs of numerous local, diocesan, and national youth organizations in the Church.[3] Many of these organizations, as well as the National Canterbury Association of Episcopal college students, are represented in the *National Convention of Episcopal Young Churchmen,* a triennial assembly of young people. Continuity of the Convention's activity is provided by a *National Commission,* representative of youth in the provinces and from college associations, which act as an advisory group to both the Division of Youth and the Division of College Work, assisting each in formulating and carrying out its programs.

The *Adult Division* of the Department exists to strengthen and develop the new program of adult education in the parishes and missions of the Church. Special study courses for adults have been produced, and their use throughout the dioceses and districts is widely promoted by the Division. Particular emphasis is placed on missionary education and the better understanding of Christian motivation in evangelism. Working closely with the Children's Division, the Adult

[3] These include parochial and diocesan units of the *Young People's Fellowship,* and local branches of such national organizations as the Junior Division of the *Brotherhood of St. Andrew,* the *Junior Daughters of the King,* the *Girls' Friendly Society,* the *Servants of Christ the King,* the *Order of the Fleur de Lis,* the *Order of Sir Galahad,* and the Church Greek-letter fraternities *Phi Sigma* and *Pi Alpha* for boys, and the sorority *Tau Delta Alpha* for girls.

Division makes available resources for family worship, coordinating its efforts for better adult education with those of the Children's Division in the direction of strengthening the influence of the Christian home.

Serving all the educational Divisions is the specialized office of the *Division of Audio-Visual Education,* responsible for distributing audio-visual aids throughout the Church and making these resources more widely known. The Division maintains a film rental service of religious moving pictures, slides, and film-strips, and at times assists in the production of suitable films. Efforts are made to train leaders and teachers in the proper use of audio-visual aids, and to keep the Church abreast of the latest developments in these modern means of communication and education.

CURRICULUM DEVELOPMENT

The *Division of Curriculum Development* has attacked one of the major tasks confronting the national Department upon its reorganization and expansion—the production of a new official curriculum for Episcopal Church schools. The ultimate objective of any sound program of Christian education of children is that they may be trained to take their place as committed and practicing Christians in the full life of the Church. In seeking this end, those responsible for the Department became convinced that an entirely new curriculum of Church school courses should be made available, together with the spread of a deeper understanding of effective Christian teaching and the careful training of teachers and leaders in the aims and purposes to which the new materials are directed.

For years, it was felt, the Church has used study methods and courses which attempted to acquaint pupils with a knowledge of the Bible, Church history, the Prayer Book, the faith and practice of the Church, and the standards of Christian living in such a manner as to place an almost impossible task upon the teacher. Not only was the teacher in a Church school expected to impart an immense amount of factual information and confront the children with all the various elements in our Christian heritage, but this had to be done in such a fashion as would bring it alive in the minds of the pupils—a difficult task at best, and one made even harder by the lack of effective parental co-operation and little or no correlation between what went on in the Church school and in the other activities of parish life. In such circumstances it was frequently beyond a teacher's capacity to relate what was being taught to anything real in the children's experience. As a result, the ultimate objective of Christian education was often unrealized, despite the most faithful and devoted efforts of many teachers.

It is exactly at this last point that the new curriculum, now produced by the Department, seeks to become a more effective instrument of proper Christian education than any of the older programs. Not only do the materials and methods provide for better co-operation on the part of parents and the creation of a new relation between the home and the Church school, but the curriculum is also intended to be related to the whole parish program. Most important of all, the new methods and courses are designed to bring alive the faith and practice of the Church in the experience of pupils at every age level. Acceptance into the family of God can be experienced by children in truly redemptive terms, no matter how simple that experience may appear. In the new curriculum, therefore, the materials of our Christian heritage are taught within the context of the pupils' acceptance as a child of God. Such is the basic method employed in the new courses. It is intended to implement the conviction that "a teaching program which would really teach must become a program which nurtures by relating a child's need to the answer and action which Almighty God has provided." [4]

LEADERSHIP TRAINING

It is clearly evident that if the new curriculum is to be adequately related to the total life of Episcopal parishes and missions, and used intelligently and effectively with Church school pupils and parents, an intensive program of leadership training must be continued throughout the Church. This is the special responsibility of the Department's *Division of Leadership Training,* which was established in 1949, and which since that time has conducted a remarkably successful training program for clergy, teachers, lay leaders, and parents in the aims, methods, and materials of proper Christian education. For a number of years clergy conferences were held at the College of Preachers, while regional meetings throughout the country reached a large number of both clergy and lay leaders.

Today the leadership program includes, among other activities, several basic elements. Training teams are sent out to assist diocesan departments in evaluating their aims and functions, and to hold conferences in the dioceses to make better known to clergy and directors of religious education the nature and use of the courses in the new curriculum. Training conferences for leaders, especially in the conduct of

[4] David R. Hunter, Director of the Department of Christian Education, in "The New Program of Christian Education," a release of the Department, September, 1953. The basic reference is to *Man's Need and God's Action* by Reuel L. Howe (Greenwich: The Seabury Press, 1953).

parents' classes, may also be held in connection with the visits of leadership teams to the dioceses and districts.

Other primary efforts at leadership training are made through the *Church and Group Life Laboratories,* two-week conferences for the clergy held in different parts of the country as training experiences in group development in the life of the Church; and in the *Parish Life Conferences,* intensive week-end meetings where preparation for full participation in the task of Christian education may be given to lay leaders and teachers in parishes. Like other aspects of the leadership training program, such conferences are designed to become the eventual responsibility of diocesan departments of Christian education. Much of the effort of the Leadership Training Division, in common with the work of many divisions of the National Council, is directed towards the strengthening of diocesan departments to the point where they may become the effective agents of the Church's work in the local scene.

CONFERENCES AND OTHER EDUCATIONAL AGENCIES

Apart from the programs of parishes, diocesan departments, and the National Council, there are numerous other agencies of education in the Episcopal Church, many of them directed towards special goals and projects. Independent organizations, guilds, societies, and publishing associations of all kinds flourish in the Church, the majority of them embracing a program in which elements of evangelism, education, and promotion are inseparably combined.[5]

One of the most important agencies of Christian group experience and education is the Church conference, camp,

[5] A brief sketch of some of these appears in Chapter XII.

or summer school, operated by a province or diocese, or under independent auspices. Nearly all the provinces conduct such conferences for adults as the *Finger Lakes Conference* of the Second Province, the *Conference of the Province of Washington* at Hood College, and the *Sewanee Summer Conference* of the Fourth Province. At their sessions of a week or more, adults undertake group study, a community life and worship, and enjoy the experience of fellowship under leaders drawn from many different parts of the Church. Other provincial conferences are held regularly for the exploration of special topics and aspects of the Church's work: conferences for college workers, for young people, and for those drawn to the ministry; vocational conferences and leadership training conferences; and conferences for better education in problems of Christian sociology.

The last few decades have witnessed the rapid growth of diocesan conferences and the establishment of permanent conference centers in many dioceses and districts. These have brought members of the diocesan family together in a reinvigorating experience of study, worship, and renewed common dedication to the tasks before the Church. Like the provincial conferences, those in the diocese are often varied in character. Most dioceses today gather their young people together in a youth conference, and if facilities permit hold conferences of church workers, adults, and other special groups. Conference centers are frequently located in an area where camp and outdoor surroundings allow the reception all through the summer of constant groups of church people who combine vacation and refreshment with a group life of prayer and study.

CHURCH BOARDING AND DAY SCHOOLS

No brief survey of Christian education in the Episcopal Church is complete without some mention of those schools where, under Church influences, the whole experience of education is oriented in a Christian direction. If, as we have seen in an earlier chapter, the Episcopal Church achieved little notable success in establishing numbers of Church colleges, this has not been the case in respect to boarding schools. The years of the Church's extension throughout the country witnessed the building of many excellent schools for boys and girls, some of them of diocesan foundation, others independent proprietary or incorporated schools whose religious auspices are those of the Episcopal Church.

Perhaps the best known group of schools of this type includes the Church's boys' schools in New England, modeled to some degree after the pattern of English public schools. Though private institutions, independently governed and endowed, their ethos is thoroughly Episcopalian, in nearly all cases their founders or early headmasters being clergymen. There are a few equally well known girls' schools in this group, nearly all located in the Atlantic seaboard states. In these institutions the services of the Church are a central feature of the school life, while the sacred studies in the curriculum reflect the doctrine and practice of Anglicanism. No longer exclusively associated with families of wealth or prominence, these schools now draw students from a broad cross section of American society. Their high academic standards and strong emphasis on Christian ideals and Christian discipline in personal character have played a significant part in shaping the aims of many other Church schools.

Another group of Church boarding and day schools, similar in general character to the private institutions but more numerous and often older in foundation, are the diocesan schools, closely related to the Church by diocesan control or ownership. Many of the dioceses maintain such schools, the majority of them having been founded by far-sighted bishops during the Church's expansion in the mid years of the nineteenth century. Minnesota and Virginia, for example, are notable among the dioceses and districts, both for the unusual number and the sturdy traditions of their schools. Throughout the country Christian education of a high order is provided by all these diocesan schools, as well as by a smaller group of equally fine schools similarly closely related to the Church and operated by Episcopal religious orders.[6]

Day schools of the Church are numerous, either independently controlled with Church affiliations or maintained by dioceses or parishes. Nursery schools, preparatory schools for young boys and girls, and a few choir schools attached to cathedrals or large parish churches make up the majority of these. In recent years, however, the new movement to establish parochial schools in which the children may receive their education with Christian orientation has gathered considerable momentum in many areas. Today nearly two hundred parochial schools are in operation throughout the Church. Though few of them have grown to the point of

---

[6] Episcopalians should be better acquainted with their Church secondary schools, both private and diocesan. The Porter Sargent *Handbook of Private Schools* (Boston, 1954) lists no fewer than ninety-three schools of these groups, operated by the Church or with Church affiliations. In many other independent schools of no denominational connection Episcopalian influence has been traditionally strong.

providing all grades through high school, they give promise of steady future expansion. While the Episcopal Church will probably never have a parochial school system on anything like the wide scale familiar in the Roman Catholic and some Lutheran Churches, there will always be local needs and conditions which can be met and fulfilled by the Church parochial school.

CHAPTER ELEVEN

Christian Social Relations and Action

FOR CENTURIES the Church has been the conscience of society, arousing men and women to their Christian duty in the care of the sick and the poor, the underprivileged and the helpless. A courageous faith has armed churchmen for an undaunted witness against all forms of social evil, injustice, and discrimination; a renewed Christian consecration has found ways of making more effective their response to God's will for a better world in which His children may live. In the Episcopal Church the stimulation and direction of this aspect of Christian witness and work is the function of the National Council's *Department of Christian Social Relations.*

Few responsibilities are more challenging than those that the Church entrusts to this Department. The torch it bears is that which lighted the philanthropic and humanitarian labors of Florence Nightingale; the zeal it arouses and directs is that which moved St. Vincent de Paul to the care of the sick in their need, the youth in trouble, and the aged in loneliness. There is an unbroken line of faithfulness to God's justice and mercy that leads from the righteousness of Israel's Prophets through the loving services of the medieval Brethren of the Common Life, the passion for social reform of Hugh Latimer and Charles Kingsley, the concern for the underprivileged that took Jean Jaques Olier into the slums of Paris and William Dolling to the dock-yards of Portsmouth—indeed, the glory of Church history is the unquenchable spirit in which generations of men and women have obeyed the injunction of their Lord. "A new commandment I give unto you," said Jesus, "That ye love one another." [1]

The work of the Department of Christian Social Relations is difficult to summarize. Inevitably its programs constantly change as the Church is aroused to new human situations on which the mind of Christ must be brought to bear. Moreover, the Department has the responsibility of stirring the Christian conscience to extend the ministry of pastoral care or the affirmation of Christian witness into new areas of men's relationships and human need. The work of this Department is not easily confined. Frequently its activities will touch all other areas of the Church's efforts; sometimes the Department of Social Relations will initiate a program that eventually stabilizes itself as the work and proper re-sponsibility of another office in the National Council.

For many years the Department has been a major instru-ment of co-operation between the Episcopal Church and other Churches, and with certain agencies of the federal government and national welfare bodies. In the church field this co-operation is with the National Council of the Churches of Christ, the World Council of Churches, and with the social welfare departments of other Anglican Churches.

The task of the Department is an exacting one. Though

[1] John, 13:34.

vastly strengthened in the last few decades, the acceptance of social responsibility on the part of many Episcopalians is still weak; programs for social education and community action are still limited and sporadic. Attitudes of many Christian people in some social situations often reflect a serious lack of understanding of the relevance of the Gospel and little knowledge of the witness of the Church in specific problems of contemporary life. Partly this is owing to lack of proper education; more frequently, however, it is owing to the partial character of the Christian commitment of many church people. The task is always one, therefore, of making the full implications of the Gospel apparent in social situations. People need a keener awareness of the reality of human community, a more firmly grounded assurance of the meaningfulness of their lives in terms of brotherhood and vocation. They must be helped to create conditions that will give equal opportunity to all men, regardless of race, color, creed, or national origin; they must be armed to wage unceasing war upon poverty, disease, and insecurity, to safeguard basic human rights and discharge the basic human duties which those rights entail, to defend and extend the freedoms of thought and speech, of belief and worship, that the supreme worth of human personality demands. These are the aims to which the activities of the Department of Christian Social Relations are directed, in the conviction that all Christians "are called by God to take their part in the life of the world and, through the power of God's grace, to transform it." [2]

---

[2] *Christian Social Relations at General Convention, 1952* (New York: The National Council), page 20.

THE WORK OF THE DEPARTMENT

Appropriations of the national Church for the work of the Department total nearly one hundred thousand dollars a year, approximately the same amount as that supplied to the College Work Division of the Home Department. On this budget the activities of the Department are necessarily limited, and they are wisely channeled into a few crucial areas. The *Division of Christian Citizenship* seeks to create a deeper sense of personal responsibility, interest, and participation in the application of Christian standards to social relations on every level. The problem of race relations, for example, is constantly explored and means sought to implement the conviction of the Episcopal Church "that we consistently oppose and combat discrimination based on color or race in every form, both within the Church and without, in this country and internationally." [3] Such affirmations are given specific application by the Division of Christian Citizenship, as for example in the statement submitted to the National Council and adopted by its members in 1954, approving the decision of the United States Supreme Court on Segregation in Public Schools. "The Court's ruling is more than a matter of law and order," ran the Division's statement, "It has to do with the welfare and destiny of human beings . . . Judged in the light of Christian principles . . . the Court's decision is just, right, and necessary."

This Division is equally involved with problems of human rights and fundamental human freedoms, relations between Church and State, ways of furthering international amity and co-operation leading towards the promotion of peace and justice among all nations, and means whereby the full

---

[3] *Ibid.*, page 15.

duties and responsibilities of Christian citizenship may be assumed by all church people.

A specific program of Christian citizenship is the encouragement of diocesan and parochial conferences on the Christian and his daily work. The Division also conducts a program of education on the ministry of the Church to alcoholics and their families.

The *Division of Urban-Industrial Work* provides an example of the response of the Department of Christian Social Relations to a new challenge to the Church's mission. The changing patterns and rapid mobility of our modern urban-industrial society have opened new areas and means of evangelism and philanthropic activity in our crowded cities. City churches, no longer able to maintain the stable parish life once familiar in them, are finding fresh opportunities today as preaching stations, educational and clinical centers, and places of Christian worship and activity where peoples of different races and ethnic origins, often underprivileged and crowded into tenement areas, may be built into a real community life. In many cities experiments in this valuable ministry are now under way, and encouraging success has been achieved.

In nearly every case the chief responsibility for urban-industrial work lies with the diocese. The Division attempts to analyze and evaluate the many new urban Church programs throughout the nation, and to make available the resources of knowledge thereby acquired. More recently the Division has been enabled to undertake a special program of urban-industrial Church research, a five-year study to assist in forging "techniques whereby relations can be made more meaningful to people in modern urban-industrial society."

The stimulation of health and welfare services is one of the chief activities of the Department of Christian Social Relations. The Episcopal Church has had a long and honorable history of the care of the sick and the aged, the destitute and the handicapped. Its hospitals, for example, range across the continent from the great St. Luke's Hospital in New York to the small Hudson Stuck Memorial Hospital at Fort Yukon, Alaska, each playing a vital part in the health services of its community. Over two hundred institutions and welfare agencies operate in the name and under the sponsorship of the Episcopal Church today—hospitals, convalescent homes, rest houses, institutions for child and maternity care, community and settlement houses, counseling agencies, chaplaincies in penal institutions and mental hospitals, rehabilitation centers for delinquents and youth in difficulties, homes for the aged and the handicapped, and others devoted to one or another human need.[4] Throughout the country thousands of men and women, boys and girls, are ministered to by this enterprise of Christian service.

A large number of these institutions are diocesan foundations, supported by the Church in a particular diocese or missionary district. A few are parochial, and most of the remainder are ventures of private philanthropy, associated with the diocese in which they are located, supported partly by endowments, partly by gifts and annual offerings. Some idea of the extent of the work may be gained from the fact that the operating costs of all our hospitals, homes, and other agencies totals nearly fifty million dollars each year.

The *Division of Health and Welfare Services* does not operate any of these institutions or services. Its function is

---

[4] The *Episcopal Church Annual* contains a full list of all services.

partly advisory and partly that of helping to keep these services efficient, adequately staffed and financed, and alert to the changing needs of people and the communities in which they live. Assistance is given to those responsible for their operation through the provision of educational material and the holding of conferences, field studies, the recruiting, training, and referral of personnel, and the general guidance of churchmen in meeting the challenges offered in the field of health and human welfare.

A national organization whose work is affiliated with that of this Division is the *Episcopal Service for Youth.*[5] This is a nationwide federation of Episcopal case work agencies, offering the services of trained social workers, clergy, and psychiatrists to the problems and difficulties of young people. Each local agency is organized on a diocesan basis, and all are linked together for the extension and development of the immensely valuable help they give in rebuilding the lives of hundreds of young men and women in tragic circumstances.

Similarly, the *Church Association for Seamen's Work,* formerly known as "The Seamen's Church Institute of America," is an affiliated organization of the Department of Christian Social Relations.[6] The seamen's institutes in Los Angeles, Boston, Michigan, New York, Philadelphia, Rhode

---

[5] In some dioceses it is known by the names of its local agency: "The Church Mission of Help" or "The Youth Consultation Service."

[6] There are a number of independent organizations in the Church whose aims and activities parallel some of the work of the Department. The *Episcopal League for Social Action,* for example, avowedly exists to bring together "for study and action those who seek to apply the principles of Christ in national and international life." The *Guild of St. Barnabas for Nurses* is a national association formed to foster the spiritual and social aspects of the life and work of hospital nurses. The *Episcopal Hospital Assembly* brings into closer contact administrators and chaplains of Church hospitals for fellowship and the sharing of experience.

Island, and South Carolina are famous for their long records of philanthropic and pastoral care of those who make their living from the sea.

THE DEPARTMENT AND THE CHURCH

By its very nature much of the work undertaken in the different fields of social service and Christian witness in social situations is the responsibility of the diocese. One major effort of the national Department, therefore, is assisting in strengthening the diocesan departments of social relations. Programs of witness and work are necessarily made ultimately effective in the life of the parishes and missions of the Church, that is, in the local situations which they are designed to meet. To a large degree final success rests with the quality of leadership given by diocesan officers. All dioceses and districts have such departments or committees, normally represented on the Diocesan Council, and many of them today show a marked increase of effective activity in this work. Just as the national Department serves the Presiding Bishop as a consultative staff in his duty to give leadership in social relations and action on the national level, so the diocesan departments assist their bishops to point up all the community-related activities and social responsibilities of their parishes and people that help make the Christian witness effectively felt.

WORLD RELIEF AND CHURCH CO-OPERATION

One of the most striking examples of the concern of Episcopalians for the needs of others is the extraordinary program of world relief and inter-Church co-operation that is supported by the whole Episcopal Church. In recent years the money thus expended has been approximately a half million dollars annually. At first this was made possible by the voluntary contributions of church people to *The Presiding Bishop's Fund for World Relief,* but now the major portion of this fund is a budget item of the national Church, though additional gifts and contributions constantly swell its total. Allocations of money are made by a committee of the National Council under the chairmanship of the Presiding Bishop; administration of these grants is placed in the hands of the Department of Christian Social Relations.

The program has considerable flexibility. In the past few years the Church has been able to meet the needs of many sudden emergencies as well as those of continuing responsibilities. Hurricane relief to the Diocese of Jamaica, flood relief to churches in Kansas, rebuilding in Singapore, assistance to the war-devastated Old Catholic Churches in Europe, the financing of an extensive program for the resettlement of displaced persons, food, clothing, and medicines to Europeans and Asiatics, scholarships for overseas students from many Churches—all these illustrate the variety of needs served by the Fund.

Normally expenditures are made in several ways: (1) through the Episcopal Church for the expenses of settling displaced persons in the United States and of providing education for overseas church workers in American institutions of learning; (2) through grants to other Anglican Churches, among them to the Church of India, Pakistan, Burma and Ceylon and the Nippon Sei Ko Kwai, and to the support of work in various Anglican missions; (3) through the Eastern Orthodox Churches, a large portion of which has been given to refugee programs and to the support of St. Vladimir's Theological Academy in New York City; (4) in co-operation with the World Council of Churches in both service programs and those of inter-Church aid; and (5) in co-operation with the National Council of the Churches of Christ in America, for its department of Church World Service, which ships vast quantities of food, clothing, and medicines to Christian agencies in Europe and Asia, and operates the central service for refugees coming to the United States.

Few efforts of our Church's social program have made Christian brotherhood a more effective reality than the work of this "Operation World Relief." Here is a striking and continuing example of the witness we bear—across all lines of nation, race, and color, across all barriers of Church loyalty—to our common humanity as the children of the One God and Father of us all.

CHAPTER TWELVE

Finance and Promotion

TWO DEPARTMENTS of the National Council discharge major responsibilities in the efficient implementation of the Church's whole program of missionary, educational, and social work on the national scene: the *Department of Finance* and the *Department of Promotion.* The first is entrusted with the care of all properties and the custody of all funds of the Domestic and Foreign Missionary Society through which the business of the national Church is transacted; on the second is laid the task of making more widely and better known, through all media of communication, the program and work of the national Church in all its various aspects. A brief consideration of the activity of these two offices in the National Council opens as well the financial and promotional activity of the Episcopal Church on other levels than that of the national work and through other agencies than those of the national Church.

FINANCING THE CHURCH'S PROGRAM

At each triennial meeting of the General Convention the National Council submits a budget containing the expenditures proposed for the work of the National Church during the ensuing three years. After careful scrutiny by the Convention's *Committee on Program and Budget,* the proposed budget is brought before the Convention for consideration and adoption. Once it is passed, the National

Council is entrusted with its administration during the triennium. As a budget adopted for a period as long as three years cannot be inflexible, the Council may, within the limits set by the General Convention, revise the appropriations in details and adapt the program to the changing needs and circumstances of the triennium.

In any triennial budget by far the largest expenditures are those for the missionary work of the Church. Out of appropriations of nearly six million dollars in 1954, for example, over four million was devoted to the support and extension of missionary activity. Of this sum, two and a quarter million went to overseas missions; one and a quarter million was expended in the missionary districts and aided dioceses in the United States; half a million was devoted to world relief and Church co-operation with other Anglican Churches, the Eastern Orthodox Churches, and the interdenominational Councils of Churches; the relatively small remainder of the missionary appropriation was absorbed by the expenses of general administration. These approximate figures mean that out of every dollar received for the support of the general program of the Church's work about seventy-five cents is devoted to missionary work in the broadest sense of that phrase.

Other departments of the National Council receive appropriations far smaller than the missionary allocations made to the Home and Overseas Departments. The next largest amount in recent years has been that granted to the rapidly expanding work of Christian Education. In 1954, for example, this department received about three hundred and thirty thousand dollars, or about six cents out of every budget dollar. The Department of Promotion was allocated two hundred and twenty thousand dollars in the same annual budget, or four cents from each dollar, while the Department of Christian Social Relations was given ninety-five thousand, or a little less than two cents out of every dollar. While these figures are from a budget of a single recent year and therefore do not represent the exact amounts appropriated at any time, yet the proportionate amounts remain much the same.

Any budget adopted by the General Convention is one of proposed and estimated expenditures. Effective implementation of the program it sets forth depends upon the co-operation of the whole Church through the dioceses and missionary districts. While a substantial portion of the funds budgeted comes from legacies, special gifts, the income of endowment funds held by the national Church, and from the gifts of churchwomen through their United Thank Offering, by far the greater part is received from the dioceses and missionary districts—that is, from the regular offerings of the people. Of an annual budget of six million dollars, five million is given by the members of the Church. Under the plan adopted by the General Convention, the National Council assigns to each diocese and district its *missionary quota*—its proportionate share of the responsibility for financing the Church's program. All dioceses and districts participate—even the overseas missionary areas to which the largest amount of support is given—and to each is assigned a just proportion of the total.[1]

[1] Quotas vary widely in accordance with the numerical and financial strength of the dioceses and districts, their expenditures, and their potential capacity to bear the proportion of the budget assigned. In recent quotas a few dioceses have paid over $200,000 annually; the next ten, between $100,000-$200,000; approximately twenty pay a sum between $50,000-$100,000; fifty have a quota between $10,000-$50,000; and of the remaining twenty, half pay between $5,000-$10,000, and half below $5,000. Naturally these are only approximate figures, conveying some impression of the distribution of financial strength among the dioceses and districts of the Church.

DIOCESAN AND PAROCHIAL RESPONSIBILITY

Responsibility for meeting the quotas lies with the dioceses and missionary districts. Diocesan officers usually report to the National Council an "expectation," that is, the amount of the assigned quota which in any given year is reasonably certain to be paid. On the basis of these "expectations," the Council revises the triennial budget from time to time. No money is spent which there is not ample assurance of receiving, for the Domestic and Foreign Missionary Society is kept free of debt. At times the difference between the total amount of diocesan quotas and the "expectations" returned for any year amounts to two or three hundred thousand dollars, but by the end of the fiscal year this gap is much reduced by the number of dioceses that have paid beyond their "expectations." Frequently dioceses overpay their quotas; in other instances it appears that the quotas assigned them are momentarily, at least, beyond their normal capacity. To fall below the quota is not necessarily a sign that the people of a diocese or district are unwilling to bear their full share in the Church's work. Increases in the national budgets have been rapid and extensive in the last few decades, and often a particular diocese finds it hard to keep pace with the advance. The local program of education in a deeper sense of stewardship lags behind the opening of new opportunities which the national program of work is designed to meet. Nevertheless, the record of the dioceses in striving to meet their assigned share in support of the General Church Program has been remarkable in recent years. In 1953, for example, seventy of the ninety-nine dioceses and districts paid or overpaid their quotas, twenty-five met or bettered their "expectations," and four failed to meet the latter. In 1954, no less than eighty-two of the dioceses and districts paid or exceeded the assigned quotas, while sixteen of the remaining seventeen met or overpaid their "expectations." Moreover the total receipts in 1954 were roughly ninety-five per cent of the amount asked in all the quotas—a record of giving never before equalled in the history of the present unified budget system.

To bring the financial needs of the Church's program to its people, the diocese, through the diocesan department or committee on finance, employs a quota system similar to that used by the National Council. The diocesan budget is apportioned among the parishes and missions, each local congregation being asked to give in accordance with its ability—the local quota being fixed with consideration to the numerical size and financial strength of the parish or mission, its expenditures for its own support, and its estimated capacity to bear a greater or lesser share in the total responsibility falling upon the diocese or district. Thus in the parochial "proposed budget" that is normally placed before the congregation by the vestry or finance committee in every local church, preparatory to the annual canvass for pledges for the ensuing year, there appear two items for the Church's work outside the parish. The first is the *Diocesan Apportionment,* the amount assigned to a particular parish as its share through the diocesan quota in the support of the national Church's program, as well as its share in the missionary, educational, and social work undertaken by the diocese within its own borders; the second, and much smaller, amount is the *Diocesan Assessment,* a proportionate sum levied on each parish and mission for diocesan expenses—support of the episcopate, diocesan convention expenses, and other costs of maintaining the administrative activity of the diocese. The use of the quota system on each level, therefore, brings every member of the Church into direct relationship to the needs and support of the Church's program in both its general and local aspects.

OTHER FUNDS AND OFFERINGS

From time to time special campaigns for funds, outside the normal budget of the national Church, have been launched on a church-wide scale, chiefly for the provision of ample capital funds to meet urgent needs in the Church's work or life. Such campaigns, for example, were that which raised the initial millions of dollars needed for the establishment of the Church Pension Fund in 1917 and the *Reconstruction and Advance Fund* of 1947 to which was given more than seven million dollars for world relief, the rebuilding of mission properties destroyed in the second World War, and the extension of missionary programs overseas and at home.

The most recent appeal to the whole Church for a special single offering was that of the *Builders for Christ* campaign in 1954-55, with a goal of slightly more than four million dollars. Half this sum was distributed among the eleven seminaries of the Church to assist in the expansion of their overtaxed facilities—dormitories, libraries, and other buildings sorely needed; the other half was divided among similar needs for schools and mission buildings in the Church overseas, the mission fields at home, and for the improvement of facilities in the schools assisted by the American Church Institute for Negroes.

In addition to the occasional special campaign, several annual offerings are regularly made throughout the Church to help meet urgent needs.[2] One of the most important is the *Theological Education Sunday Offering,* an opportunity on the Sunday nearest January 25—the feast of the Conversion of St. Paul—for the people of the Church to share in the maintenance of the seminaries for the education and training of their clergy. None of the seminaries described in an earlier chapter of this volume is supported by appropriations from the funds of the national Church; all of them depend upon endowment incomes, tuition charges, and special gifts and grants. As a result of the pioneer efforts of a number of alumni of the General Theological Seminary to win recognition for this valuable method of assisting the seminaries to meet increasing expenses in educating candidates for the ministry and to bring wider knowledge of their work to the congregations of the Church, the General Convention of 1940 established Theological Education Sunday.

The success of this offering has been phenomenal. In 1943 about fifteen hundred parishes made an offering that totaled a little less than fifty thousand dollars. By 1950 the number of parishes and missions contributing had almost doubled while the total offering had multiplied nearly five times. In 1954, only fourteen years after its establishment, close to forty-five hundred congregations gave to the seminaries over four hundred thousand dollars.[3] This is the more remarkable in view of the success of the Builders for Christ cam-

---

[2] The women's *United Thank Offering* is one of these. Another is the *Good Friday Offering* throughout the Church, the greater part of which is devoted to the support of Anglican work in Jerusalem and the Near East.

[3] The theological offering is a "personalized" one—that is, most parishes and missions send their offering to the seminary from which their rector graduated. In 1954 the largest amounts were given to the Virginia and the General seminaries, with about $90,000 and $61,000 respectively. The Episcopal Theological School, Bexley Hall, and the Church Divinity School of the Pacific received between $33,000-$37,000 each; six other seminaries, between $20,000-$29,000 each.

paign in the same year, a large part of which was devoted to the capital needs of the seminaries of the Church. In a very real sense the Theological Education Sunday Offering has made the seminaries truly the care of church members.

One of the latest ventures in financing extraordinary activities in the life and work of the Episcopal Church was the establishment of the *Episcopal Church Foundation* in 1950. An independent corporation approved by the General Convention of 1949 and controlled by a board of lay directors under the chairmanship of the Presiding Bishop, the Foundation seeks to accumulate funds from generous donors "to enable the Church to expand its operations beyond the range of its annual budget" and to provide out of special gifts the resouces by which the Church "may enter new and broadening fields of service over and above its regular work." The Foundation administers gifts given for specific uses within the range of the Church's normal work, as well as making loans and grants of the income from undesignated donations to needs and opportunities which the Church has no ordinary funds to meet. Immensely valuable assistance is given to the implementation of the Church's mission from this reservoir of sacrificial offerings and generous donations.

AGENCIES OF SPECIAL AID

In addition to the regular channels for support of the Church's program in its various aspects, a large number of independent societies and corporations exist in the Episcopal Church, devoting their interest and funds to particular projects. The *Church Society for College Work,* for example, whose functions have already been described, assists in the maintenance of college work and workers. At least four organizations devote their resources to the financial assistance of candidates studying for the ministry: the *Society for the Increase of the Ministry,* which grants aid both to college seniors and to seminary students; the *Church Scholarship Society,* a loan-granting agency with affiliations to the Diocese of Connecticut; the *Protestant Episcopal Education Society,* an organization closely related to the Virginia dioceses; and the *Evangelical Education Society,* founded "to educate for the ministry of the Protestant Episcopal Church young men who are in hearty and practical sympathy with the Evangelical teaching of this Church." Loans and grants of aid made by these agencies are often of great assistance to men preparing for the ministry of the Church.

The *American Church Building Fund Commission,* established by the General Convention in 1880 and incorporated in the State of New York in the following year, is a nonprofit corporation operating solely for the benefit of the Episcopal Church. The Commission makes gifts and loans, the latter generally at lower rates than normally prevail, for the erection, improvement, or repair of churches, rectories, and other parochial buildings.

One of the most valuable services to the Church is rendered by the *Bible and Common Prayer Book Society of the Episcopal Church,* an organization founded nearly a century and a half ago, which out of its income from endowments and special gifts distributes free Prayer Books and Bibles to missions, congregations, institutions, and chaplains who are without adequate means to purchase these books. The yearly distribution of the society often totals nearly twelve thousand Prayer Books and two thousand Bibles.

The limitations of space make it impossible here to enumerate all the societies and agencies in the Episcopal Church which serve particular needs or special interests.[4] But two corporations which are subsidiaries of the Church Pension Fund deserve notice. One is the *Church Life Insurance Corporation,* which offers low cost insurance and annuity contracts to clergy, lay workers in the Church, and their immediate families; the other is the *Church Fire Insurance Corporation,* providing insurance of property belonging to the Church or to its affiliated institutions at unusually low rates. As these corporations are not operated for private profit, both of them perform an immensely useful service in making adequate insurance coverage available within the Church at costs considerably lower than usual.

PROMOTING THE CHURCH'S PROGRAM

The effective promotion of the Church's program of evangelism and work is one of the heaviest responsibilities on those who are entrusted with leadership on any level of the Church's activity. Promotion, publicity—what may be called "Christian propaganda"—if rightly designed to prepare the ground for the Gospel in people's hearts and minds, to popularize Christian truth, and to deepen men's understanding of the nature and work of the Church, is truly an evangelistic responsibility of primary importance. As such, all means of modern communication—radio, television, the press, the drama, advertising, publications, movies, filmstrips, and other visual aids—may be properly open to use by the Church. In the modern world these means of communication have become immeasurably powerful instruments for influencing thought and conduct in human

[4] The pages of *The Episcopal Church Annual* contain summary descriptions of most such organizations.

society. They are, in fact, often the strongest weapons in the hands of unscrupulous men and nations. Christian propaganda cannot afford to ignore or to use these agencies ineptly in the furtherance of truth and the advance of the Church's mission.

The National Council's Department of Promotion has the task of presenting winningly and persuasively the whole work of the Church to the world in which we live. In effect the Department is a service agency for all other departments and divisions of the Council, and it is organized to carry on its work in four divisions. The *Publications Division* is charged with editing and publishing all the printed materials of the National Council, with the exception of those of the Department of Christian Education.[5] Therefore this Division, for example, undertakes the preparation and publication of such materials as the Overseas Department may find useful in the promotion of wider knowledge and support of missions. The pamphlets in the series called *Building the Church Around the World,* each dealing with a particular mission area, and the newer booklets on great missionaries of the Episcopal Church called the *Builders for Christ Series,* are both edited and published under the supervision of the Publications Division. Books, materials, and pamphlets for other departments and divisions are similarly prepared in this office.

One of the most important promotional publications is the monthly magazine *Forth,* successor to the old *Spirit of Missions,* the pages of which are devoted to an attractive presentation of the Church's work, particularly in the missionary centers. *Forth* has the widest circulation of any of

[5] Publications of the Department of Christian Education are published by The Seabury Press.

the magazines in the Episcopal Church, and its challenging picture of the various aspects of the Church's work wins many to their support. Another periodic publication is *Churchways,* a bulletin of material, methods, and ideas for everyone who takes an active part in parish life. *Parish Helps* is a useful triennial catalog of all the educational and promotional materials available from the departments of the National Council; and the *Partly Printed Parish Papers,* leaflets issued for each Sunday of the year, contain pictures and articles on the General Church Program, designed to be supplemented by matter of parochial interest and used as a parish bulletin.

Another division of the Department of Promotion, that of *Stewardship and Missionary Information,* prepares and supplies to the field departments of the dioceses and to the parishes of the Church materials useful for the annual Every Member Canvass in which pledges are made for the support of the Church and its program. Methods of conducting parish canvasses are made available, and the Division holds provincial conferences to help train diocesan leaders and parish canvass chairmen in both the basic principles of Christian stewardship and the practical organization of an effective canvass. This laymen's training program has been one of the most successful means of extending education in the demands of true stewardship, and of winning a wide acceptance for the Every Member Canvass in the parishes and missions throughout the Church.

The work of the other two divisions of the Promotion Department may be briefly summarized. The *Division of Public Relations* exists chiefly for the provision of proper publicity through the Church and the secular press. The Division seeks to implement a program of effective news services and releases at the national, diocesan, and parochial levels of church life, in order that the Episcopal Church may be more forcefully brought to the attention of people in the communities where its evangelism and work are done. The *Division of Radio and Television* strives to promote a wider use of the facilities of radio and television by the Church. The Division works closely with the National Council of Churches in order that the Episcopal Church can have an effective voice in the programs sponsored by that Council, and it conducts workshops for the training of clergy in the use of these important media of communication in the diocese and at the parish level.

PROMOTION IN THE DIOCESE

As the diocese or missionary district assumes initial responsibility for a particular share in the support of the national Church's program, as well as undertaking to finance its own evangelistic, educational, and social work, the character of diocesan promotional activity is often a decisive element in the successful advance of the Episcopal Church. Each diocese has a field or promotion department, composed of clergy and lay members and represented on the Diocesan Council or Executive Committee. Sometimes this department is known as that of "publicity" or "evangelism," or the words "strategy" and "stewardship" are occasionally employed in its designation—all of which terms indicate the breadth of responsibility involved in the promotion of the Church's total program.

The diocesan department is the essential link between the National Council's Department of Promotion and the local parishes and missions. Acting closely with the finance department or committee of a diocese or missionary district, the field or promotion department educates the diocesan family in the principles of stewardship, assists in fixing the diocesan apportionments to the parishes and missions, and promotes the effective use of the Every Member Canvass.

Beyond that, the responsibilities of a diocesan department of promotion may embrace all the activities of the national Department—the use of radio and television, publications, press relations and publicity—depending upon the resources and facilities available in the local scene for proper promotion. One of the most valuable means of education and promotion among the parishes and missions of a diocese is the diocesan magazine. Nearly every diocese and district in the Episcopal Church publishes a monthly periodical, and many of these are notable for their attractive and interesting presentation of the Church's program.[6] Often containing pictures, articles, book reviews, general and local news, and other material of wide interest, the diocesan periodical today is one of the most useful means both of uniting the people of a diocese in their common efforts to advance the Church, and of arousing their informed support of the Church's work within and without the diocese.

INDEPENDENT AGENCIES OF EDUCATION AND PROMOTION

To a large degree the manifold activities of the Church are inseparable one from another. Evangelism, education, and promotion are all part of the advancement of the Church's total mission, and in the Episcopal Church there

[6] The California *Pacific Churchman,* Chicago's *Advance,* Maine's *Northeast, The Nebraska Churchman, The Maryland Churchman,* Massachusetts' *Church Militant, The Bulletin* of the diocese of New York, and *The Pastoral Staff* of Western Massachusetts are typical examples chosen at random of excellent diocesan papers. Many of the other diocesan periodicals today achieve the same high standard of effective education and promotion.

are numerous independent organizations existing to interest and educate people in particular aspects of church life and thought, to arouse and maintain their loyalties as churchmen, or to promote special concerns of Christian devotion and witness. Thus most of these organizations and agencies combine in their programs activity which is partly evangelistic and devotional, partly educational and promotional.

Though too numerous to describe in detail, these organizations fall into several more or less well defined groups. First, there are those that seek to spread a wider appreciation of and loyalty to particular emphases in the heritage of the Episcopal Church. Best known among such societies, perhaps, are the *Episcopal Evangelical Fellowship* which affirms this Church to be "Catholic in its inclusiveness, Liberal in its essential spirit, and Evangelical in its witness for the Gospel of Christ," and seeks to further greater loyalty to Evangelical principles; the *American Church Union,* among the avowed aims of which are the maintenance and defense of the Catholic heritage of Anglicanism and the furtherance of loyalty to the doctrine, discipline, and worship of the Episcopal Church as expressed in its official formularies; and the *Anglican Society* which strives to promote a central churchmanship based on the unifying power of strict obedience to the Prayer Book.[7] The existence and activity of these organizations is sometimes deplored, more especially when their enthusiastic support of a particular cause leads their members to indulge in acrimonious controversy or promote their ends in a partisan spirit. On the other hand, their witness to different aspects of our total heritage in the spirit of truth, humility, and charity may be one of the most

[7] Among other organizations in this category are the *Catholic Clerical Union,* the *National Guild of Churchmen,* and the *Evangelical Education Society.*

valuable ways in which the comprehensive character of the Anglican tradition is forcefully affirmed.

More avowedly ecumenical in their purposes are such organizations as the *Orthodox and Anglican Fellowship* which aims at establishing closer fellowship between members of the Orthodox and Episcopal Churches; the *Fellowship of St. John of Jerusalem* and the *Catholic Evangelical League,* both existing to promote wider contacts between Episcopalians and members of the Old Catholic, Polish National, and Eastern Orthodox Communions; and the *International League for Apostolic Faith and Order,* a branch of which in the Episcopal Church bears witness to its world-wide effort to increase understanding among Christians everywhere of the essential place of Apostolic faith and order in the life of the Church.

Among the groups dedicated to promote special concerns of Christian witness are the *Episcopal Pacifist Fellowship,* formed of Episcopalians who conscientiously believe a pacifist witness to be the vocation to which they are called; and the *Fellowship of St. Luke* and the *Order of St. Luke,* both of which seek to spread a better understanding and more effective practice of the ministry of spiritual healing.

Finally, societies for the promotion of a fuller devotional life among members of the Episcopal Church may be illustrated by the following: the *Guild of All Souls,* encouraging constant prayer for the repose of the faithful departed and firm adherence to Christian customs and Church practice in the burial of the dead; the *Confraternity of the Blessed Sacrament,* which seeks to spread a deeper appreciation of the centrality of the Eucharist in the life of Christians; and the *Order of St. Vincent for Acolytes,* a national guild of boys and men who are united by their common activity as servers in the Church services, and bound together by a rule designed to strengthen their devotional life. One of the most active devotional organizations is that of the *Companions of the Holy Cross,* a society of women who live under the discipline of intercessory prayer and simplicity of life. The Companions maintain Adelynrood, a retreat house and conference center at South Byfield, Massachusetts, familiar to many church people through the retreats and educational conferences that are frequently held there.

· CHURCH PRESS AND PUBLICATIONS

In addition to the publication of the official monthly *Forth* by the National Council, the Church press comprises a number of weekly or fortnightly magazines published independently: *The Living Church, The Episcopal Churchnews, The Witness,* and *The Churchman.* All of them are important agencies of promotion and education in the life of the Church, but none has the circulation that a national Church periodical or weekly should possess, despite the fact that their format and pictures, news coverage, feature articles, book reviews, and editorials are generally of a reasonably high standard of interest. Most Episcopalians are not avid readers of Church papers, though they might be made so if it were possible to publish a magazine or newspaper with a subscription cost low enough to bring it within reach of the majority of Church families.

There are two quarterly periodicals in the Episcopal Church, chiefly of interest to students and scholars. One is the *Anglican Theological Review,* a journal reflecting the Church's theological and intellectual activity; the other is the *Historical Magazine of the Protestant Episcopal Church,* the publication of the Church Historical Society, an official agency of the General Convention for the collection and preservation of the records and historical documents associated with the life and growth of the Church.

The publishing house established by the National Council as an agency of the Department of Christian Education is known as *The Seabury Press.* Started on September 1, 1951, with offices in Greenwich, Connecticut, the Press exists to publish both the materials of the Department of Christian Education and general religious books. In the latter field, The Seabury Press has made notable advances since its foundation, and today some of the most popular religious books bear the imprint of this press.

CHAPTER THIRTEEN

Our Place in Christendom

NO ADEQUATE summary of the manifold activities of the Episcopal Church can be complete without some consideration of our relation to other Christian bodies. One of the dramatic manifestations of the power of the Holy Spirit has been the response throughout the world to the challenge of divided Christendom. A half century ago the cause of Christian reunion was regarded as the peculiar fad of a few; today it is a primary concern of thousands of men and women of nearly every Christian allegiance. It may well be that the ecclesiastical history of our times and the years immediately ahead will be written in terms of the unifying power of the Lord in His Church.[1]

Efforts to increase co-operative activity among Christian Communions, and to explore as well the areas of both underlying unity and serious difference among them, are known today as the work of the *Ecumenical Movement.* In this connection the word "ecumenical" means simply "world-wide in extent and influence." Once, in the days of the undivided Church, the term could properly mean "pertaining to or representing the whole Church," and in that sense it is used, for example, to describe the great councils of the Early Church which formulated the Creeds of Chris-

---

[1] See *Chapters in Church History,* pages 252-254.

tian faith.[2] Today in divided Christendom the word is employed to signify the world-wide outreach of inter-Church activity that seeks to bring all Christians more closely together in their life of work, worship, and witness.

The Episcopal Church, like all other Churches of the Anglican Communion, has played an important role in the Ecumenical Movement. Largely because the Anglican tradition, as we have seen in an earlier part of this book, embodies elements in its church life that are both Catholic and Evangelical and possesses variety within its own unity, the Anglican Churches have often borne witness in the Ecumenical Movement to the necessity of seeking to embrace the whole of Christian truth and spiritual experience in any approach to church unity.

Repeatedly the Anglican Churches have affirmed their thanksgiving for the "signs of a growing movement towards Christian unity in all parts of the world," and the Lambeth Conference of 1920 issued a famous *Appeal to All Christian People,* "acknowledging all those who believe in our Lord Jesus Christ, and have been baptized into the name of the Holy Trinity, as sharing with us membership in the universal church of Christ which is His Body." The *Appeal* continued: "We believe that God wills fellowship . . . that it is God's purpose to manifest this fellowship, so far as this world is concerned, in an outward, visible, and united society, holding one faith, having its recognized officers, using God-given means of grace, and inspiring all its members to the world-wide service of the Kingdom of God." [3] Recognizing that Anglicanism has many ties of common

[2] *Ibid.,* pages 36-38. See also *Twenty Questions About the Episcopal Church and the Ecumenical Movement* (New York: The National Council).

[3] The *Appeal* was repeated in the Lambeth unity report in 1930. See the *Report of the Lambeth Conference 1930,* pages 130-131.

faith and tradition with other ancient episcopal Churches in both East and West, and equally close historical and spiritual affinities with many non-episcopal Communions, and acknowledging that the causes of division should arouse men continually to penitance and charity, the *Appeal* set before Christendom the vision "of a Church, genuinely Catholic, loyal to all Truth, and gathering into its fellowship all who profess and call themselves Christians, within whose visible unity all the treasures of faith and order, bequeathed as a heritage by the past to the present, shall be possessed in common, and made serviceable to the whole Body of Christ."

The bishops at Lambeth in 1948 again called attention to the claim which the *Appeal* of 1920 makes upon the vocation of Anglicanism, and in the Anglican Congress of 1954 the representatives of all the Churches of the Communion identified themselves with the *Appeal,* reaffirming its four "principles of unity"—that is, "(1) the Holy Scriptures as the record of God's revelation of Himself to man, and as being the rule and ultimate standard of faith; (2) the Creed, commonly called Nicene, as the sufficient statement of the Christian faith, and either it or the Apostles' Creed as the Baptismal Confession of belief; (3) the divinely instituted sacraments of Baptism and the Holy Communion, as expressing for all the corporate life of the whole fellowship in and with Christ; (4) a ministry acknowledged by every part of the Church as possessing not only the inward call of the Spirit, but also the commission of Christ and the authority of the whole body." [4]

---

[4] *Report of the Anglican Congress 1954,* pages 195-196. Presented in this form, these four elements in the life of the Church are known as the "Lambeth Quadrilateral," and were contained in the unity pronouncement of the bishops at Lambeth in 1888. That was a slightly revised statement,

Constantly strengthened by this vision of unity set before the whole Communion, the Anglican Churches have labored diligently and prayerfully in the cause of reunion during the last few decades, participating with increasing effectiveness in the various phases of the Ecumenical Movement.

THE ECUMENICAL MOVEMENT

Co-operation among the Churches on an international scale was stimulated first by the extent of the missionary advance in the nineteenth century. Gradually the Churches perceived the urgent need for the establishment of agencies for "research and conference regarding missionary work and problems," through which their missionary experience might be shared and policies determined for the more effective evangelistic activity of all Communions.[5] This movement culminated in a world missionary conference held in Edinburgh in 1910, out of which came the

---

reworded again in the 1920 *Appeal,* of the same points of the original "Chicago Quadrilateral," set forth by the House of Bishops of the Protestant Episcopal Church in 1886.

The Chicago pronouncement asserted that Christian unity could be found only by "a return to the first principles of unity exemplified by the undivided Catholic Church during the first ages of its existence." These principles were said to embrace "the substantial deposit of Christian Faith and Order committed by Christ and his Apostles to the Church . . . and therefore incapable of compromise or surrender . . ." The four elements of the Quadrilateral were affirmed to be "inherent parts of this sacred deposit, and therefore essential to the restoration of unity among the divided branches of Christendom . . . The Holy Scriptures . . . The Nicene Creed . . . The two Sacraments, Baptism and the Supper of the Lord . . . The Historic Episcopate." *Journal of the General Convention 1886,* pages 79-80. That the phrase used in the *Appeal* of 1920: "a ministry acknowledged by every part of the Church," means "the historic episcopate" was made clear in the Lambeth Conference of 1930. *Report of the Lambeth Conference 1930,* pages 114-115.

[5] The *World Student Christian Federation,* organized in 1895, is actually the oldest movement for co-operation in church work. In the Episcopal Church our relation to the Federation is through the Division of College Work.

formation of the *International Missionary Council,* founded in 1921, now the chief agency of inter-Church missionary co-operation. Under its auspices four world-wide missionary conferences have been held: Jerusalem, 1928; Madras, 1938; Whitby, 1947; and Willingen, 1952.

Meanwhile the same years witnessed the growth of two other movements. One was the *Life and Work Movement,* an attempt to bring the Churches together for the exploration of problems and challenges presented by other areas of church life than that of missions. The issues were practical ones, touching on political, social, moral, economic, and educational matters in which a stronger witness to Christian principles might be made by joint action. Discussion of doctrinal differences among the Churches or questions of their reunion were not topics of the Life and Work Movement.

Two world conferences gave impetus to this effort "to unite the different Churches in common practical work, to furnish the Christian conscience with an organ of expression in the midst of the great spiritual movement of our time, and to insist that the principles of the Gospel be applied to the solution of the contemporary social and international problems." [6] The first was held at Stockholm in 1925, under the brilliant leadership of the Swedish Archbishop Nathan Söderblom; the second at Oxford in 1937, where William Temple, then Archbishop of York, made strongly felt the extraordinary influence that soon gave him pre-eminence in the Ecumenical Movement.

But many Christian leaders, particularly among Angli-

---

[6] Leonard Hodgson, *The Ecumenical Movement* (Sewanee: The University Press, 1951), page 13.

cans, were concerned to raise the question of differences of belief among the Churches. Neither missionary co-operation nor common Christian witness in social and international affairs could be long separated from the fundamental issue of church unity, and under the influence of Charles Henry Brent, then Missionary Bishop of The Philippines, our own General Convention of 1910 was aroused to this aspect of ecumenical activity. A resolution of that Convention, proposed in the House of Deputies by William T. Manning, rector of Trinity Church, New York, and later Bishop of New York, launched a movement "to bring about a Conference for the consideration of questions touching Faith and Order, and that all Christian communions throughout the world which confess our Lord Jesus Christ as God and Saviour be asked to unite with us in arranging for and conducting such a conference." That was the genesis of the *Faith and Order Movement* which has played such a vital part in bringing about the exploration of areas of both difference and agreement in the deepest issues on which the Churches of Christendom are divided. Three world conferences have been the scenes of searching and courageous grappling with the problems of Christian disunion: Lausanne in 1927, Edinburgh in 1937, and Lund in 1952. At them have been representatives from all the major Christian bodies and Communions, both East and West, except the Roman Catholic Church.

In this world-wide faith and order activity of the Ecumenical Movement Anglican influence and participation has continued to be notable, and among the Anglican Churches the Episcopal Church has produced a number of influential leaders from the days of Brent's first inspiration to the present time. Strong and whole-hearted Anglican participation, often reinforced by the presence of representatives from the great Churches of the Eastern Orthodox Communion, has kept before these world conferences the true goal of the movement for church reunion: the unity of *all* Christendom, Catholic and Protestant alike. Faithful to the ultimate goal expressed in the Lambeth *Appeal* as "a Church, genuinely Catholic, loyal to all Truth, and gathering into its fellowship all who profess and call themselves Christians," Anglicans have never been content to envisage any final and successful achievement of Christian unity that will not embrace the Roman Communion. Despite the refusal of Roman Catholics to participate in the faith and order activity of the rest of Christendom, and, indeed, in the face of an intransigeant hostility sometimes displayed by Rome, Anglicans still hold the conviction expressed by their bishops at Lambeth that "there can be no fulfillment of the Divine purpose in any scheme of reunion which does not ultimately include the great Latin Church of the west, with which our history has been so closely associated in the past, and to which we are still bound by so many ties of common faith and tradition." [7]

THE WORLD COUNCIL OF CHURCHES

The encouraging widening of ecumenical concern and the continued activity of all these various movements led to their co-ordination in a single *World Council of Churches,* within the framework of which the different aspects of the Ecumenical Movement might be more closely directed and related to each other. In 1937 the Life and

[7] *Report of the Lambeth Conference 1930,* page 131.

Work Movement at its Oxford Conference and the Faith and Order Movement at its Edinburgh Conference began the steps leading to their closer relation, and in 1948 the World Council was fully organized at its first Assembly at Amsterdam. The Amsterdam Assembly, attacking its study-theme "Man's Disorder and God's Design," was a thrilling experience in ecumenical encounter. Truly an international and interracial gathering, it brought together Christians of all the principal non-Roman Churches for worship and prayer, work and study, under the conviction that "Here at Amsterdam we have committed ourselves afresh to Him, and have covenented with one another in constituting this World Council of Churches. We intend to stay together."

The second World Assembly was held in 1954 at Evanston, Illinois. "Christ the Hope of the World" was its main theme, and again the Churches made plain their intention to stay close to one another in their efforts to find greater unity through all difficulties and discouragements, trusting the guidance of the Holy Spirit to bring the Ecumenical Movement along the path of God's purpose for the eventual reunion of His Church throughout the world.

Anglican leadership in the World Council has been evident from the beginning. The Archbishop of Canterbury, Geoffrey Francis Fisher, was a member of its presidium from 1948 to 1954, when his place was taken among the new presidents by the Presiding Bishop of the Episcopal Church, Henry Knox Sherrill. Among the American members of the Central Committee, which is the governing body of the World Council between Assemblies, were two Episcopalians, the Bishop of Washington, Angus Dun, and Dr. Nathan M. Pusey, President of Harvard University.

THE NATIONAL COUNCIL OF CHURCHES

The ecumenical organization immediately at hand in the United States is the *National Council of Churches of Christ in the U.S.A.*, constituted in 1950 by the consolidation of the Federal Council of Churches, Church World Service, the United Council of Church Women, various missionary councils, and a large number of other agencies of interdenominational co-operation. To it belong thirty Churches, including all the major denominations in the United States except the Roman Catholics. Episcopal delegates are sent regularly to its General Assembly; its first president was the Presiding Bishop of the Episcopal Church.

The National Council of Churches undertakes to direct or sponsor such co-operative projects as the resettlement of displaced persons, Christian evangelism through radio and television networks, the provision of institutional chaplaincy services on an interdenominational basis, the publication of educational materials for Church schools and vacation Bible schools, missionary education, the publication of the Revised Standard Version of the Bible, the development of programs for more effective Christian witness in issues of social and economic concern, and the furtherance of the Christian life of prayer and worship.

Member Churches contribute to the support of the work of the National Council of Churches, but in no way do they abnegate their own freedom or independence by membership in its organization. The Episcopal Church, for example, is not committed to every statement or activity of this ecumenical agency, and like all other member Churches, may at any time refuse participation in activities that are not in accordance with its own faith or practice. The purpose of our membership in the Council, like that of any Church, is to make a stronger impact on American society by co-operation in those areas of work and witness where all Christians may freely stand side by side.

ACHIEVEMENTS IN UNITY

The various councils and conferences of the Ecumenical Movement do not devise plans or programs for reuniting separated Churches. The function of faith and order study is simply to explore paths which the Churches may themselves decide to follow. Any achievement of unity rests with the separate Christian bodies. But here striking advances have marked the ventures of Christian reunion in the last thirty or forty years.[8] Steady progress, for example, has been made in healing divisions among denominations that belong to the same great family of Christian Churches. For the most part these breaches are the kind that lend themselves most readily to healing. Division is not rooted in serious difference in doctrine or church order, yet often an immense patience, a willingness to sacrifice some long-cherished customs and traditions, and a spirit of consecration to the primary things of Christian allegiance have been the qualities of mind and will essential to any achievement of unity.

Examples of such efforts in the United States are those that resulted in the formation of the *Congregational Christian Fellowship* in 1931, out of the Christian and Congregational Churches; the *Evangelical and Reformed Church* in 1934, from the two bodies in its present name; and the *Methodist Church* in 1939, a union now including millions

---

[8] See *Towards Church Union 1937-1952* by Stephen Neill (London: Faith and Order Commission, 1952).

whose allegiance was once divided among three Methodist bodies. Other reunions might be instanced both in the United States and abroad—the *United Lutheran Church* in America, the *Reformed Church of France,* the *Dutch Reformed Church* in the Netherlands, and many more. Negotiations looking towards the joining together of separated bodies of the same doctrinal position—"intra-confessional" unions—are constantly in progress throughout the world.

Far more difficult are "trans-confessional" achievements in corporate reunion, that is, the uniting of Churches whose theological heritage or principles of ministry and church government are different. Yet here the Ecumenical Movement measures its greatest success. In Japan, for example, the *Church of Christ in Japan,* a union of Presbyterians, Methodists, Congregationalists, and other smaller denominations made under severe pressure from the Japanese Imperial government in 1941, has nevertheless held together, and today is probably the largest Christian body in that country. The *United Church of Canada* brought into a single body former Presbyterian, Methodist, and Congregational Churches, while the *South India United Church* was formed by the union of Presbyterian and Congregationalist missions in the vast peninsula of southern India.

The trans-confessional union of chiefest concern to Anglicans, and perhaps also to the whole Christian world because in it episcopal traditions have been merged with non-episcopal traditions—Catholic with Protestant elements—is the *Church of South India,* inaugurated in 1947 by the union of the South India United Church, the Methodist Church in South India, and the four southern dioceses of the Anglican Church of India, Pakistan, Burma and Ceylon.

These four dioceses have left the Anglican Communion to take the episcopate and other elements of the Anglican heritage into a union with Churches of Protestant traditions. The difficulties attendant upon such a daring experiment are such that at present the Church of South India is not in communion with Anglican Churches. Fuller exploration must be made of problems of faith and order which are raised by the South India union, but the Lambeth Conference in 1948 expressed the hope that one day "there shall be full communion between the Church of South India and the Churches of the Anglican Communion."[9] This hope was again affirmed in the Anglican Congress of 1954.

THE EPISCOPAL CHURCH

Like all the independent Churches participating in these movements towards greater Christian unity, the Episcopal Church has conducted its own negotiations with other bodies which have responded to invitations to explore the difficulties in the path of union. Some years ago, for example, conversations were held with the Congregationalists. From 1937 until 1946 prolonged and intensive negotiations were carried on with the Presbyterian Church in the U.S.A. Both Churches initially declared their purpose to achieve organic union, but successive proposals to implement this original intention proved to be unacceptable, largely because many Episcopalians felt them to be contrary to the terms of the Lambeth Quadrilateral. The negotiations terminated in the General Convention of 1946, where again the elements of the Quadrilateral were declared primary in any statement of faith and order upon which the Episcopal

Report of the Lambeth Conference 1948 (Part I), page 38.

Church might proceed towards intercommunion or organic federation with any other Christian body. More recently the Convention's Joint Commission on Approaches to Unity has opened discussions with representatives of the Methodist Church, but as yet no specific proposals for possible union have been produced for study and action.

If our negotiations with Protestant Communions have been fruitful thus far only of increased understanding and friendly co-operation, on the side of episcopal Churches of Catholic heritage the ecumenical gain has been greater. The Churches of the Anglican Communion are in full intercommunion with the Old Catholic Churches, a group of small episcopal Churches which separated themselves from the Roman papacy, rejecting the dogma of the infallibility and universal supremacy of the Pope, as well as other Roman doctrines. In 1931 the famous Bonn Agreement between the Church of England and the Old Catholics set a model for the closer relation of such free Catholic Churches. By this agreement each Communion recognized the catholicity and independence of the other, and agreed to admit each other's members to participate in the Sacraments, recognizing that "intercommunion does not require from either communion the acceptance of all doctrinal opinion, sacramental devotion, or liturgical practice characteristic of the other, but implies that each believes the other to hold all the essentials of the Christian faith." [10]

While most Old Catholic Churches are in Europe—in Holland, Switzerland, Germany, and Austria—the *Polish National Catholic Church* in the United States belongs to this Communion. When by 1946 both the Polish National Catholics and the Episcopal Church had accepted the Bonn

[10] Neill, *Towards Church Union 1937-1952,* page 36.

Agreement, intercommunion between them was established. Today it is an increasingly common sight to see Old Catholic bishops and clergy participating in special services in the Episcopal Church, and to discover places where isolated Polish Old Catholics are ministered to in our parishes.

Our relations with the *Philippine Independent Church* are of a specialized kind. When the Independent Church was formed by the separation of a number of clergy and congregations from Roman Catholicism, ministerial succession was continued without the historic episcopate. The consecration in 1948 of three Filipino bishops by Episcopal bishops has already been described in an earlier chapter. No formal union has taken place between the Independent Church and our own Church in the Philippines, but limited intercommunion is practiced, and many of the candidates for the priesthood of the Independent Church are trained for ordination in St. Andrew's Seminary in Manila.

The Episcopal Church enjoys the same close friendship and co-operation with both the Eastern Orthodox Churches and the lesser Eastern Churches as do all Anglican bodies. Formal intercommunion has not yet been reached, though from time to time informal arrangements have been made for its limited practice. Several of the Orthodox Churches have issued important irenical pronouncements on the faith and order of Anglicanism, and the increasing understanding between the two Communions gives hope of the eventual possibility of some mutual official recognition like that between Anglicans and Old Catholics.

Limited though many of these steps in the direction of the unity of "all who profess and call themselves Christians" may appear, encouraging progress has been made in a remarkably brief time. Four centuries of separation lie behind many of the Churches of the Western world, and even older divisions sunder East and West. These deeply rooted breaches cannot be healed in a few years. Nevertheless, Episcopalians, like all other Anglicans, have maintained firmly their belief in the special vocation of Anglicanism in the ecumenical activity of Christendom. The response to the challenge of Christian division grows deeper and stronger as the years pass, and ever nearer looms the time when we may play our part in God's purpose for the union of all His children in "a greater Church into which we may bring our gifts and lay them at His feet along with Christians of other traditions." [11]

---

[11] *Report of the Anglican Congress 1954,* page 208.

APPENDIX OF MAPS AND TABLES

THE ANGLICAN

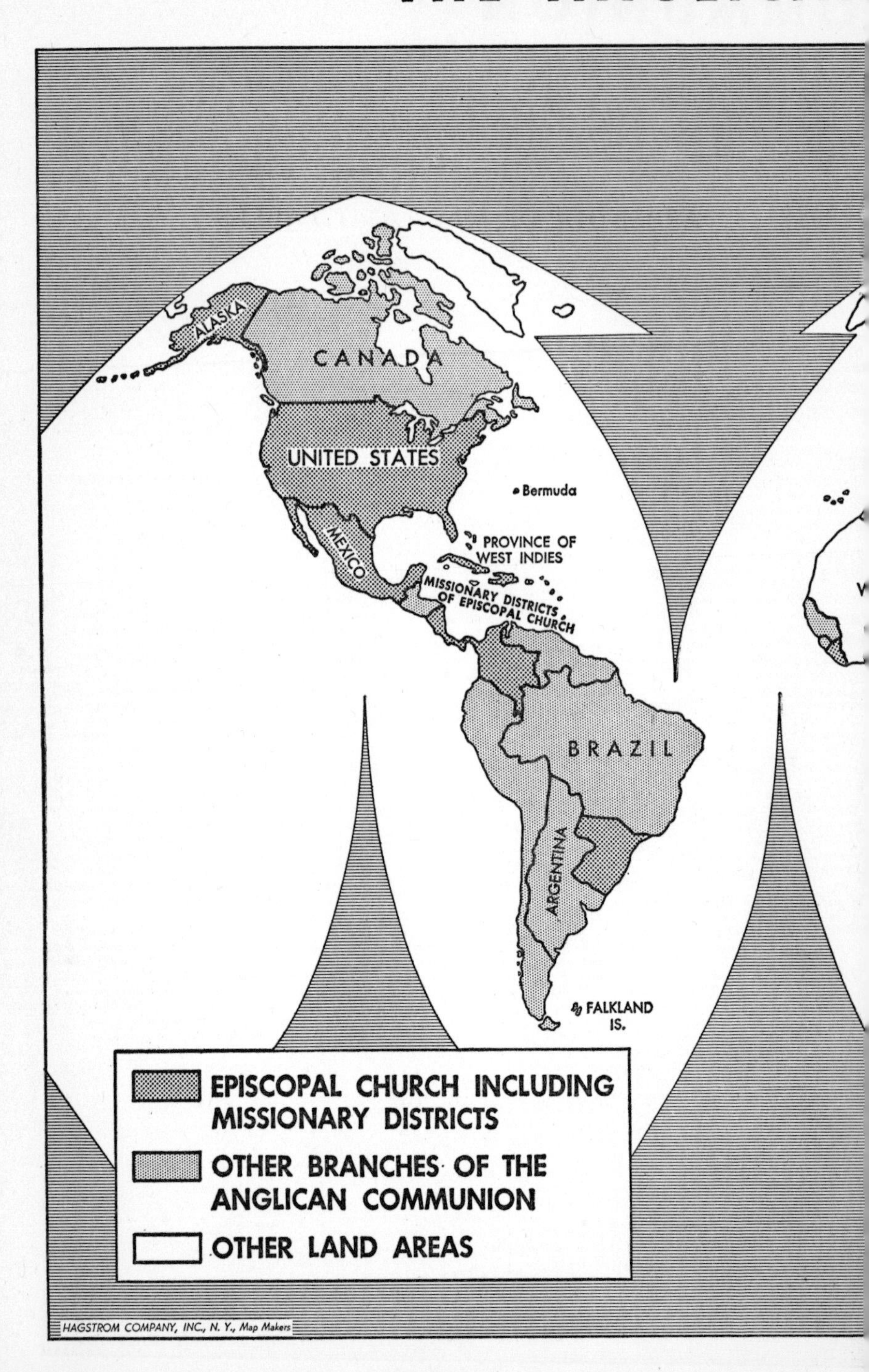

OMMUNION

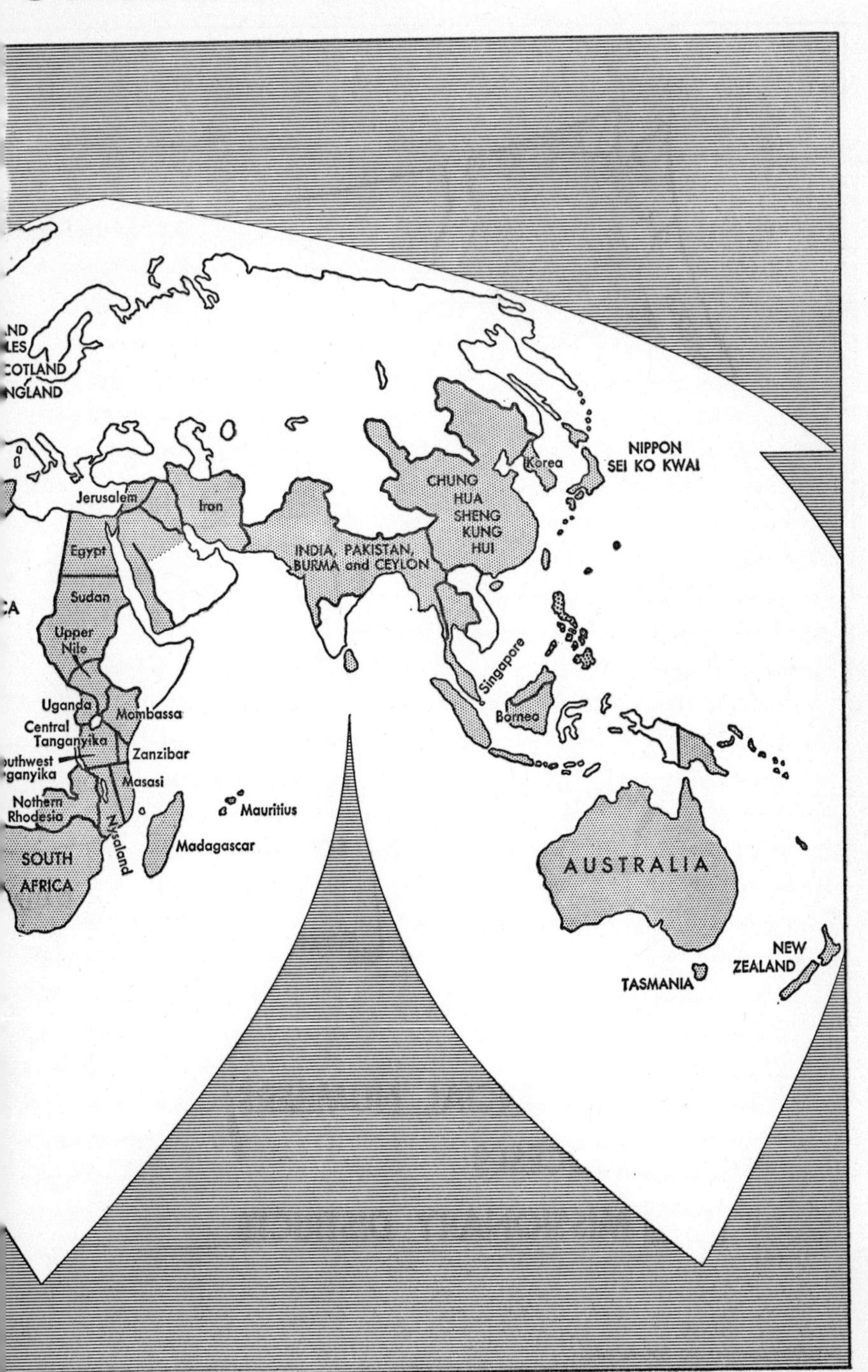

NIPPON SEI KO KWAI
Korea
CHUNG HUA SHENG KUNG HUI
Jerusalem
Iran
Egypt
INDIA, PAKISTAN, BURMA and CEYLON
Sudan
Upper Nile
Singapore
Uganda
Mombassa
Borneo
Central Tanganyika
Zanzibar
Masasi
Mauritius
Nothern Rhodesia
Nysaland
Madagascar
SOUTH AFRICA
AUSTRALIA
NEW ZEALAND
TASMANIA

THE EPISCOPAL CHURC

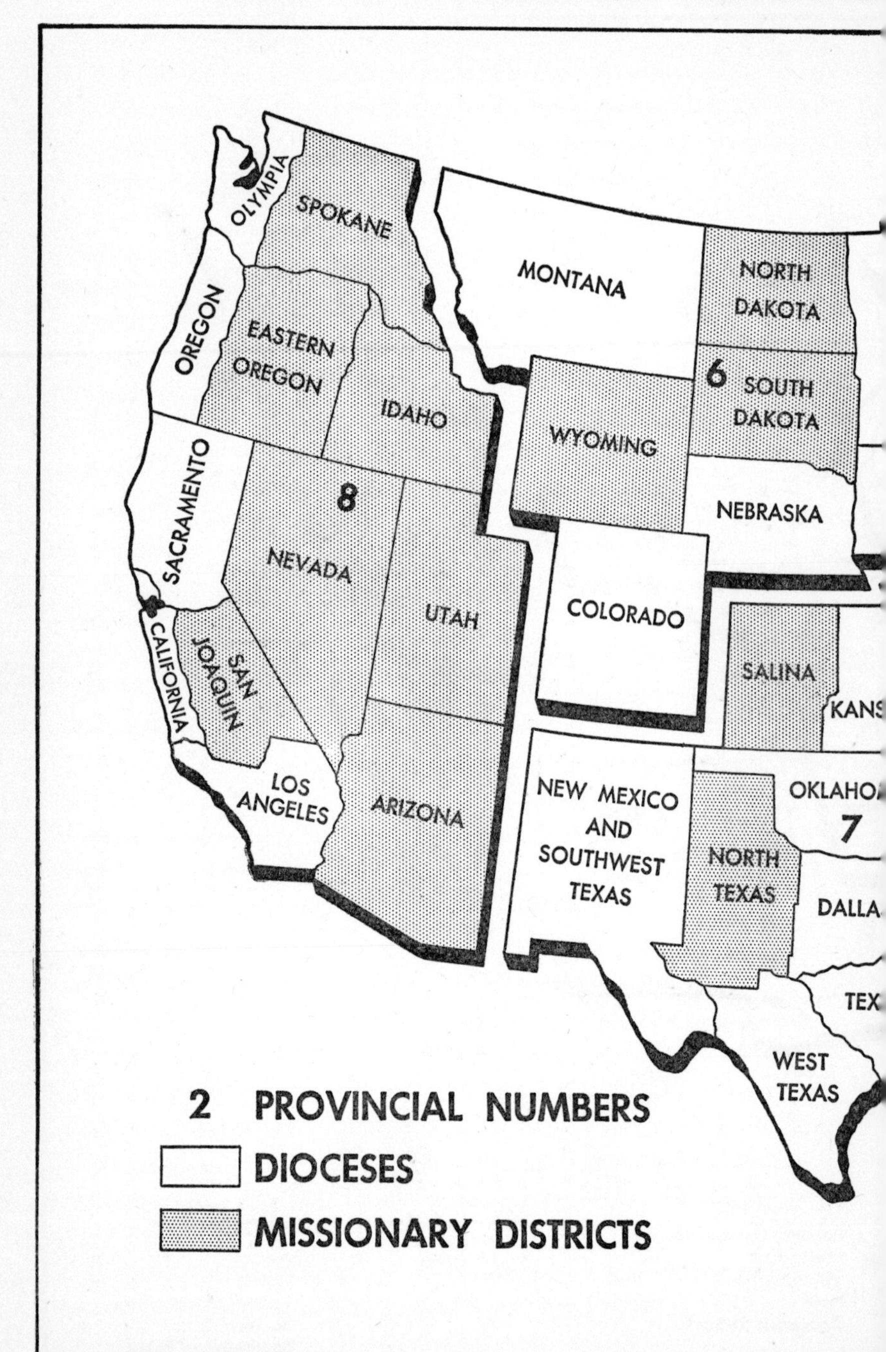

N THE UNITED STATES

THE EPISCOPAL CHURC

IN THE ATLANTIC

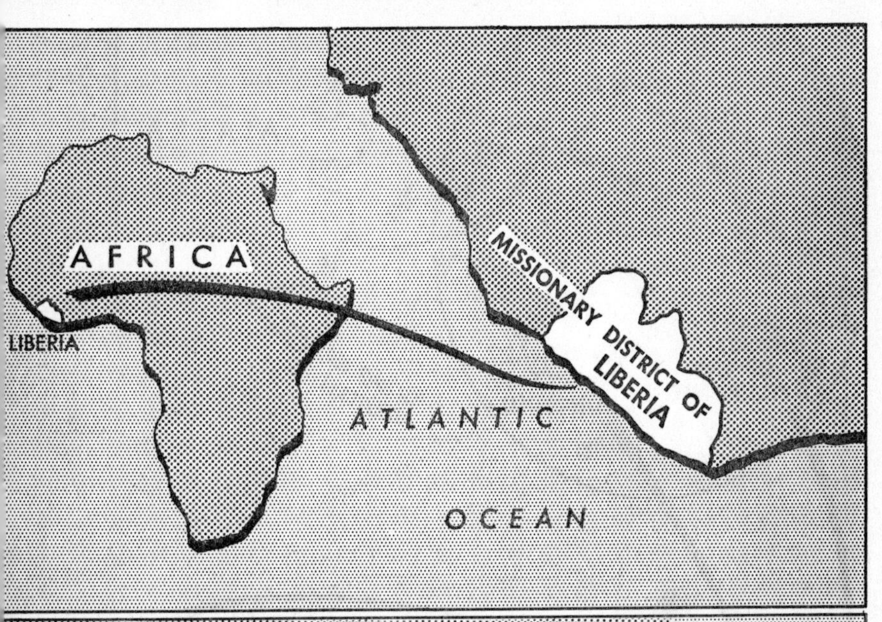

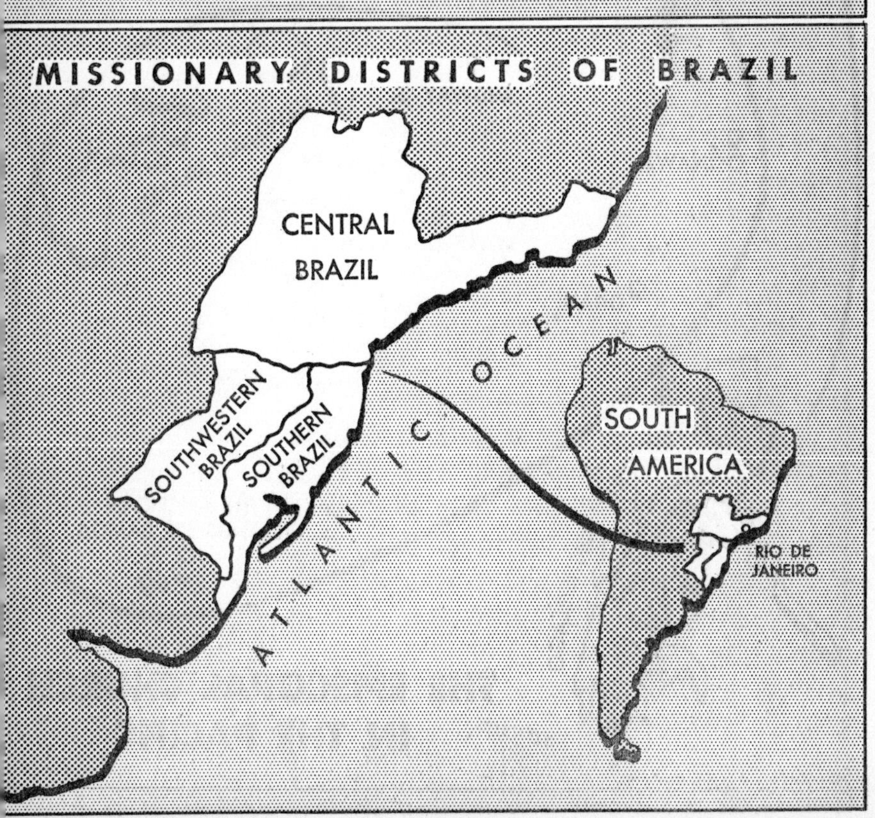

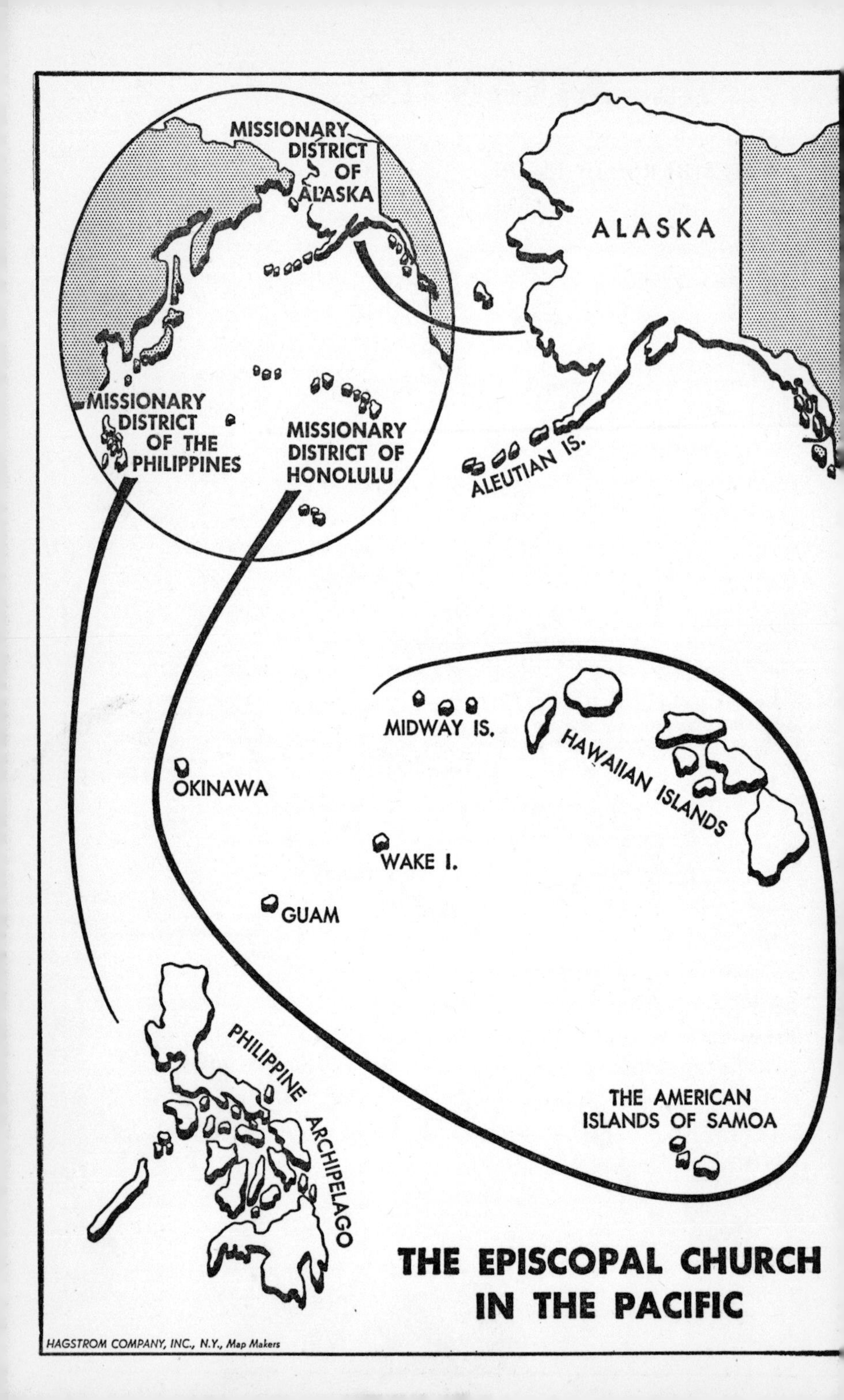
MISSIONARY DISTRICT OF ALASKA
ALASKA
MISSIONARY DISTRICT OF THE PHILIPPINES
MISSIONARY DISTRICT OF HONOLULU
ALEUTIAN IS.
MIDWAY IS.
HAWAIIAN ISLANDS
OKINAWA
WAKE I.
GUAM
PHILIPPINE ARCHIPELAGO
THE AMERICAN ISLANDS OF SAMOA
THE EPISCOPAL CHURCH IN THE PACIFIC
HAGSTROM COMPANY, INC., N.Y., Map Makers

MEMBERSHIP IN THE LARGER AMERICAN CHURCHES

(*Approximate figures for those numbering over one million adherents*)

Roman Catholic Church	31,470,000	Eastern Orthodox Churches	2,100,000
Baptist Churches	17,990,000	Disciples of Christ	1,900,000
Methodist Churches	11,640,000	Churches of Christ	1,500,000
Lutheran Churches	6,610,000	Christian Scientists	1,500,000
Presbyterian Churches	3,640,000	Congregational-Christian Church	1,280,000
Protestant Episcopal Church	2,900,000	Latter-Day Saints	1,210,000

See the statistics in the *Yearbook of American Churches* (New York: National Council of Churches), and in *The World Alamanac and Book of Facts* (New York: World-Telegram).

WORLD STATISTICS

(*Approximate round numbers*)

Roman Catholics	423,000,000	Anglicans	40,000,000
Eastern Orthodox	160,000,000	Baptists	40,000,000
Lutherans	68,500,000	Methodists	30,000,000
Presbyterian and Reformed	41,000,000	Congregationalists	5,000,000

These figures are based on a statement issued by the Archbishop of Canterbury at the Anglican Congress of 1954. See the *Report of the Anglican Congress 1954* (Greenwich: The Seabury Press, 1954), page 52. The difficulty with Church world statistics is that there is no universally acknowledged standard by which to measure the exact numbers of adherents to different Christian Communions. Some figures give an unrealistic picture regarding adult members since calculations are frequently based on those presumed to belong on general grounds of geographical boundaries. For another discussion of world statistics see G. K. A. Bell, *The Kingship of Christ* (Penguin Books, 1954), pages 178-181.

ANGLICAN STATISTICS

It is impossible to break down accurately the forty million Anglicans into the numbers belonging to each of the fourteen separate Churches and Provinces of the Anglican Communion and the extra-provincial missionary dioceses. While reasonably exact membership statistics of the Protestant Episcopal Church, the Church of England in Canada, the Scottish Episcopal Church, and some other Anglican bodies that do not have the associations of "National Churches" are readily obtained, with other Anglican Churches and Provinces it is difficult to arrive at precise numbers of adherents. No accurate statistics can be easily compiled of active membership in the Church of England, for example; on the other hand, for different reasons it is impossible to obtain knowledge of the membership today in the Chung Hua Sheng Kung Hui.

The Church of England, however, is clearly the largest single Church in the Anglican Communion. Either the Protestant Episcopal Church in the United States of America or the Church of England in Australia and Tasmania comes in second place, their total memberships being sufficiently close to make the decision difficult. The Australian Church reports about one hundred thousand more adherents than the Episcopal Church, but owing to the fact that the Australian Church has retained some characteristics of a "National Church" in the Commonwealth, the figures reported may not be as accurate as those given by the Episcopal

Church. Listed in the order of their size, as far as may be determined with such information as is available, the fourteen independent Churches and Provinces of the Anglican Communion would be arranged thus: the Church of England, the Church of England in Australia and Tasmania or the Protestant Episcopal Church in the United States, the Church of England in Canada, the Church of the Province of New Zealand, the Church of the Province of West Africa, the Church of the Province of the West Indies, the Church in Wales, the Church of Ireland, the Church of India, Pakistan, Burma and Ceylon, the Church of the Province of South Africa, the Episcopal Church in Scotland, the Chung Hua Sheng Kung Hui [?], and the Nippon Sei Ko Kwai.

STATISTICS OF THE PROTESTANT EPISCOPAL CHURCH 1954

Church Members (Baptized persons)	2,907,321
Communicant Members	1,816,611
Church School Children	678,935
Parishes and Missions	7,912
Clergy	7,367
Candidates for Holy Orders	666
Postulants for Holy Orders	1,195

Complete statistics for the Episcopal Church may be found in the latest edition of *The Episcopal Church Annual* (New York: Morehouse-Gorham). As the ratio statistic is of special significance in estimating the growth of the Church, the following table is reprinted, by permission of the Morehouse-Gorham Company, from *The Episcopal Church Annual,* 1955, page 26:

RATIO OF COMMUNICANTS OF THE EPISCOPAL CHURCH

TO THE POPULATION OF THE [CONTINENTAL] UNITED STATES SINCE 1830

Year	Communi-cants	Population	Ratio
1830	30,939	12,866,020	1-415.851
1840	55,477	17,069,453	1-307.685
1850	98,655	23,191,876	1-235.08
1860	150,591	31,443,321	1-208.799
1870	231,591	38,558,371	1-166.493
1880	341,155	50,155,783	1-147.017
1890	531,525	62,947,714	1-118.428
1900	742,569	75,994,575	1-102.34
1910	930,037	91,972,266	1- 98.89
1920	1,073,832	105,710,620	1- 98.442
1930	1,261,167	122,775,046	1- 97.35
1940	1,437,820	131,669,275	1- 91.57
1950	1,640,101	150,697,361	1- 91.883

The figure given for the population in each instance is from the official U. S. census for the year indicated. The figure for communicants is taken in most instances from the Church's year book dated two years later. The reason for this is that the statistics in the 1952 *Living Church Annual,* for example, are compiled in 1951 from diocesan journals containing information for the year 1950. Thus the figures in the 1952 *Annual* are the ones comparable with those of the 1950 census.

For the years 1830 and 1840 no reliable annual statistics are available, and the figures are therefore taken from the average for three years reported in the Journals of General Convention.

All figures are for continental United States, excluding Alaska and the Panama Canal Zone. They are therefore somewhat smaller than those given in other tables under "Communicants—Domestic"—a classification that includes all dioceses and missionary districts under the American flag.

About the Author

THE REV. POWEL MILLS DAWLEY, PH.D., is Professor of Ecclesiastical History and Sub-Dean at the General Theological Seminary. He was formerly Associate Rector of St. David's Church, Baltimore, and Dean of St. Luke's Cathedral, Portland, Maine. A graduate of Brown University and the Episcopal Theological School, he received his Ph.D. from the University of Cambridge, England. He is co-author of *The Religion of the Prayer Book,* and author of *The Words of Life, John Whitgift and the Reformation* (The Hale Lectures for 1953), and *Chapters in Church History,* Volume II in THE CHURCH'S TEACHING series.

OTHER MEMBERS OF THE AUTHORS' COMMITTEE
AT THE TIME THIS BOOK WAS PREPARED

THE REV. STANLEY BROWN-SERMON, D.D., the late Dean and Professor of New Testament Language and Literature at the Protestant Episcopal Theological Seminary in Virginia.

THE REV. ROBERT CLAUDE DENTON, PH.D., Professor of Old Testament Literature and Interpretation at the General Theological Seminary and author of Volume I in THE CHURCH'S TEACHING series, *The Holy Scriptures.*

THE REV. JOSEPH F. FLETCHER, S.T.D., Professor of Christian Ethics at the Episcopal Theological School.

THE REV. JOHN HEUSS, D.D., Rector of Trinity Church, New York and co-chairman of the Authors' Committee.

THE REV. DAVID R. HUNTER, ED.D., Director of the Department of Christian Education of the National Council and co-chairman of the Authors' Committee.

LEON MCCAULEY, Publisher, The Seabury Press.

JOHN D. MIDWORTH, Executive Secretary, Adult Division, the Department of Christian Education of the National Council.

THE VERY REV. JAMES A. PIKE, J.S.D., Dean of the Cathedral of St. John the Divine, New York, and co-author of Volume III in THE CHURCH'S TEACHING series, *The Faith of the Church.*

THE REV. W. NORMAN PITTENGER, S.T.D., Professor of Apologetics at the General Theological Seminary and co-author of Volume III in THE CHURCH'S TEACHING series, *The Faith of the Church.*

THE REV. MASSEY H. SHEPHERD, JR., S.T.D., Professor of Liturgics at the Church Divinity School of the Pacific and author of Volume IV in THE CHURCH'S TEACHING series, *The Worship of the Church.*

THE REV. CHARLES W. F. SMITH, D.D., Professor of New Testament at the Episcopal Theological School.

THE REV. C. WILLIAM SYDNOR, JR., Executive Secretary, Division of Curriculum Development, the Department of Christian Education of the National Council.

THE REV. THEODORE O. WEDEL, PH.D., Warden of the College of Preachers, Washington, D. C.

THE REV. M. MORAN WESTON, PH.D., Executive Secretary of the Division of Christian Citizenship, the Department of Christian Social Relations of the National Council.

Books for Reference

Books listed here have been selected to provide suggestions for further reading on the subjects discussed in this volume. As in many instances the summary treatment made necessary in this volume by the limitations of space will appear insufficient, the following books and pamphlets will be of use to those interested in various aspects of the general subject. By far the greater number of titles included here are of books that present a popular treatment of their material. This bibliography is intended for the layman, not the expert.

Reference should be had to the earlier volumes in this series and their bibliographies:

THE CHURCH'S TEACHING SERIES

I. *The Holy Scriptures* by Robert Claude Dentan (Greenwich: The Seabury Press, 1949).

II. *Chapters in Church History* by Powel Mills Dawley (Greenwich: The Seabury Press, 1950).

III. *The Faith of the Church* by James A. Pike and W. Norman Pittenger (Greenwich: The Seabury Press, 1951).

IV. *The Worship of the Church* by Massey H. Shepherd, Jr. (Greenwich: The Seabury Press, 1952).

BOOKS FOR PART I

THE ANGLICAN HERITAGE

A History of the Church in England by John R. H. Moorman (London: A. & C. Black, 1953). A new and very readable history of the English Church.

Everyman's History of the English Church by Percy Dearmer (New York: Morehouse, 1915). Older, but designed for more popular reading. Profusely illustrated.

The English Reformation to 1558 by T. M. Parker (New York: Oxford [Home University Library], 1950). An admirable brief survey of the Reformation from Henry VIII to Elizabeth I.

The Reformation in England by L. E. Elliott-Binns (London: Duckworth, 1937). A clear account of the whole movement.

Highlights of Church History: The Reformation by Powel Mills Dawley (Philadelphia: Church Historical Society, 1949). An introductory booklet.

The Anglican Tradition by A. T. P. Williams (New York: Macmillan, 1947). A concise summary of post-Reformation Anglicanism.

The Churchman's Heritage by E. G. Knapp-Fisher (Greenwich: The Seabury Press, 1952). The heritage of Anglican thought.

The English Religious Tradition by Norman Sykes (London: S. C. M. Press, 1953). An excellent brief survey of the character and influence of the English religious tradition.

A Brief Sketch of the Church of England by G. K. A. Bell (New York: Morehouse, 1929). A handbook of the organization of the English Church.

The Claims of the Church of England by Cyril Foster Garbett (New York: Morehouse, 1947). An attractive and able apologetic for Anglicanism, together with a discussion of the life of the English Church.

Magnificent Heritage by H. G. G. Herklots (London: S.P.C.K., 1950). Very readable. Especially designed for use by study groups.

Why I Am Not a Roman Catholic by Kenneth N. Ross (London: Mowbray, 1953).

Infallible Fallacies. An Anglican reply to Roman claims by some priests of the Anglican Communion (New York: Morehouse, 1953).

THE ANGLICAN COMMUNION

The Reports of the Lambeth Conferences (See especially *Report 1930* and *Report 1948,* London: S.P.C.K). The encyclical letters, resolutions, and reports of the Anglican bishops on matters of interest and concern to the whole Anglican Communion.

The Anglican Communion by J. W. C. Wand (New York: Oxford, 1948). A volume of essays, each one devoted to one of the Churches of the Anglican Communion.

The Expansion of the Anglican Communion by John S. Higgins (Louisville: Cloister Press, 1942). The spread of the Anglican Communion, briefly told.

The Mission of the Anglican Communion by Edmund Robert Morgan and Roger Lloyd (London: S.P.C.K., 1948). Essays on different aspects of church life in various parts of the Communion. Chiefly misionary.

Christian History in the Making by J. McLeod Campbell (London; Church Assembly, 1946). The inspiring story of the missionary expansion of the Anglican Communion.

New Horizons by J. McLeod Campbell (London: Church Assembly, 1952). A companion volume to *Christian History in the Making.*

Report of the Anglican Congress: Minneapolis 1954 (Greenwich: The Seabury Press, 1954). Report of the proceedings and activities of the Congress representing the whole Anglican Communion.

EPISCOPAL CHURCH HISTORY

A History of the American Episcopal Church by William Wilson Manross (New York: Morehouse, 1935). Full and detailed, especially in the colonial period.

The Episcopal Church in the United States 1789-1931 by James Thayer Addison (New York: Scribners, 1951). Excellent and very readable.

Three Hundred Years of the Episcopal Church by George Hodges (*Philadelphia: Jacobs, 1931*). Brief, but well done.

Men and Movements in the American Episcopal Church by Edward Clowes Chorley (New York: Scribners, 1946). Topics and personalities presented in some detail.

The Episcopal Church: A Miniature History by Walter H. Stowe (Philadelphia: Church Historical Society, Second Edition, 1952). An excellent introductory booklet.

Early English Churches in America: 1607-1807 by Stephen P. Dorsey (New York: Oxford, 1952). Description and excellent photographs of colonial churches and those of the Federal period.

THE AMERICAN RELIGIOUS SCENE

Religion in America by Willard Sperry (New York: Macmillan, 1946). An interesting sketch of the Churches in the United States.

Religion in Colonial America by W. W. Sweet (New York: Scribners, 1942). A study of the religious life of the colonial period.

The Story of Religion in America by W. W. Sweet (New York: Harpers, 1939). An historical treatment for general reading.

The Christian Heritage in America by George Hedley (New York: Macmillan, 1946). Addresses on various Christian bodies.

They Have Found a Faith by Marcus L. Bach (New York: Bobbs-Merrill, 1946). A brief introduction to some of the smaller sects.

The Small Sects in America by E. T. Clark (Nashville: Abingdon, 1937).

These Also Believe by C. S. Braden (New York: Macmillan,

1949). Modern American cults and minority religious movements.

The Story of American Protestantism by A. L. Drummond (London: Oliver & Boyd, 1949).

The Story of American Catholicism by Theodore Maynard (New York: Macmillan, 1948).

American Idealism by Luther A. Weigle (New Haven: Yale, 1928). The influence of religion on American life. Profusely illustrated.

BOOKS FOR PART II

INTRODUCTION TO THE EPISCOPAL CHURCH

The following books will provide a general introduction to the organization and life of the Episcopal Church:

The Episcopal Church: Its Message for Men of Today by George Parkin Atwater (New York: Morehouse, New and Revised Edition, 1954).

The Episcopal Church by George Hodges (New York: Macmillan, 1925).

The Episcopal Church by Latta Griswold (New York: Morehouse, 1938).

An Introduction to the Episcopal Church by Joseph B. Barnadin (New York: Morehouse, 1940).

I Chose the Episcopal Church by Chad Walsh (Greenwich: The Seabury Press, Revised and Enlarged Edition, 1954).

What Does the Episcopal Church Stand For? by W. Norman Pittenger (New York, 1946).

CONSTITUTION, CANON LAW, ETC.

Constitution and Canons of the Protestant Episcopal Church (Printed for the General Convention. New York: The National

Council). The official edition of the Constitution and canon law.

Annotated Constitution and Canons for the Government of the Protestant Episcopal Church, edited by E. A. White and J. A. Dykman, 2 vols. (Greenwich: Seabury Press, 1954). Detailed commentary on the Constitution and Canons of the Episcopal Church.

Journals of the General Convention (Printed for the General Convention. New York: The National Council).

The General Convention: Offices and Officers 1785-1950 by C. Rankin Barnes (Philadelphia: Church Historical Society, 1951). Invaluable reference.

The Canon Law of the Church of England (London: S.P.C.K., 1947). Interesting to students of canon law.

Western Canon Law by Robert C. Mortimer (Berkeley: University of California Press, 1953).

The Ancient Canons (Riverside, N. J.: Burlington, 1952). An interpretation of the ancient canon law and the extent of its operation in the Episcopal Church. Contains an excellent full bibliography.

LITURGY AND WORSHIP

The books listed here will provide an introduction to the liturgy, worship, and allied activities in the Episcopal Church:

Church Services and Service-Books before the Reformation by Henry Barclay Swete (London: S.P.C.K., New Edition, 1930).

The Religion of the Prayer Book by Walden Pell and Powel Mills Dawley (New York: Morehouse, Revised Edition, 1950).

The Story of the Prayer Book by Percy Dearmer (New York: Oxford, 1933).

The Story of the Prayer Book in England and America by Verney Johnstone (New York: Morehouse, 1949).

The American Prayer Book by Edward L. Parsons and Bayard H. Jones (New York: Scribners, 1937).

The Oxford American Prayer Book Commentary by Massey H. Shepherd, Jr. (New York: Oxford, 1950).

The Worshipping Community by H. C. L. Heywood (New York: Morehouse, 1938).

At All Times and in All Places by Massey H. Shepherd, Jr. (Greenwich: The Seabury Press, 1953).

The Prayer Book Speaks in Our Uncertain Age (Greenwich: The Seabury Press).

Prayer Book Studies (New York: The Church Pension Fund). Prepared by the Liturgical Commission of the Episcopal Church:

I *Baptism and Confirmation* (1950)
II *The Liturgical Lectionary* (1950)
III *The Order for the Ministration to the Sick* (1950)
IV *The Eucharistic Liturgy* (1953)
V *The Litany* (1953)

Prayer Book Interleaves by William Palmer Ladd (New York: Oxford, Second Edition, 1943).

The Living Liturgy by Massey H. Shepherd, Jr. (New York: Oxford, 1946).

The Singing Church by C. Henry Phillips (Toronto, Ryerson, 1945).

In Every Corner Sing by Joseph W. Clokey (New York: Morehouse, 1945).

Good Housekeeping in the Church by Katherine M. McClinton and Isabel M. Squier (New York: Morehouse, 1951).

An Altar Guild Manual by Edith Weir Perry (New York: Morehouse, 1934).

Church Needlework by Hinda M. Hands (London: Faith, 1950).

MINISTRY IN THE CHURCH

Books and pamphlets on various forms of ministry in the Episcopal Church:

What Is the Priesthood by John V. Butler and W. Norman Pittenger (New York: Morehouse, 1954).

Stewards of the Mysteries of Christ by W. Norman Pittenger (Greenwich: The Seabury Press).

Clothed With Salvation by Walter C. Klein (Evanston: Seabury-Western Theological Seminary, 1953).

Religious Communities in the American Episcopal Church (West Park: Holy Cross Press, 1945).

Guide to the Religious Communities of the Anglican Communion (New York: Morehouse, 1951).

Guide for Lay Readers (New York: The National Council).

Handbook on Layman's Work (New York: The National Council).

Women in the Life of the Church (New York: The National Council).

I Am a Vestryman by Theodore R. Ludlow (New York: Morehouse, 1945).

What Every Warden and Vestryman Should Know by Henry Anstice (New York: Morehouse, 1924).

HANDBOOKS AND REFERENCES

The Episcopal Church Annual (New York: Morehouse). Indispensable guide to the dioceses, parishes, statistics, and organizations of the Episcopal Church. Published annually.

Stowe's Clerical Directory (New York: The Church Pension Fund). Biographical data on the clergy of the Episcopal Church. Revised every three years. Latest issue: 1953.

BOOKS FOR PART III

MISSIONS

Our Expanding Church by James Thayer Addison (New York: The National Council, Revised Edition, 1944). A survey of the work of the Episcopal Church in its missionary fields.

Building the Church Around the World (New York: The National Council). A series of pamphlets describing the fields of missionary activity of the Episcopal Church. Bibliographies in each pamphlet. Titles in the series:

A Half Century in the Philippines (Philippine Islands)
Beyond the Eight Horizons (China)
Brazilian Destiny (Brazil)
Eden of the Americas (The Carribbean)
Land of Contrasts (Mexico)
Liberian Palaver (Liberia)
On the Trail to Tomorrow (American Indian Missions)
Partners in Africa (Africa)
That Great Land (Alaska)
The Door Is Open in Japan (Japan)
Threshold of the Pacific (Hawaiian Islands)

Builders for Christ Series, edited by Powel Mills Dawley (New York: The National Council). A series of pamphlets on great missionaries of the Episcopal Church. Titles of those published to date:

William Ingraham Kip by George W. Barrett
Lucien Lee Kinsolving by Anson Phelps Stokes, Jr.
Alexander Viets Griswold by David W. Norton, Jr.
Bravid Washington Harris by John M. Burgess
Jackson Kemper by W. Norman Pittenger
James Lloyd Breck by Robert S. Bosher
Philander Chase by Richard G. Salomon

EVANGELISM AND EDUCATION

Two books are widely used for their approach to basic principles involved in both evangelism and education:

The Christian Gospel and the Parish Church by Charles D. Kean (Greenwich: The Seabury Press, 1953).

Man's Need and God's Action by Ruel L. Howe (Greenwich: The Seabury Press, 1953).

Other useful books on aspects of evangelism:

Preach There Also by E. Dargan Butt (Evanston: Seabury-Western Theological Seminary, 1954).

Effective City Church by M. H. Leiffer (Nashville: Abingdon, 1949).

The American City and Its Church by Samuel C. Kincheloe (New York: Friendship Press, 1938).

Church Work in the City by Frederick A. Shippey (Nashville: Abingdon, 1952).

Priest-Workman in England (London: S.P.C.K., 1951).

The Missionary Spirit in Parish Life by Abbé Michonneau (Westminster: Newman Press, 1952).

Revolution in a City Parish by Abbé Michonneau (Westminster: Newman Press, 1949).

An Outline of Christian Sociology by William G. Peck (London: J. Clarke & Co., 1948).

The following books will provide an introduction to problems and methods of Christian education:

A Parish Workshop in Christian Education, edited by Donald W. Crawford (Greenwich: The Seabury Press, 1953).

Religion and the Growing Mind by Basil A. Yeaxlee (Greenwich: The Seabury Press, Revised Edition, 1952).

Children and Religion by Dora P. Chaplin (New York: Scribners, 1948).

Education into Religion by A. Victor Murray (New York: Harpers, 1953).

The Clue to Christian Education by Randolph Crump Miller (New York: Scribners, 1950).

These Are Your Children by Gladys G. Jenkins, Helen Shacter, and William W. Bauer (New York: Scott, Foresman and Co., 1953).

Faith and Nurture by H. Shelton Smith (New York: Scribners, 1941).

Projected Visual Aids in the Church by William S. Hockman (Boston: Pilgrim Press, 1947).

Audio-Visual Materials: Their Nature and Use by Walter A. Wittich and Charles F. Schuller (New York: Harpers, 1953).

Tips to Teachers by Vernon McMaster (New York: Morehouse, 1946).

It's Fun to Teach by Victor Hoag (New York: Morehouse, 1948).

FINANCE, ORGANIZATION, AND PROMOTION

Tell Us About the National Council (New York: The National Council).

The Finances of a Church by Robert Cashman (New York: Harper, 1949).

The Business Administration of a Church by Robert Cashman (Chicago: Willett, Clark, 1937).

How to Raise Funds by Mail by Margaret M. Fellows and Stella A. Koenig (New York: McGraw-Hill, 1950).

More Power for Your Church by Willard A. Pleuthner (New York: Farrar, Straus, and Young, 1952).

Public Relations Manual for Churches by Stanley I. Stuber (New York: Doubleday, 1951).

How to Make Publicity Work by Jack Ramsberger (New York: Reynol and Hitchcock, 1948).

See also the publications of the *National Publicity Council for Health and Welfare Services* (New York) on promotion and public relations, many of which may be adapted for Church use.

THE ECUMENICAL MOVEMENT

Short popular introductions to the Ecumenical Movement will be found in:

One Christ, One World, One Church by Norman Victor Hope (Philadelphia: Church Historical Society, 1953).

The Ecumenical Movement by Leonard Hodgson (Sewanee: The University Press, 1951).

The Quest for Christian Unity by Robert S. Bilheimer (New York: Haddam House, 1952). Also contains brief sketches of various Christian traditions.

Twenty Questions about the Episcopal Church and the Ecumenical Movement (New York: The National Council). A useful pamphlet.

More detailed treatment of various aspects of the Movement will be found in the following:

The Kingship of Christ by G. K. A. Bell (Penguin Books, 1954).

Christian Unity: The Anglican Position by G. K. A. Bell (London: Hodder and Stoughton, 1948).

Towards Church Union 1937-1952 by Stephen Neill (London: Faith and Order Commission, 1952).

Index